Grauballe Man

Pauline Asingh

Grauballe Man
– portrait of a bog body

Moesgård Museum | Gyldendal

Pauline Asingh: Grauballe Man

© 2009 by the author, Moesgård Museum and

Gyldendalske Boghandel, Nordisk Forlag A/S, Copenhagen

Illustration editing: Pauline Asingh

Cover design and graphic layout: Jørgen Sparre

Typesetting with ITC Legacy Book

Translation: Anne Bloch and David Robinson

Editor: Lisbeth Frimodt

The book is published in cooperation with Moesgård Museum, Århus

The book is printed by Korotan, Slovenia, 2009

1st edition, 1st printing

ISBN 978-87-00-79655-3

Content

Foreword

Few discoveries from Denmark's prehistory enjoy the attention afforded by the public and the media to Grauballe Man, the well preserved Iron Age bog body exhibited at Moesgård Museum, south of Århus. Grauballe Man has a prominent place in the Danish national soul, is admired for his indestructibility and endures in the role of national treasure and world class prehistoric find. First and foremost, Grauballe Man is a human being of flesh, skin, bones and hair, handed down from a distant past in the first centuries of the Iron Age, before Caesar was born. The story of Grauballe Man is an account of a life lived in the Iron Age that ended so suddenly and dramatically by a small bog near Grauballe in Central Jutland more than 2000 years ago.

There is also the golden moment when Tage stuck his shovel into Grauballe Man's shoulder one April day in 1952, and the rebellious shock of red hair appeared in the bog, causing such a stir. It is the account of the first bog body to be investigated scientifically, conserved and exhibited, while the world looked on curiously and open-mouthed and someone in the Museum world predicted "Now there will be trouble". But there wasn't, because the principal character in Grauballe Man's cultural-historical afterlife, Professor P. V. Glob, gave the bog body a dignified and enthralling life after death.

In 1969, the book The Bog People was published, in which P. V. Glob so vividly and poetically described the fascinating Iron Age people from the bogs. As the 50th anniversary for the discovery of Grauballe Man approached the time was ripe to ask new questions of science which is today able to decipher the story of lives lived in the past.

This book is a presentation of our knowledge of Grauballe Man, his life, his afterlife, his bog and an interpretation of him and his time. It is also an account of prehistoric people and the natural environment in which their lives unfolded, back to the time when lakes and bogs played a very special role – out between water and land – as the gateway to another spiritual world.

From Grauballe Man's diary

*"I took the shovel up with the peat that sat on it.
There was the head, just as fine as you like.
I had to kneel down to see if it really was a human head."*

On Saturday 26th April 1952, peat was being cut in Nebelgaard bog, a kilometre south of the village of Grauballe in Central Jutland. Local contractors had bought the turbary rights to the small kettle bog lying among the hills northeast of Silkeborg. In addition to two drivers with Jutish draught horses hitched to carts, Tage Busk Sørensen and a couple of other labourers were busy in the bog that morning.

It was Tage who found him

Peat extraction in the bog had been going on for almost two seasons. Knud Kristian Nielsen from Grauballe was involved the whole time. "Major production in the area began just after the war, but only for private use. That's why there were so many small peat cuttings in the area," recalls Knud Kristian one spring day in 2000 by the bog that has today been converted into a small lake with willows growing around the edge and a couple of families of ducks scuttling around on the shore.

In the company of a genuine "bog trotter", everyday life 50 years ago comes alive again as he narrates: "The water level had to be lowered right to the bottom so people could walk all the way out here, and so they could drive out with the cart when they took out the peat slurry. They brought a peat press out here. One man was at the bottom and one above so they could mix the peat to the correct consistency. And when they were finished, they moved to the next baulk. Then it went on the conveyor belt up to a press, and the peat blocks were pushed out. One man stood there to take them and place them on the cart. Then a man with a horse came to collect the cart and leave an empty one. Then that one was filled up, and that's the way it continued all the time, with two drivers to take out the loads. Sometimes it was a long way when they had to go all the way to the top of the hill. One man unloaded the peat at the drying site. When

FROM GRAUBALLE MAN'S DIARY   9

The man in the bog.
27th April 1952.

that was finished, he took a fork and the peat blocks were divided up into five. After they had lain at the site for a fortnight, the women and children came and stacked them up into long rows, each with 1000 blocks. This is the form in which they were sold. There was oak in that bog, great trunks. It wasn't very common here in the Grauballe area where there was mostly pine, great Scots pines. The bottom had been reached and one peat baulk was left, five metres in and then three metres across."

Frederik Pedersen, who had worked in the peat bogs for 25 years, tells about that April day in 1952: "I was down there myself. First, I found two great ox horns down there. We pressed the last peats on the ground. I went and cut away the topsoil with a pointed peat spade and then we continued to work inwards. It was Tage Busk who stuck his shovel in the shoulder. That shows how high up he lay. And then the hair appeared. And then I said: Here is the hide from the ox. We had one of Hans' farmhands with us, and he drove down there, and he almost jumped out of his skin. He was so scared when he saw that head. That was Saturday about two o'clock."

"Aye, it was me who dug into him," remembers Tage, one autumn day in 2001. "We had just moved the elevator, I stood round the back and dug. I stood on the shovel. I couldn't understand it, it was as if it sprang back a bit. And a root was hard, you know, when you dug into it. So I took the shovel up with peat that sat on it. There was the head, just as fine as you like. I had to kneel down to see if it really was a human head. Then I realised that it really was. Then the village postman came, just as we had found him. He was cycling past, and he often came down into the bog to chat with us. He jumped on his bike and rode down to Nebelgaard and rang Dr Balslev in Aidt. He had something to do with such matters. We covered him up and worked the rest of the day."

The local doctor, Ulrik Balslev, attended the stranger in the bog that same evening. With a suspicion that the discovery in the bog did not fall under his professional responsibilities, but rather his passionate interest in archaeology, he did not move the find and rang Professor P.V. Glob. The professor was, however, on archaeological business near Randers and was first able to visit the site on the Sunday.

Several people had, of course, heard the rumours about the strange discovery in the bog and many people came in the evening to visit the man, who still lay unguarded up to his neck in peat. During the crush in the dark, one of the visitors accidentally stepped on the sack that Tage had laid over the corpse's head. This blunder was reported in the national newspapers a couple of days later when the bog man, on the same occasion, was hailed as a world-wide sensation.

"The find became of significantly less value as a person who had been out to look at it at night or early in the morning had, by accident, come to tread on the face and squash it, so the actual head no longer has its natural shape!" wrote the newspaper *Silkeborg Avis* on 28th April under the headline: "2000-year-old Iron Age man found in a bog at Grauballe."

More important than a packed lunch

The peat workers' accounts from the scene of the day one of the greatest treasures of Danish prehistory was discovered, give little indication of enthusiasm. The impression is more of wonderment at apparently having stood at the epicentre of an event that would come to enthral the whole country and would reverberate throughout the coming decades. One man in the bog – more or less – shouldn't interfere with the team's work ethic. Peat work was piece-work, and peat extraction was firmly on the agenda that day – like every other day in the bog. When asked what he felt deep down inside when he suddenly stood face to face with the red-haired man he had dug out with his own bare hands, Tage answered: "Just when I first saw him, I was a little frightened, but it didn't really affect me, there was work to be done!"

Far more enthusiastic and full of great expectations, Professor P.V. Glob arrived at the bog the next morning. "The bog lay in the bright, slanting morning light, the dew-drops sparkling like millions of diamonds," wrote Glob in 1969, with poetical devotion, in *The Bog People*, a book which sparked an archaeological awakening and provided an insight for many people into the wonderful bog people of the Iron Age. "A large crowd of the local inhabitants had already gathered. As it was Sunday they had time off from their work on the land. They were tightly grouped in a ring around a dark-coloured human head, with a tuft of short-cropped hair, which stuck up clear of the dark brown peat. Part of the neck and shoulders was also exposed. We were clearly face to face once again with one of the bog people," concluded Glob that morning in the bog.

A macabre sight

Two years previously, in the spring of 1950, Glob had stood in Bjældskovdal bog, just 20 kilometres distant, face to face with the most beautiful of them all, Tollund Man, whose serene and delicate facial features give the impression of a man sleeping through eternity. Tollund Man was in the care of Silkeborg Museum, and from here he was sent to the National Museum in Copenhagen for investigation and conservation. However, he returned home to Silkeborg much later in a severely amputated state. Only his well-preserved head and his right foot were deemed worthy of conservation. The rest of his body was left to slowly dry out. On conservation-related and probably, in particular, ethical grounds, Johannes Brøndsted, the National Museum's director, found the human body unsuitable for conservation and future storage as a museum artefact, and absolutely not for exhibition to the public. "It is, you know, a pretty macabre sight," was the view of a like-minded senior curator.

Such ethical scruples did not disturb the professor from Jutland. With his never failing foresight, Glob was aware from the very first moment how sensational this unique find of a human being was for archaeology. He did not doubt for an instant that the bog man should not only be subjected to scientific analysis, but also conserved and exhibited to the public. Firstly though, he should, by the most secure means available, be transported to the Prehistoric Museum in Århus, still encased in the peat that surrounded him. Then the actual excavation could take place indoors under optimal conditions.

"When Glob came, we did the heavy work," remembers Tage. "And then Glob stood there with his trowel and dug right at the end. He did not leave the man's side, and had his packed lunch lying on top of him."

Before the body was transported to Århus, it was important for Glob to establish exactly how it lay in the bog, and how it related to the surrounding peat layers. This was important with respect to, among other things, determining the point in time at which it had been deposited in the bog. The corpse apparently lay in an old peat cutting about 30 metres out from the edge of the bog. Light-coloured fibrous sphagnum peat extended both under and over the body, and was clearly different from the surrounding dark, compact peat. The size of the peat cutting could not, however, be determined, as the

edges on three sides had already been cut away. Only at one side was the original edge preserved. Here, the light-coloured fibrous peat continued for more than a metre beyond the dead man's outstretched leg, from where the edge of the cutting continued evenly up to the surface exposed by the peat extraction. That year, about a metre of the overlying peat had already been cut away before Tage struck him with his shovel. The peat layer had, however, originally been much thicker, but had been steadily dug away through centuries of extraction, as now became apparent in the complete jumble of old peat cuttings in the bog.

The corpse lay slightly at an angle in the bog, with its head and upper body highest, and resting approximately on the base of the old peat cutting. It could already be seen that the man lay on his chest with his left leg extended and his right arm and leg bent.

When Glob had satisfied himself that the corpse lay alone and that there were no accompanying items of any kind, a metal sheet was pushed in from one side, through the peat and under the man. This enabled him to leave the bog inside the entire block of peat that still enclosed him. Tage was involved: "We attached something securely down along the sides and bound it up with rope. The lorry could not drive out into the bog, so we hitched up the horses. He was pulled out on a wooden sledge. It took probably eight or nine of us to lift him up onto the lorry." Knud Kristian was at the back:

"And then a great big tuft of hair fell off and I picked it up and said to Glob: "You'd better take this, too." "No, you can just stuff that in your pocket," said Glob, "which of course I didn't. I should have done just that." On the other hand, Tage, Knud and the others were each given 50 *kroner* as a reward. "People stood all the way round and looked down into the bog, even though it was raining. It was a Sunday, you see," remembers Tage.

A gateway to Århus

A conservation department had been set up at the Prehistoric Museum in Århus shortly before the discovery. Glob had insisted on an emergency entrance of sufficient width that possible future bog bodies could be invited indoors for tender, loving care from the museum's newly appointed conservator, Gunnar Lange-Kornbak. It was important for Glob to be able to take care of the find himself, and not risk having to send him to Copenhagen, where professional enthusiasm for bog bodies as research objects was extremely limited.

During the subsequent "excavation" inside the museum, no traces were found either of clothes or other items together with the corpse. Clothes of wool or leather associated with the corpse, such as those found together with other similar discoveries, would have been preserved if he had had any. Textiles of linen or other plant fibre are likely to have decayed, but they would probably have left impressions on his skin, which was smooth and well preserved almost all over. Glob concluded that he was laid in the

Grauballe Man was laid in the bog just as naked as he came into the world.

bog just as naked as when he came into the world. Even though there was no immediate archaeological basis for a dating, he had no doubt that here he stood with a bog body from the Iron Age, corresponding to those which, in large numbers, and especially during and between the two world wars, had been found during peat extraction in Northwest European bogs.

Stories from the bog archives

Despite no artefacts being found that could help archaeology towards a date beyond that provided by experience and intuition, help was still at hand. Dating by way of the radiocarbon method, a scientific revolution in archaeological dating, was at that time in its infancy. The method was developed by an American professor, W.F. Libby, at the end of the 1940s, and is based on modern atomic physics. At the newly established Zoo-physiological Laboratory, which later became associated with the National Museum, trial dating procedures were being carried out at this time with the aim of improving and becoming more familiar with this dating method, which promised to open up completely new perspectives in archaeology.

Another dating method involves looking in detail at the peat layers within the bog, as these represent an archive of the Danish flora through the millennia. The climate, and therefore also the vegetation, changed many times during prehistory. Through pollen analysis, a technique involving identification of microscopic pollen grains, produced by the surrounding herbs and trees, that have become preserved in the various layers of the bog, it is possible to discover from which vegetational or pollen zone, and therefore which time period, the individual peat layers originate.

In the days following the discovery, Dr Svend Jørgensen of the National Museum carried out a thorough investigation of the peat in Nebelgaard bog, including a study of the peat layers within which the corpse was found. On the basis of his investigations, he could draw an exact picture of the vegetation of the bog and the surrounding landscape at the time the body was deposited. In his 50 m-long vertical and sharply-cut section through the bog, Svend Jørgensen could see tremendous peat cutting "activity" precisely during the vegetational period characterised by the light-coloured, fibrous peat layer. This is more poetically referred to as "dog's flesh", and is peat which was formed in the latter part of the Bronze Age, on the threshold to the Iron Age, around 7-600 BC. At that time there was a marked change in the climate, from warm and dry to considerably wetter and cooler. This climatic change is reflected in the formation of light-coloured fibrous peat in our peat bogs.

Svend Jørgensen reached the conclusion that a considerable amount of peat cutting had taken place in the bog, beginning around the birth of Christ and continuing up until the present day. This extensive peat cutting posed great problems for his interpretation, as he could not be sure that those layers lying deepest were also oldest. He therefore had difficulty in finding out precisely when the oldest and therefore the first peat cutting in Nebelgaard bog took place. Pollen diagrams, showing curves for the occurrence of pollen, produced from three of the oldest peat cuttings, including the one in which the body was found, suggested that peat began accumulating again in the peat cuttings shortly after the birth of Christ. Svend Jørgensen based his interpretation on observations of rye pollen, the presence of which had, at that time, i.e. the 1950s, not been demonstrated prior to the first centuries AD. The low values of beech pollen suggested, furthermore, that the body must have been placed in the bog during the Early Roman Iron Age, AD 0-400. This is the period during which Iron Age societies in Northern Europe received many cultural impulses from the expanding Roman Empire

to the south. Beech was at that time, which in terms of vegetation history is referred to as the sub-Atlantic, slowly expanding. Due to the presence of rye pollen and the low values of beech pollen, Svend Jørgensen concluded that the peat cuttings in Nebelgaard bog could be dated to the centuries just after the birth of Christ. Pollen dates such as this, based solely on a relative chronology and the current (1952) status of research into vegetation history, became quickly overtaken by the absolute dating framework provided by the radiocarbon method, as will become apparent below.

P.V. Glob during investigations and survey at Bjældskovdal bog where Tollund Man was found in 1950.

A handshake from the past

Already on the day after the discovery the Danish media bellowed forth such that the reverberations reached the international press. Grauballe Man, as he had now been christened, dominated the front pages. In reality, he should have been named after Nebelgaard bog, where he was actually found. But as there seemed to be so much more blood, flesh and power in a Grauballe Man than a Nebel Man, Glob named him after an extensive area of bog lying behind the hills a couple of kilometres away.

"2000-year-old man with a red beard and black nails found in bog in Jutland," was the headline in the newspaper *Ekstrabladet* on Monday morning. The professor took the media by storm with news of the sensational discovery. Not just his bones, but also his skin, muscles and his thick reddish-brown hair, facial stubble and eyebrows, even the furrows of his brow were preserved. The fine patterns of his palm and fingertips and the rounded, albeit black, nail crescents were a warm handshake from the past and grist to the mill of science. He was decidedly the best preserved bog body found so far.

While Grauballe Man still lay partially enclosed within his acid peat soil inside the museum, the professor pronounced him as a sacrifice to the supernatural. "Red-haired young man sacrificed to goddess," was the headline *Nationaltidende* splashed across its front page on Monday morning. With his untiring desire to narrate and his formidable ability to communicate details of prehistoric society, Glob enveloped the bog man in a fabulous story, which elevated him to the level of a research icon for science, for the public – and for the Prehistoric Museum in Århus.

This tall, well-built young man from the Grauballe area was a temple servant for the goddess of fertility, Nerthus, Mother Earth, who, according to Glob, people began worshipping at this time during the Iron Age. The Roman historian Tacitus describes Nerthus worship in his work *Germania*, dating from the first century AD. The goddess lived in a sacred grove of trees. Every spring, her statue was driven around in its sacred wagon, drawn by oxen, in order to visit all the people in the surrounding area and bring them fertility. During this time, no fighting was allowed, all weapons were to be hidden away, peace and happiness should reign. When her tour was over, a purification ceremony took place in which the goddess, her wagon, and her clothes were cleansed. This ceremony ended with those who had participated in the cleansing being sacrificed to the goddess, naked and often, as in this case, deposited in a nearby bog. Glob continues the story: "How the man who was to be sacrificed was chosen, whether he was a servant at the shrine or just an ordinary member of the community, we do not know. Although his beautiful hands, unused to work, suggest that he was not chosen from the farming community's ordinary members. Grauballe Man was a magnificent example of strength and size. Probably, he went voluntarily to his death to spare his companions death from starvation, as it was seen as an honour and a blessing to sacrifice one's life to a deity."

This interpretation appealed to Danes in the post-war years; National Romanticism was dusted off and backs were straightened. Just think – we Danes are descendants of a people who practised such a noble tradition as to sacrifice to the goddess of love. And one of the chosen sacred offerings, for whom the act of sacrifice was an honour, has now emerged from the earth of Central Jutland. Glob reckoned that Grauballe Man, just like Tollund Man, had been hanged, and that the remains of the rope would be found as the excavation proceeded. Hanging was, according to Tacitus, seen as being an honourable death. It was first with the advent of Christianity that it became a demeaning way to die. A good Christian view, which had the aim of doing away with ungodly human sacrifices.

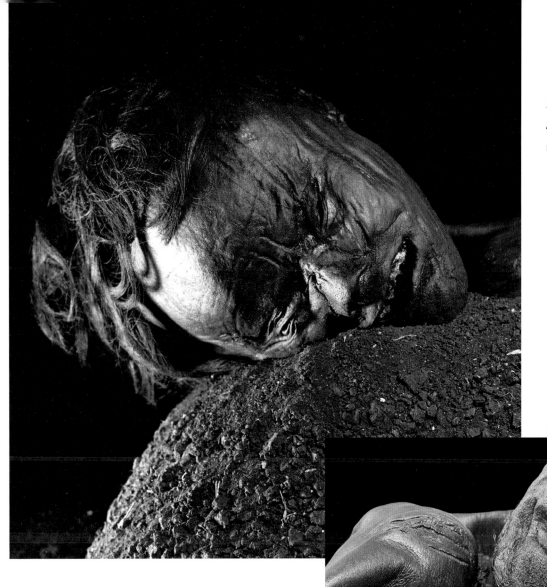

Even his beard, his eyebrows and the furrows of his brow were preserved.

Inside the museum, work was proceeding apace with the excavation of Grauballe Man from his encasing block of peat. Conservator Lange-Kornbak took part in the excavation and was also given responsibility for the future preservation of the treasure. This involved him finding, or rather inventing, a method of conserving an entire, intact human body. This had never been attempted before. So it was a rather nervous conservator who was forced to accept Glob's decision immediately to invite the public in to stand face to face with one of our own ancestors, and a magnificent example of such into the bargain. Glob told the Danish newspapers: "He was a beautiful and imposing figure, approximately of the height required of a guardsman and very well built, and any possible presumption of a certain roughness in our Germanic ancestors from the Iron Age is refuted by the fact that he had such beautiful hands and almond-shaped nails."

Lying in state

Despite the very substantial conservation considerations to the contrary, the public had to be given a share in our common past before scientific investigation of the body got under way. Accordingly, fully exposed and still resting on an underlay of bog peat he was laid in a glass coffin, as newspapers expressed it, and exhibited in the middle of the floor in the museum's Bronze Age gallery.

It was the very first time that a well-preserved human corpse had, in this way, been exhibited to the public. Although thousands of Soviet citizens did file past Lenin's dead body in 1924, but the Soviet state stood behind that decision and it was not open to discussion. It is true that Glob was a self-confessed communist and scientist, but that did not prevent him from seeking views on ethical opinions in higher places. For there were disapproving voices from outraged fervent Christians, who thought that Grauballe Man should be reburied in consecrated ground. They maintained that science had merely become the modern person's religion and that its priesthood now demanded

"Everyone joined the queue: school children, young and old, even mothers with crying babes at arms."

The queue to see Grauballe Man at the Prehistoric Museum in Århus. 4th May 1952.

sacrifices to the gods, as the priesthood had done in Grauballe Man's time. The Earl of Bothwell lay exposed to the public in God's own house, in Faarevejle church on Zeeland, but that was, so to speak, acceptable, and besides, he was mummified beyond recognition.

The parson in Grauballe Man's parish raised no ethical or religious objections at the prospect of one of his flock being exhibited in Århus. "I don't think the Church should have any right to take up opposition to science. Grauballe Man is considered to be much the same as other things people visit a museum to see. And his resting place at the

*"One is gripped with wonderment
and veneration for this unusual
glimpse from a distant past."*

Prehistoric Museum in Århus is much more noble than that in Nebelgaard bog," was the view expressed on the matter by the Reverend Møller Rasmussen of Svostrup parish. Neither did the diocesan bishop, Christian Baun, see any reason to demand that Grauballe Man be handed over and given a resting place in Christian soil: "One is faced with something which can hardly be said to be sacred, but something which is, however, so great and so decisive for human life that respect for the dead can lose some of its significance. The temptation for the viewer to become, how should I say – a little cynical – is probably present in this respect." The museum reserved its right to one restriction during the exhibition of Grauballe Man: children could only enter if accompanied by an adult. It was up to parents to decide how much their children were allowed to see.

The exhibition of Grauballe Man was a great success and it was neither cynicism nor popular entertainment that characterised the intense atmosphere around the display case in the museum's Bronze Age gallery. The interest was enormous. Already on the first day of the exhibition there was a queue running the length of the street Museums-gade. All day long, a steady stream of people passed through the otherwise so quiet museum. Everyone joined the queue: school children, young and old, even mothers with crying babes at arms. A reporter from *Aarhus Stiftstidende* felt enriched by the experience: "One enters through a side door, deposits 50 *øre* with a welcoming lady, and is led along ropes through half the museum. After an hour, one has reached the display case housing this fascinating prehistoric discovery. Grauballe Man is no marvel of beauty. His cramp-like twisted posture, unruly red hair and black-tanned skin lead one's thoughts in the direction of a cover illustration for a sombre detective novel, and now and then one of the spectators is heard to utter an "Ooooh! Dear me!" But once one has come to terms with the "horror" and has had the opportunity to study details at close hand, one is gripped with wonderment and veneration for this unusual glimpse from a distant past. And when one once again stands out in the spring sunshine, one is an experience richer." After the first two days, 5000 people had seen Grauballe Man. Despite the fact that the success and the tumult could, seen from the street, perhaps begin to resemble a sideshow, visits to the display case took place under extremely dignified circumstances, some people even removed their headgear as they passed the 2000-year-old Iron Age man.

"Flock to see Body 2000 Years Dead," wrote *The Cleveland Plain Dealer* and *The Washington Post* served up the sensation under the headline "Body of Unshaven Dane found Preserved after 2000 Years." The news continued to circulate the globe and at home in Århus everyone wanted to see him. The exhibition, which was originally planned to last three days, was extended. Grauballe Man's carer, conservator Lange-Kornbak, was not happy with this decision. Lange-Kornbak was responsible for Grauballe Man's future preservation and he had to resign himself to all the publicity the discovery had attracted, and the danger that the treasure would suffer damage as a result. The diary entries for the days of the exhibition contain simple but numerous accounts of watering and more watering of the corpse. At the same time there was the conflict of interests – between the required high humidity of around 90% in the display case and the formation of condensation and the consequent lack of visibility for the public. The temperature rose in the overcrowded exhibition gallery and Grauballe Man was put on ice.

On the morning of the seventh exhibition day, Lange-Kornbak discovered small "creepy-crawlies" running about, and white spores had begun to spread over the skin. Stronger measures were employed and local application by brush of a 0.5% phenol solution halted the beginnings of decay. Every evening, when the exhibition closed at 8 pm, the conservator started his night shift with an inspection of the body – spraying with water, covering with a sheet and oilcloth, taking the temperature and placing bowls of ice and water under the tablecloth. All this for the sake of the public, and only to then, early next morning, repeat the ritual once again, in reverse order, each time with a trembling heart. The last small "creepy-crawlies", in a small puddle held in a fold of skin, were removed with a sponge on the morning of the tenth exhibition day. And with it, the conservator's first nightmare was over, and he could look forward to the end of the final day of exhibition.

Glob was delighted – 18.000 people had seen Grauballe Man in the course of the ten days the exhibition lasted. He had now been exposed to the great Danish public. And the exhibition had brought in almost 10,000 *kroner* in entrance fees – not an insignificant sum. Through his lying in state he had earned the costs of his coming exhibition case and conservation, and hereby his continued existence as a national treasure.

He touched the soul of the nation

One can quite rightly ask what it was about the bog man, back then in the 1950s, which attracted such great attention from the general public? He was not an especially beautiful representative of our ancestors. And he was not significantly different from the other bog bodies that had turned up in bogs in previous decades. The attention given to Tollund Man is easier to comprehend. But despite the latter's undoubtedly beautiful appearance, the most beautiful from all of prehistory, he did not receive anything like the same attention, when found two years previously. And, as already mentioned, the National Museum was not impressed when Tollund Man arrived by train from Jutland for examination and possible conservation. It was only because it was so important to the museum authorities in Silkeborg that his head and one of his feet were conserved. Grauballe Man, on the other hand, tugged at the heartstrings of the Danish public right from the very moment on that spring day we he again saw the light of day after more than 2000 years in the bog.

Professor Glob had, since the discovery of Tollund Man, had a pious hope that yet another bog body would turn up and that it would come into his custody. Glob was a charismatic person, an animated storyteller and a friend of the people. He described prehistoric societies on the basis of the people who created them. This stood in sharp contrast to the research tradition prevailing at the National Museum where the spirit of the museum's founder, C.J. Thomsen, still ruled and where the study of the typological development of artefacts alone was an accepted research basis for the description of prehistoric cultures. Tufts of hair, teeth and other human remains were stored together with accompanying artefacts where this was thought appropriate. But as individual objects, it was unethical and inappropriate to study them. Glob was of a different mould and also a communist of political persuasion. He was interested in prehistoric people of flesh and blood. He interpreted the bog bodies as sublime offerings to the powers above and considered them to be worthy representatives of Iron Age society. In bog bodies, Glob saw evidence that we once lived in close contact with nature, reconciled with death and in a social fellowship according to the motto: All for one and one for all. He was as brilliant a story-teller as his friend Martin A. Hansen, who gifted Danes their prehistory through his portrayals in the novel *Orm og Tyr*, and who trans-

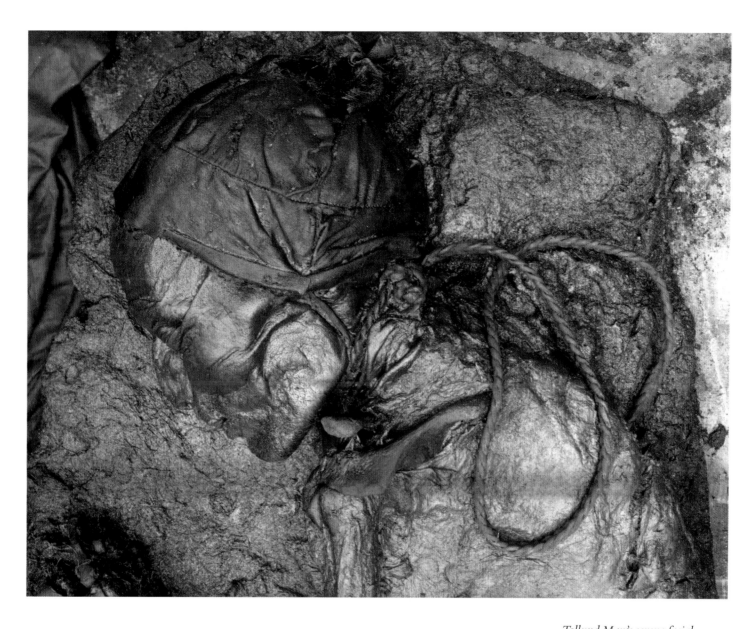

Tollund Man's serene facial expression gives the impression of a man sleeping through eternity under his tightly-fitting cap. However, the noose around his neck leaves no doubt as to his sudden death.

fixed entire audiences in village halls across the land with his lectures. In 1960, the artist Asger Jorn visualised these stories in a series of paintings, in which human sacrifices were also depicted, inspired by the stories in *Orm og Tyr*: "In poor times, tools, cattle and people, thralls, prisoners, even the king, were offered to Odin, the god of fire, who had long been neglected in favour of the earth." Glob was, however, more in favour of the goddess of love, Nerthus, than the god of war, Odin. But they both have in common the fact that they transgress the boundary between life and death – humans become reconciled with death. This was an interpretation the Danish people could understand.

Grauballe Man turned up in the post-war years, at a time when national self-respect had difficulty in finding a fertile substrate. Grauballe Man came to us as a representative of the Danish mentality. He was the proof that Danes belong to a different tradition and do not possess a primitive warlike mentality. We are descendants of a people who practised the ultimate, to sacrifice in the name of love and fellowship. What is more, this was an offering tradition through which we were reconciled with death. Where death's essence was beautiful and the sacrifice pure and clear. This thought took root in the soul of the Danish people and Grauballe Man was the tangible proof, recovered from the depths of our own Jutish bog. We needed a common identity to cling to in post-war times; we stood together, and Grauballe Man became an icon for the Danish national mentality.

A national treasure

Glob's idea of inviting the public in to meet Grauballe Man, freshly dug up from the bog, was crucial for the role the bog man came to play as a national treasure – and continues to play as an important part of our common cultural heritage. The experience of standing beside Grauballe Man's display case during those ten days in May 1952 is still within living memory, and is retold from one generation to the next. The effect of the exhibition can be compared to that of Zarafa's wanderings through the streets of Paris in 1824, as recounted by Michael Allin. Everyone wanted to see the giraffe – the celebrity!

It was, in particular, Grauballe Man's cultural history in recent times, that gifted to him by Glob, and which the public accepted with open hearts, that made him a part of Danish history. Today, we do not question his role among heritage gems. The fact that he is one of our crown jewels is deeply rooted in our national history. And he attracts the attention of the public and the media every time archaeologists and other scholars lay a hand on him. As the philosopher Arno Victor Nielsen says: "He is ugly as sin, but we love him, as only a mother can love him, because he is one of us."

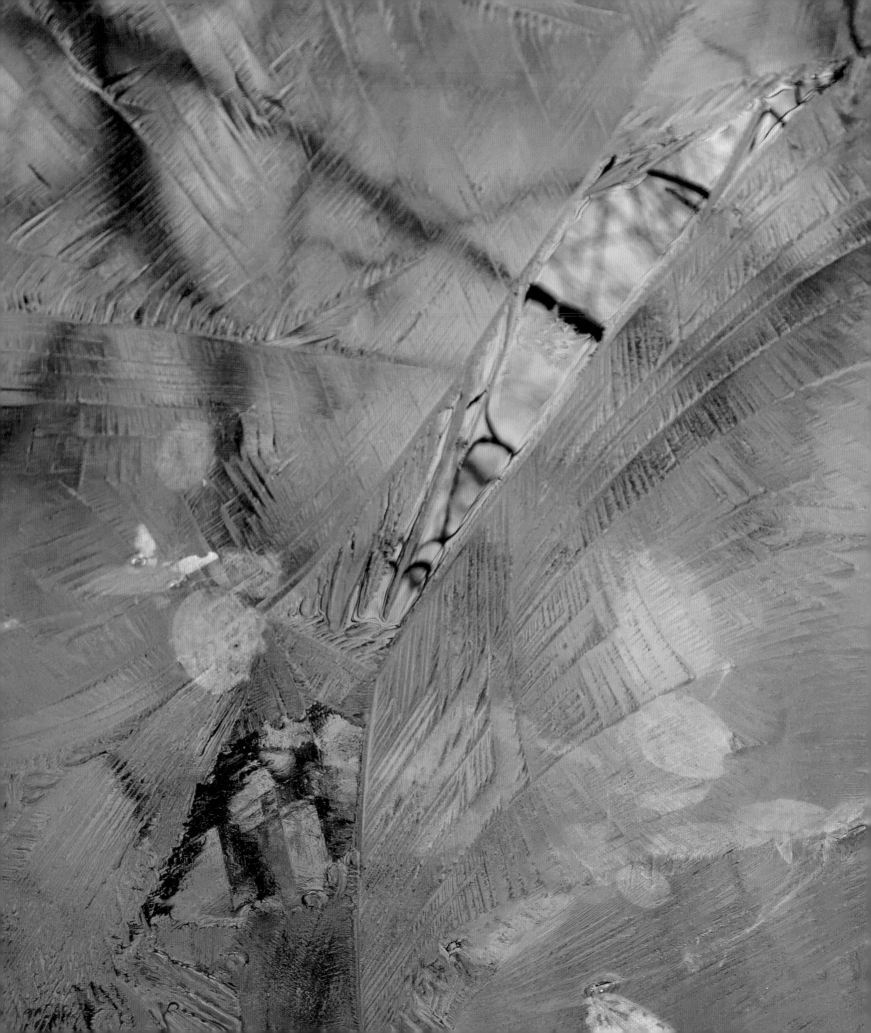

In the spotlight of science

"It should be made clear that the work is being done in the name of science and with due veneration."

Conservator Lange-Kornbak must have heaved a great sigh of relief when the door finally closed behind the last museum visitor at 8 pm on Sunday 11th May. The temperature in the display case had been critically high that day, bringing with it the danger of the beginnings of serious decay behind the glass. The public had now to live on memories and recollections in the coming years while conservation was in progress. It was science and conservation that took precedence. An ambitious programme had already been planned, according to which he was to be investigated from every possible angle.

Doctors queuing up

On Monday, the early watering was skipped as the morning was dedicated to photography and documentation of Grauballe Man, before doctors and other specialists began to turn their attentions to him. At 3 pm, forensic pathologist, Professor Willy Munck from Århus District Hospital came visiting. He carried out what could probably be termed a preliminary inquest report, and promised also to execute the subsequent autopsy. It was the first time that forensic work of this nature had been undertaken. Investigation of such a well-preserved body from the distant past had not previously been attempted, either in Denmark, or elsewhere in the world. Not even the Egyptian mummies had offered such opportunities as the ancient Egyptians had themselves removed the internal organs and conserved their dead prior to burial.

Willy Munck's description was carried out on the basis of Gruaballe Man in the position in which he was found, as the body had not yet been lifted from the peat on which he was transported. The skin is described as being dark brown all over, firm, as if tanned. The head was, like the rest of the body, somewhat flattened as a consequence of pressure from the overlying peat mass. The latter had rested with its full weight on the

*The delicate patterns of his skin
and his rounded nails with the
light "crescents" are a wonderful
handshake from the past.*

*There was not the slightest trace
of scars or cuts on the
well-preserved soles of his feet.*

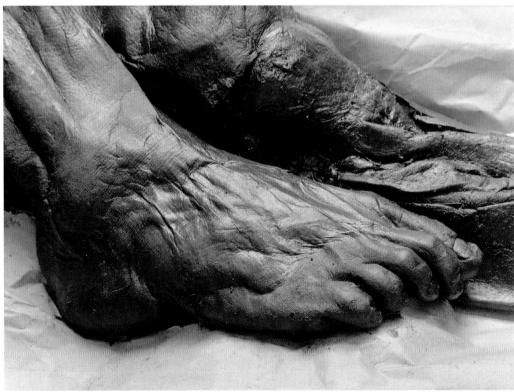

corpse after the water in the bog had been pumped away in the interests of peat extraction. Willy Munck reports the body's rather twisted position: "The corpse is lying in prone position, with its head turned slightly to the right. The back turns almost vertically upwards, but there is a forward curvature of the vertebral column. The right arm is slightly bent and the lower arm is turned such that the palm faces backwards. The left arm lies alongside the body, the hand is clenched. The right leg is strongly bent at the hip and, notably, at the knee. The left leg is more extended."

Hair was preserved on the crown and the left side of the head. It was 15 cm long and reddish brown in colour. Munck remarks that this is unlikely to be its original colour, but is due to colouring agents in the bog water, just like the colouration of the skin. In a subsequent investigation of the hair it was thought that a strong brown pigmentation could be detected that did not originate from the bog water. On this basis, it was assumed that he was dark-haired. On the upper lip and chin there was 3-10 mm of stubble. The eyes were screwed up and the eyeballs could just be glimpsed. Even though the colour of the iris could not be judged with certainty, it seemed likely that he had dark eyes. The nose was pressed flat to the right. In behind the slightly open mouth, the teeth could just be seen – black and worn on the masticating surfaces. The forensic pathologist's observations must correspond closely to the details that 18,000 museum visitors already had imprinted on their retinas.

On the following day, detective inspectors C.H. Vogelius Andersen and H.C. Andersen of the Forensic Team, Århus Police, arrived. Attention was now turned to the unusually well-preserved hands and feet. Andersen and Andersen were certainly used to seeing fingerprints, but they had never previously been in a situation where the victim's fingerprints were clearer than their own. The so-called papillary lines in the skin of the fingers were the oldest and also the clearest ever seen. Wax impressions were carefully taken of the fingers of the right hand and the sole of the right foot. "The pattern on the right thumb could be read directly as whorls, a so-called double-loop pattern, whereas the right middle finger proved to contain an ulnar loop." These professional terms refer to the patterns formed by the fine lines on the skin of the fingers. Exactly these types of pattern have survived through the millennia and are now seen on the fingertips of the male Danish population with a frequency of 11.2% and 68.3%, respectively. The almost pristine state of preservation of the papillary lines on the surface of Grauballe Man's hands must be taken as evidence that he was not someone involved in heavy manual work. There were, so to speak, no signs of wear on his hands. This piece of evidence fitted very well with the interpretation of him as a noble sacrifice – of aristocratic origin. Today, 50 years on, we know that the outer skin and, consequently, also the hard skin of the toughest workman's fist is simply dissolved away by being in bog water. What remains is, right enough, the knife-edge-sharp pattern of the inner layer of skin.

Arrival with the Danish Salvage Corps Falck at Aarhus District Hospital on 16th May 1952. Lange-Kornbak (to the left) and Glob (furthest away) help carry him in.

On the morning of Wednesday 16th May, an out-patient X-ray investigation at Århus District Hospital by Professor Carl Krebs and Dr Erling Ratjen was listed on the programme. After his morning watering, Grauballe Man was pushed, together with the last remains of the peat, over on to a soap-covered sheet of block-board that functioned as a stretcher. At 12.15 pm, the Danish Salvage Corps Falck intervened. At no time did Lange-Kornbak leave Grauballe Man in the care of others, and he went in the ambulance, with his water sprayer, to the radiology department. The entire radiological staff of white-coated men and women, and more, were there to receive Grauballe Man at the department. He was wheeled along the corridors on his block-board, flanked by the astonished personnel. Judging from the facial expressions seen on the press photographs, he was perceived as a visitor from another world – which was also true. The smell of the boggy depths also still clung to him, as most people held their noses. A group of Irish doctors, on a study visit to see how work proceeded in a modern radiology unit, had not quite expected to find a 2000-year-old under the modern X-ray apparatus that day.

After five hours of hard work, and the taking of 100 radiographs, during which the greatest care had to be exercised in order not to damage the fragile body, he was almost fully documented internally. It was not possible, however, to achieve satisfactory results for the pelvis as long he lay on the metal plate used in his recovery from the bog.

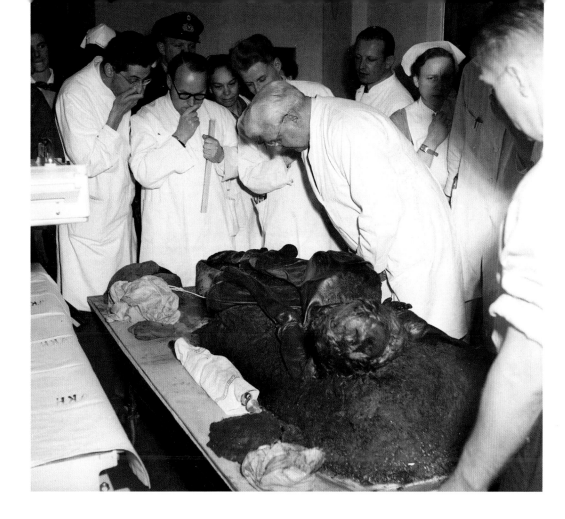

Medical examination of Grauballe Man at Aarhus District Hospital.

The many images had now to be analysed, together with supplementary pictures. Already on the following day the newspapers printed a picture of his cranium containing a well-preserved but shrunken brain. On this it was still possible to discern the two cerebral hemispheres and the convolutions of the brain surface. Even though his bones were soft and de-calcified from their time in the bog, the pictures still revealed their fine net-like structure enclosed within the shadows of the skin.

Signs of the cause of death were, of course, searched for. As yet, no observations had been made that could document fractures to the vertebrae of the neck or to the vertebral column as a consequence of the presumed hanging. The radiographs did, however, reveal a fracture to the cranium by the left temple and a fracture to the left tibia.

Prior to the autopsy, and a further X-ray examination, it was necessary to turn Grauballe Man over. At the same time, it was important to ensure that, once the conservation process had been completed, he could be exhibited in exactly the same position as that in which he was found. Therefore, it was necessary in the first instance to manufacture a closely fitting plaster cover in order to be able then to turn the body. For the first time in a week, Lange-Kornbak was able to confirm that the regular treatment with 0.5% phenol solution had had the desired effect. It was no longer possible to observe white spores, the beginnings of mould formation, on the skin.

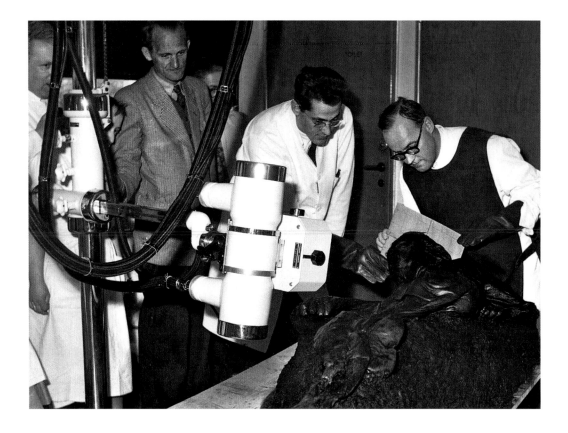

On Saturday morning the entire colossus, comprising corpse, peat and plaster support, was turned, but not without difficulty as it was a very heavy item to manoeuvre.
Neither were remains of clothes or other items found when his last covering of peat was
removed. He had been placed in the bog naked. First now, 21 days after his discovery, the
cause of his death was revealed. This had left much more formidable traces than any
presumed hanging. There, on his neck, where it was expected to find the mark of a rope,
such as that which Tollund Man still had around his neck when he was found, was
instead a great gaping wound stretching from one ear to the other. The wound was so
deep that the vertebrae of the neck could be glimpsed within the dark depths. It must
undeniably have been a shocking discovery, and one that greatly surprised the experts.
The wound has given rise to both terrible and sombre thoughts about how Grauballe
Man met his death. The always calm, collected and strictly professional conservator
does, however, subsequently record dryly the discovery in his diary. His entry is otherwise more pre-occupied with the ventral side of the corpse which, after thorough wash-
ing, proved to be even better preserved than the dorsal side.

Judging from the accounts given in the newspapers, Glob was not present on this
occasion. He was in Southern Jutland, searching around for other offerings to the gods
at Gallehus, in order to locate the find site for the famous Golden Horns. The exact

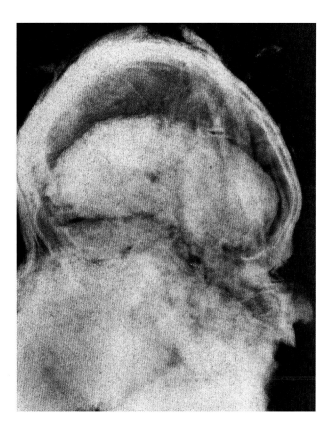

Radiograph of Grauballe Man's head. Even though his brain has shrunk to less than half its original size, the two cerebral hemispheres and the convolutions of the brain are visible after more than two thousand years in the bog.

position of these golden horns, which first nourished Danish nationalist sentiment and later, one is almost tempted to say, again and again, took it away from us, was apparently wrongly marked in the landscape. The correct place, "where prehistoric society offered rich gifts to their gods," actually lay under a scrubby thicket and a building. "So the stone commemorating the finds will continue to be in the wrong place," Glob told the newspaper *Demokraten* that Saturday.

On 20th May, the body was again taken by Falck to Århus District Hospital's radiological department. This time the principal character was followed by a film crew from *Politikens Filmjournal*, who recorded the funeral procession on its journey through the town and into the path of the X-rays. It was thought fully justified to film the man and to show him to the entire world as it was only here, in northernmost Europe, that such ancient well-preserved corpses could be encountered. It was the last time he was exposed in a intact state. The decision concerning his autopsy had been taken. This was probably not without a good few ethical deliberations, but scientific interests and his continued preservation had a high priority. It was planned to use his liver for radiocarbon dating – a recent revolution in archaeological dating. There was also interest in what lay hidden within his gut. What had he eaten for his final meal? It was hoped to gain new information on Iron Age diet and agriculture and to try to determine the

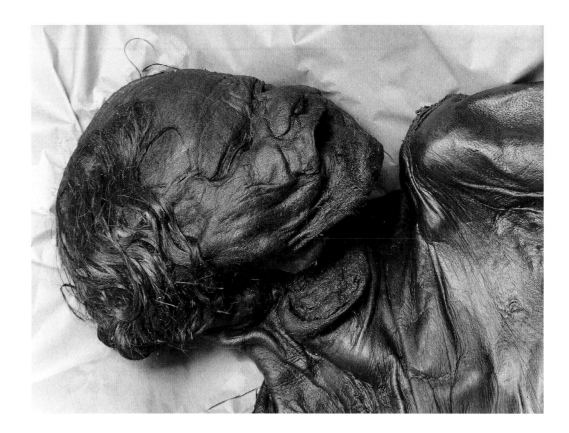

Where it was expected to find a noose there was a gaping wound to the throat, cut from ear to ear.

extent to which his Last Supper was of a ritual nature. A similar investigation had been carried out, as the first, on the contents of the large intestine of a bog body found in the bog Borremosen in Himmerland in 1946. This had shown that it was still possible to detect and identify seeds and plant remains, even after passage through the digestion system and two thousand years in a bog. Seen pragmatically, the decision concerning the autopsy was also necessary with respect to his conservation, *i.e.* to remove the easily decomposed internal organs in order to be able to carry out a successful conservation. This was something the Ancient Egyptians had also learnt.

On 31st May, pro-sector Professor Willy Munck arrived with his assistant and his secretary and carried out the autopsy at the museum. Munck made a cut extending from just under the middle of the sternum, down to the symphysis and out into the right groin area, where a wound had already been detected. Inside the rib cage were the remains of the lungs. The liver could be readily identified as an encapsulated mass measuring 10 by 15 centimetres. It was selected for radiocarbon dating. The stomach and intestines were removed in one. They clearly contained a gruel-like, dark reddish-brown mass. The entire alimentary tract was sent to be washed out by archaeobotanist Hans Helbæk, who had previously analysed the still undigested remains of Tollund Man's last meal. The other organs could not be identified. Further confirmation was provided that this was indeed a Grauballe *man* in that a flat "object" was found inside the scrotum, presumed to be a testicle. The latter was, according to a press photographer who was present, solemnly dropped into a jar of alcohol with the comment: "One 2000-year-old testicle." It has not been seen since.

Normally, we mortals prefer not to have anything to do death certificates. We prefer them to be hidden away in filing cabinets. We would rather not hear too much about the work of forensic scientists and post-mortem examiners. It can seem unnecessarily macabre. But in the case of Grauballe Man, through the medium of the press, it became legitimate to deal with these subjects. Professor Munck must have thought things through in this respect, as he stated to the newspaper: "that there is neither curiosity nor a desire for sensation behind the work that is now being carried out. It should be made clear that the work is being done in the name of science and with due veneration." It must, nevertheless, have given rise to certain ethical and humane scruples when Glob so single-mindedly handed Grauballe Man over to science. Seen with modern eyes, this was a ground-breaking, cross-disciplinary piece of work, the like of which we have first acquired a tradition for during recent decades.

After the exhibition closed and science took over, the daily newspapers followed the sequence of events very closely and put pictures and news on the streets every day. The

Several of Grauballe Man's molars were worn down to their roots.

public were able to follow the investigations and gain an insight into the researchers' considerations throughout the whole process. This is where it was made known that the man died from a blow with a blunt object to the temple, causing a fractured skull. Subsequently, his throat was cut using a sharp instrument. He had also a fracture to his left tibia, presumed to originate from the time of his death, and there were traces of an earlier fracture to the left humerus. Readers must have been very confused by the many gruesome but also conflicting pieces of information the newspapers printed about his terrible death. Unanimously, however, they informed the public that his cut throat was a sensation, as the several bog bodies found previously had all been hanged.

The experts' own interpretations of the results of their investigations were first published at the end of the year in The Jutland Archaeological Society's own journal *Kuml*. With reference to his age, state of health and final moments, they concluded that he was about 30 years of age when he died, apparently healthy, though with the beginnings of arthritis. The cause of death was a deep cut high up on the throat, running from ear to ear and extending all the way back to the vertebrae of the neck, causing his carotid artery also to be severed. In connection with his death, or immediately afterwards, his skull was fractured at the right temple, presumably with a blunt instrument. The oblique fracture to his left tibia was thought to have been caused by a direct blow while he was still alive.

The head of Vendsyssel Historical Museum, Holger Friis was a keen amateur archaeologist and, furthermore, a dentist by profession. He was extremely interested in analysing Grauballe Man's teeth and, on 23rd May, he arrived at the museum in Århus

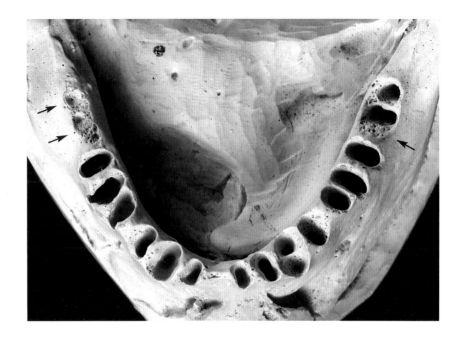

Plaster cast of Grauballe Man's gums, after his teeth had been removed. He lost an incisor from his lower jaw long before his death. He had lost molars from both his lower and upper jaw due to periodontitis.

together with local dentist Eigil Warrer. Seven teeth remained in place in Grauballe Man's upper jaw, in the lower jaw there were only five. But there were clear apertures in the jaws where a further fourteen teeth had sat. Nine of the missing teeth lay loose in various places inside his mouth. No signs were found of the man having had wisdom teeth. The teeth were dark and very small and the crowns were worn. The teeth that were still in place in the jaws were pulled out by the dentists and put into tap water. All 21 teeth were taken away by them to Warrer's school dentistry clinic in Risskov in order to be X-rayed. Out of consideration for orthodontological investigations, plaster casts were made of Grauballe Man's gums. The many dental examinations involving the taking of casts, and probably also the many previous displays of his dentition, had resulted in his lips and the soft tissue around his mouth becoming loose, and ever since then he has had an open and slightly pained expression around his mouth. When he was discovered, his mouth was closed.

Unfortunately, detailed investigations of his teeth were never carried out, but on the basis of a preliminary evaluation it could be established that he had lost an incisor from his lower jaw some time before his death. "In a couple of other teeth, periodontitis and cavities could be demonstrated, which would, for some time, have caused him terrible toothache." The plan was for Grauballe Man's teeth to be returned to where they rightly belonged. They were, however, mislaid at the Dental College and were not returned to the Prehistoric Museum until 1963 – in a desiccated state. As they had shrunk considerably, the idea of replacing them was abandoned. Posterity has therefore had to live with Grauballe Man's open-mouthed, toothless expression.

The last meal

Grauballe Man's last meal, or rather meals, judging from the 610 cubic centimetres of gut contents which was recovered, were still so well preserved that archaeobotanist Hans Helbæk was able identify what he had eaten two thousand years ago. Helbæk was one of the great pioneers of archaeobotany, *i.e.* the scientific investigation of plant remains found in an archaeological context. His many years of research in Denmark, including finds of grain and seed stores from numerous Iron Age settlements and the Viking fort of Fyrkat, plus his work in the Near East, made him world famous.

Patiently and persistently, he analysed his way to an understanding of the agricultural and cultivation practices of prehistoric cultures. The gut contents from the two bog bodies, Grauballe Man and Tollund Man, probably represented one of his greatest challenges. In contrast to almost all the other material that Helbæk investigated over the years, the bog bodies' gut contents were not preserved by charring, *i.e.* as a result of fire having had a preservational effect. In the case of the bog bodies, it was conditions in the acid and anoxic bogs that ensured the un-charred plant remains deep in their gut systems did not decay.

When the peat-brown sludge washed out of the gut had settled, it occupied 610 cubic centimetres. Subsequent months of analysis, involving sorting and identifying the species present under the microscope, revealed a remarkable spectrum of plant remains comprising more than 60 species. These were mostly cultivated plants and arable weeds, but also included species which today grow in permanent pasture and woodland. The meal contained six cereal types: wheat species emmer and spelt, rye, naked and hulled barley, as well as oats. Further to these were more than 30 weed species, including corn spurrey and persicaria which are thought to have been cultivated in Iron Age fields, together with fat hen, buttercup, lady's mantle, black nightshade, yarrow, scentless mayweed, and hawk's beard. Further to these were seeds of 13 species of grass, including Yorkshire fog and rye grass. The meal also contained a few bone fragments, which were not ascribed great significance at the time, as well as hairs of mice – a dietary supplement which Glob ascribed no further significance other than that they were probably mixed in by chance in grain and seed stores. Other organic remains found by Helbæk included spores and sclerotia of various fungi, including ergot and smuts.

In addition to cultivated species, Helbæk's plant list also includes a number of species not found today in arable fields but which belong more to permanent pastures, meadows and open woodland. His explanation was that, in addition to exploiting arable fields and fallow areas for the collection of seeds, use was also made of grassland and woodland. Glob believed it showed that the people who were chosen to be sacrificed were given a special meal, intentionally composed of the seeds of wild and cultivated plants before they were, through death, wedded to the deity responsible for the plants of the field.

A comparison of the remains of the consumed meal with coffee grounds is very descriptive of their consistency. There are millions of individual components and there can be no doubt that part of the meal had been ground before it was eaten in the form of porridge or gruel. The latter is the most likely, as the meal also contained charcoal, sand and small stones which, under normal circumstances, would not be expected to be found in a meal. So it is probably not too wide of the mark when Helbæk writes "that the food was swallowed without any conscious chewing."

There were no traces in the gut contents of the herbs and berries of spring, summer or autumn, and this should probably be taken as an indication of a winter meal. This conclusion is consistent with the perception that he was laid in the bog in winter or the early spring, when the bog water was so cold that its preserving qualities overrode the processes of decay.

On boggy ground

There was, however, one person who almost derailed the learned experts and Grauballe Man's triumphal progress. It was Jensine Jensen who started all the trouble. Her intentions were well enough meant. Jensine was an elderly farmer's wife from the Grauballe area, and she knew her local area and its inhabitants through a long life spent there. When she saw the pictures of Grauballe Man in an article in the magazine *Billed Bladet*, she immediately recognised an old acquaintance from her childhood. It was Kristian, Red Kristian, as he was known with his red hair and beard.

Kristian worked in the peat bogs around Grauballe. Jensine could remember that one evening, after working in the bog, he went to Grauholm to ask for help in cutting peat the next day. It was dark when he wanted to go home and the farmer at Grauholm said he had better follow the road around the bog. But Kristian was tired and thought he knew the bogs well enough to take a short cut. No-one has seen him since. Kristian was 42 years old, and that was in 1887, she clearly remembered. It was not until 1955 that Jensine went public with her speculations. By that time, Grauballe Man lay in his conservation vat and waited for the day he could be declared stable and well-preserved for posterity.

Already during the autopsy, Grauballe Man's liver was removed and sent under refrigeration to the newly-established radiocarbon-dating laboratory in Copenhagen. It was not that Glob doubted his status as Iron Age man, but with the aid of this very new dating method it was now possible to obtain an objective date for archaeological finds.

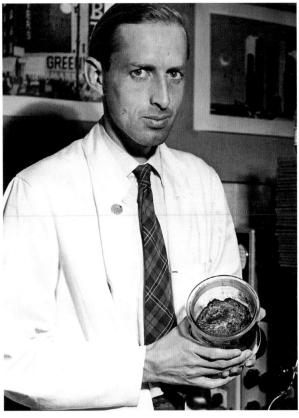

Civil engineer Henrik Tauber with the advanced analytical equipment in his new radiocarbon laboratory.

Grauballe Man's liver and some of his muscle tissue were removed for radiocarbon dating.

The laboratory in Copenhagen was established in 1952 as the first outside the United States.

The radiocarbon dating method is based on the fact that all living organisms, while they are alive, constantly take up carbon. Carbon is taken up *via* photosynthesis by plants that are then eaten by animals and humans. Some of the carbon is in the form of a radioactive isotope, ^{14}C, although this isotope occurs in such small quantities that it does not represent a health hazard. While an organism (plant or animal) remains alive, the proportion of radioactive carbon (^{14}C) it contains is constant. Once it dies, it no longer takes up new carbon and the radioactive proportion begins to decline. This is because the radioactive carbon atoms decay with time. As the rate of this decay is known, it is possible, by measuring how much remains in a sample from the organism, to determine how long ago it died and, accordingly, determine the age of the sample – be it from plant, animal or human being.

The result of Grauballe Man's radiocarbon dating was delayed because atomic bomb tests in the United States and the Soviet Union had polluted the atmosphere to such a extent that the radioactive dust penetrated cracks into the laboratory's premises in Juliane Mariesvej in Copenhagen. The laboratory's measuring equipment had to be modified so the dating process could, in the future, proceed within closed systems. But this took time. The samples had, from then on, to be combusted and converted to carbon dioxide. This had then to be purified, after which the radioactivity in the carbon dioxide itself could be measured with the aid of a Geiger-Müller counter, intended for the measurement of radioactive gasses. Everything had to take place in sealed glass tubes within a 20 cm-thick iron cabinet, so that the samples at no time came into contact with the atmosphere and its content of atomic dust.

Meanwhile, the rumours about Red Kristian and the incompetence of science continued to circulate. And a quick-witted journalist invited Jensine to the Prehistoric Museum in Århus, where she could meet her past in person. When she saw the bog man with his unruly red hair, she exclaimed: "Yes, it is him!" Her exclamation was heard by everyone and made the following day's headlines.

Johan Poulsen was, with his 84 years, one of the oldest inhabitants in Grauballe. He was knowledgeable about archaeology and had submitted several prehistoric finds to Silkeborg Museum. In 1887 he was employed at the inn in Svostrup, Svostrup Kro. It was the evening on which Kristian disappeared. Johan was in the taproom and was told to put drinks on the table for a couple of men who had come in and who – the other guests whispered – had been poaching in the large woods on the other side of the river Gudenå. One of these late customers was Red Kristian. The two men were not completely sober when they, late that night, left the taproom, and Kristian was warned against taking the route home through the bog, as he would be risking his life. But he chose that route anyway, and disappeared without a trace.

As to which of the two accounts of Kristian's movements was true, the local inhabitants were in some disagreement. But Kristian did not return to his idyllically situated home at Grauballe Vestergård, pictures of which appeared in all the newspapers. A lot of people believed most of all in the Iron Age man. Partly because so many clever people had come to see him, and partly because he had such fine, delicate fingers that never in his life could he have been a peat worker. This they could see with their own eyes, people who had worked in the bog for decades. And as one of them pointed out, "he is the only sensation we have, so we don't want to give him up." People talked and the gossip circulated and, by the way, Johan had seen and heard something at Svostrup churchyard, where some people one day stood gathered at a family grave, "Yes, Kristian is missing," they said. And who were these people, and why did it all first emerge now, so many years after someone had disappeared in Nebelgaard bog? That is what people asked one another.

Despite the fact that Glob was sure of his facts, lack of confidence in the experts grew, and soon the public were divided into two camps – for and against Red Kristian. The situation was not improved by a museum foreman publicly expressing his scepticism. He thought, moreover, that Grauballe Man's very light-coloured hands and skin were unusual for a bog body. The bog bodies he had seen were dark as a consequence of the effect of tannin on the corpse. He was definitely not convinced of the antiquity of the famous discovery. Neither could natural science come to Glob's aid in this matter. Geologist Dr J. Troels-Smith and museum curator Svend Jørgensen of the National Museum, who had carried out pollen analysis of the peat layers Grauballe Man was discovered in, found no unequivocal evidence for Grauballe Man being particularly ancient. Pollen analysis had, so to say, given up in favour of an exact date.

Growing scepticism among the general public, attempts to ridicule the experts in newspapers and magazines and the widespread composition of sarcastic verses about the professor and his misinterpretation, now called in earnest for a scientific date. If they really had dragged the body of a peat cutter into the museum for exhibition, autopsy and conservation and proclaimed him a sacrifice to the gods, then archaeology would suffer a severe loss of credibility.

The liver was to prove his age. It was, however, far from adequate, as at least seven grams of pure carbon was needed to obtain a date, and his liver did not contain that much. "Send more material," wrote civil engineer Henrik Tauber, who was to carry out the dating process as soon as the problem of atomic dust had been solved. The poor conservator, who was also responsible for the man's future, had to cut another lump off the corpse. This time, according the conservator's diary entry, muscle tissue from his abdominal cavity was chosen.

So, finally, on 7th May 1956 came the judgement, and *Politiken* broke the news everybody had been waiting for under the headline "Atoms knock out Red Kristian." The experts received their well-deserved rehabilitation and Grauballe Man had manifested his cultural origins – he was an Iron Age man and had his time on earth at the beginning of the fourth century after the birth of Christ. He died, in scientific terms, in AD 310 ±100.

Grauballe Man was by this time already conserved and exhibited, and visitors to his display case could ponder and reflect on the exceptional properties of the bog and mirror themselves in an Iron Age life.

A sought after research object

That very same month it was reported in a couple of Danish daily newspapers that an American professor of anthropology, Dr William B. Laughlin, was visiting Grauballe Man on his way to Greenland. Laughlin lectured in anthropology, the study of humans and their various races, at the University of Wisconsin. He was working on a research project on the cultural origins of the population of Greenland. On the basis of a deter-

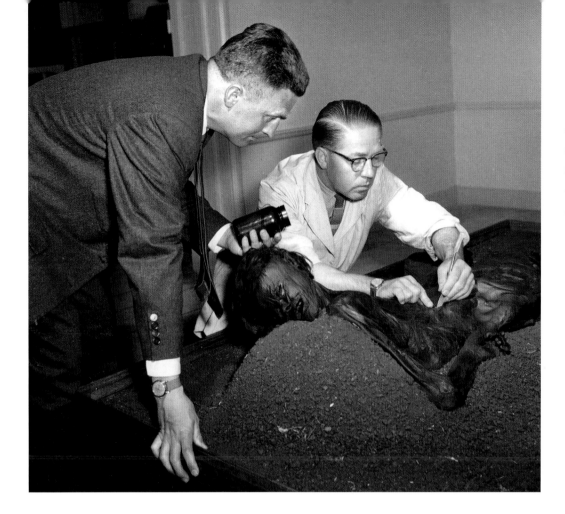

mination of the blood groups of 112 Greenlandic shipyard workers from Holsteinsborg, Laughlin could document, according to *Politiken*, "that Greenlanders today are nothing like the mixed products of Eskimos and Europeans, especially Danes, previously thought to be the case". The results of his investigations support the theory that the Inuit originated from Siberia and Asia and that they arrived *via* Alaska across the Bering Strait to Greenland, and not, as some thought, from the Indians in the West.

Laughlin was on his way north in order to take samples for investigation from the Greenlandic mummies. On his way there, he wanted to ask for bone and skin samples from Grauballe Man for similar blood group determination. Through this procedure, according to Laughlin, "it possibly can be ascertained whether the Danes of Grauballe Man's time were of the same type as modern Danes." Research into racial affiliation was at that time still a widespread science. Lange-Kornbak "executed the operative procedure," wrote *Politiken*. No-one heard anything more about Grauballe Man's blood group, but the "lump of bone" turned up in a remarkable way 50 years later, as will become apparent below.

Conservation of Grauballe Man

"Grauballe Man is now being kept in an artificial bog at the museum. The natural oak-bark tanning will be continued under controlled conditions for 18 months."

The Iron Age man should be conserved intact and in his entirety. This was the conclusion of long ethical and conservation-related deliberations. A conservator had never before faced this kind of professional challenge. And relative to the research agendas and ethics of the time, it was definitely not an obvious outcome.

Status of the preservation debate

The majority of the several hundred bog bodies encountered in Northwest European bogs over the years have subsequently been lost to posterity. Or, more correctly, there was not at the time an understanding of the cultural-historical value of these discoveries. The finders simply informed the judicial authorities as it was thought a crime had been committed. As a forensic inquest never succeeded in identifying the deceased or solving the mystery of the murder, the body was simply buried in the nearest churchyard. In other cases, bodies were hastily re-buried in the bog or simply just allowed to desiccate, becoming lost to posterity and surviving only as a note on a piece of paper. Only very few were taken in to museums where most of them were allowed to languish on a shelf in the museum stores.

It was the Danish archaeologist J.J.A. Worsaae who demonstrated the cultural-historical context of bog bodies. His first scholarly piece of work concerned the interpretation of a woman's body found in 1835 in a bog at Haraldskær near Jelling. Historians maintained the body was that of Queen Gunhild, Eric Blood-axe's cunning and quick-witted spouse. Worsaae contested this and maintained that the female corpse must be seen in the light of other discoveries of a similar nature from bogs and could not be identified as any particular historical figure. The experts' scholarly polemic prompted amusement among the general public, not least after the performance of J.C. Hostrup's

Huldremose Woman's comb, which accompanied her into the bog.

comedy *En Spurv i Tranedans* (A Sparrow Doing a Crane Dance) from 1846, in which Queen Gunhild of the bog rises up onto the stage.

Despite Worsaae's clear convictions concerning the cultural origins of bog bodies, it was apparently not commonly acknowledged throughout his own National Museum in the Prince's Palace, Copenhagen. In 1913, the Institute of Forensic Medicine in Copenhagen received a box containing a corpse from the judicial district office in Kolding. It had been found in Vester Torsted bog near Kolding. On the upper part of the torso of the corpse were the remains of a "leather shirt" or, more correctly, a leather cape made of pieces of hide sewn together, with a casing at the neck. The body was intact when it was found, but had suffered somewhat from being dug out of the bog. It must have been the body of a man, judging from the stubble on the chin. The corpse showed no signs of violence and the cause of death could not be ascertained. Curator J. Olrik of the National Museum's Second Department contributed to the case with a cultural-historical conclusion that includes the following: "As these finds (bog bodies) definitely do not constitute a discrete group, which does not belong in prehistory – the prehistoric archaeologists will have nothing to do with them – and neither will the civil community in Christian times, the burial practices of whom are well known, it seems most obvious to assign them to the gypsies, who were not members of the civil community and who are also known to have allowed individual persons who caused them trouble to disappear very quickly. Also the fact that these finds only occur in Jutish bogs indicates the same. If this assumption is correct, none of the bog bodies can be older than about AD 1500. The hypothesis advanced that the corpse was that of a labourer who died around 1860 suffers from the same improbability. A labourer of the civil community can hardly be conceived at that time to have been dressed in such a patched animal-skin waistcoat such as that which the corpse from Torsted bog was wrapped in. The museum concludes that the body is that of a gypsy, whose origin it is futile to investigate." He also remarks that "at another of these finds, which otherwise, due to the lack of accompanying items, are difficult to date, a comb was found which does not resemble those combs known from prehistory."

The comb must be that of Huldremose Woman. Her well-preserved Iron Age corpse, was found, wrapped in clothing, in 1879 in a bog of the same name on Djursland. According to the description, the cape on the corpse from Vester Torsted corresponds closely to leather capes seen on other bog bodies. It was science's loss that Worsaae's conclusions were not common knowledge in all departments of the museum, not even 70 years after he had clearly presented his interpretation of bog bodies. Had that been the case, the "gypsy", and his skin cape, would probably not have gone the way of all flesh.

This is roughly how many bog bodies ended their earthly afterlife. At the time, methods were not available to date the finds more closely. Methods from the natural sciences, such as botanical pollen analysis, had not yet been invented and for many years there was a reluctance to accept the cultural-historical context of the bodies. Re-burial of these corpses in consecrated ground continued even up to the middle of the last century. However, an expansion in peat extraction during World War II and subsequent years, brought with it several further finds of bog bodies. The corpse of a man from Borremose in Himmerland, found in 1946, was termed the best preserved example "in living memory". In 1948, another bog body was discovered in Borremose, and in 1950, Tollund Man turned up in Bjældskovdal bog, west of Silkeborg.

The bodies from Borremose were taken to the National Museum where they subsequently were kept in zinc boxes filled with water to which formaldehyde had been added. This was the same recipe as that used by medics for long-term preservation of dead tissue. Shrinkage and bacterial growth are avoided, but in the long term it is not a good storage method as the tissue parts do, with time, become somewhat flaccid. There was never any intention to conserve the bodies from Borremose permanently, and there was no thought whatsoever of exhibition.

When Tollund Man was taken to the National Museum in 1950, no conservators had yet been appointed in Jutland. A conservation compromise was entered into, even

The female corpse from the bog Borremosen in Himmerland, Jutland.

Tollund Man from Bjældskovdal bog near Silkeborg.

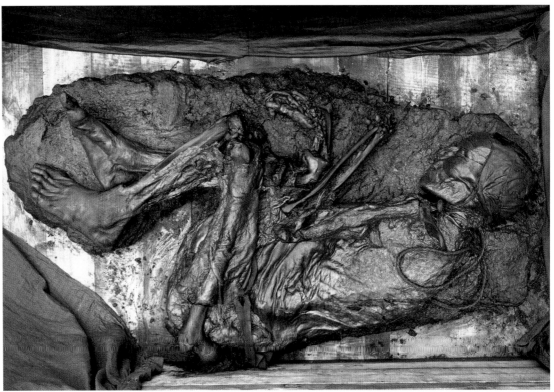

though chief curator Therkel Mathiassen was very sceptical with respect to the Jutes' desire for conservation and subsequent exhibition of the body. The head and the right foot were cut off for the conservation experiment. The remainder of the corpse was allowed to dry out. Today, Tollund Man lies exhibited at Silkeborg Museum. His exceptionally handsome head, with his serene facial expression and delicately shaped lips, is all his own, as is his right foot, whereas the remainder of the body has been reconstructed and is made of plastic.

Conservation of a human being

At the time Grauballe Man was discovered methods were not yet available for the conservation of large waterlogged items of skin, hair, bone and soft tissue. It was therefore somewhat of a challenge that awaited conservator Lange-Kornbak. The conservator was fully aware that the body would suffer if it was allowed to dry out even slightly. It had been difficult enough to keep the corpse stable at the desired atmospheric humidity, close to 90%, since its discovery two months previous. *The San Francisco Chronicle* remarked in astonishment: "A peculiar way of keeping him from disintegrating. Every second hour he was sprayed with water." The conservator was also fully aware that, out of consideration for a possible radiocarbon date, it was only permissable to stabilise the fluid balance of the body with water. Chemicals containing foreign carbon atoms would disturb any dating attempt.

Ever present, and with his water spray under his arm, the conservator had even so to note several times that the humidity crept down close to critical levels. The worst situation came when the police took prints from his fingers and foot. These almost dried out completely during the procedure. Then there was mould growth. After serious deliberations it was found necessary to brush the corpse with a weak phenol solution, only the stomach and internal organs were avoided as they had been selected for dating.

A plaster cast was made of Grauballe Man's ventral side. This cast corresponded to his position in the bog and was to be used in the coming exhibition in which he was to be displayed in a position as close as possible to that in which he was found. The cast was also to be used to check that he "maintained" his dimensions after conservation.

Lange-Kornbak was more than relieved when Grauballe Man, after two months of full exposure – including to micro-organisms and the doctors' heavy-handed touch and operative procedures – could be immersed in water to which 1% phenol had been added to keep micro-organisms in check.

But how could he now be maintained in the state that the bog had so cleverly created? No-one knew of anyone previously having attempted to "conserve an entire skinny corpse, intact and without desiccation," observed the media with concern. The art of

A plaster cast of Grauballe Man's position in the bog was made to ensure that, following conservation, he could be exhibited in exactly the position in which he was found. Lange-Kornbak and Glob.

embalming and conserving corpses extends far back in time. The Ancient Egyptians knew of this refined craft, but they took the formula with them to the grave. The embalmers organised themselves into guilds, and guarded their secret severely; nowhere is it revealed in the Egyptian texts. Elsewhere around the globe people also had methods for the immortalisation of their nearest and dearest, for example in Peru and Mexico, where recently deceased corpses were dried in the air or buried in sand. The Inca rulers were, however, embalmed by alchemy. In Australia and Africa corpses were, in some places, dried over a fire. The secret of drying the bodies was to remove water from the body as quickly as possible in order to hinder the growth of bacteria. In this way, corpses were preserved for posterity, but in a shrunken state.

Use was considered of the method that Knud Thorvildsen and B. Brorson Christensen had employed a couple of years previously on Tollund Man's head and foot. They had first dehydrated the bog body parts with concentrated alcohol, after which paraffin was allowed slowly – in a vacuum oven – to replace the alcohol. Their method corresponded to that used by biologists when preparing specimens for microscopy. The National Museum's experience of the paraffin method was known to Lange-Kornbak. He was also aware of attempts to use a variant of the method in 1876 in Austria for the preservation of whole corpses of the recently deceased. Despite the

exceptionally fine results, it could be established that Tollund Man's head had, after conservation, shrunk by 12-14%. Such marked shrinkage was not acceptable in the case of Grauballe Man and the method's large consumption of alcohol would, furthermore, represent an unacceptably expensive solution.

Among the many enquiries concerning Grauballe Man's continued existence, some were more-or-less of an occult nature. A French newspaper reader sent a detailed recipe for cosmic conservation. A pyramid constructed completely of wood, and placed with one corner towards magnetic north, was to be lowered over Grauballe Man. The pyramid would then capture cosmic rays and ensure mummification.

The conservator leaned, however, towards solutions of a more scientific nature, and had no faith in inexplicable miracles originating in ethereal regions. During forensic pathologist Munck's autopsy, he had had the opportunity to study the cross-section of the skin and had observed a clear stratification into layers of a "light-coloured core, somewhat loose and jelly-like, while the outer and inner surfaces were of a dark and firm character." This observation, and a collegial discussion with conservator Karl Schlabow of the Museum at Gottorp Castle, lead him on the trail of the correct conservation method. Schlabow knew of attempts in recent times to tan fresh human skin using oak bark. Lange-Kornbak reached the conclusion that the process responsible for preserv-

Tollund Man's head had shrunk 12-14% after its otherwise very successful conservation with paraffin.

Lange-Kornbak stuffs Grauballe Man with fresh oak bark prior to conservation.

ing the body in the bog was the first stage of a tanning process, which it now was his task to complete. But there was a long way from idea to result. "A pickled bog body," was how one newspaper, in astonishment, described the planned conservation.

"The reason that our Grauballe Man has survived for 2000 years is due to a tanning process that has taken place with the aid of the bark *etc.* of trees incorporated into the bog. As nature's own tanning process has been able to preserve Grauballe Man for so long, I now intend to complete this process with nature's own tanning agent, oak bark," wrote Lange-Kornbak in a letter to master tanner Aabye at the Tanners' Association's Research Station in Copenhagen, after having entered into negotiations with tanning experts both nationally and in the local Århus area. After examining a couple of skin samples from Grauballe Man, and some bog peat, the master tanner was able to conclude that tanning of the skin really had begun. But this could not be attributed solely to oak bark in the bog. "Humic acid" and "perhaps also certain iron compounds" were a part of the secret behind Grauballe Man's preservation.

An artificial bog

It was now a matter of finding a method whereby the tanning process could be advanced. It certainly was not possible to convert the museum into a surrogate bog and let him lie there for a further millennium. On the other hand, it was also necessary for the skin to be able to keep up with the tanning process which the fresh oak bark would initiate. The tanning experts recommended a treatment time of 18 months in a tanning

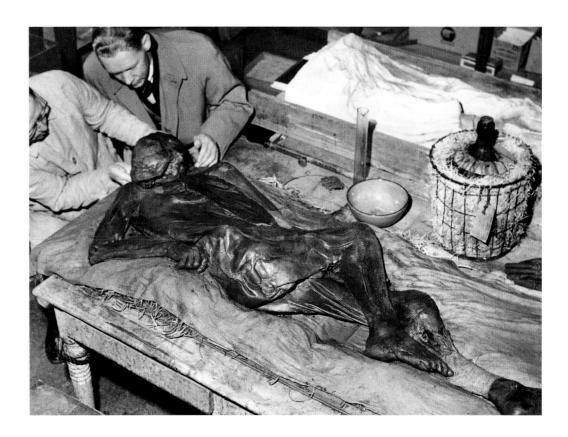

bath, in which the concentration of oak bark was steadily increased each time the bath water was replaced.

First, the conservator filled the abdomen and rib cage with fresh oak bark. The body was then wrapped in cloth in order to avoid pressure marks from the bark. On a grid cushioned with wood wool, he was then lowered into the tanning box, which had a layer of bark at its base. The box was packed and filled up with bark and, finally, water was added. The tanning box was made of wood; there is no mention of whether it was oak wood. A message went out to the public from the conservation laboratory: "Grauballe Man is now being kept in an artificial bog at the museum. The natural oak-bark tanning will be continued under controlled conditions for 18 months."

In the beginning, when bulletins had not been released by the museum for quite some time, people began to think that he had disappeared, swallowed up perhaps by his new boggy existence. He had not, of course, disappeared by any means. At first, he lay in his new bog for a period of three months and then for two further periods each of eight months. Between each bath of tanning brew, as the fluid is termed, he underwent a thorough inspection by the experts. Each time they were happy that everything was proceeding in the right direction. The skin became saturated with the tanning fluid and he slowly changed character to leather.

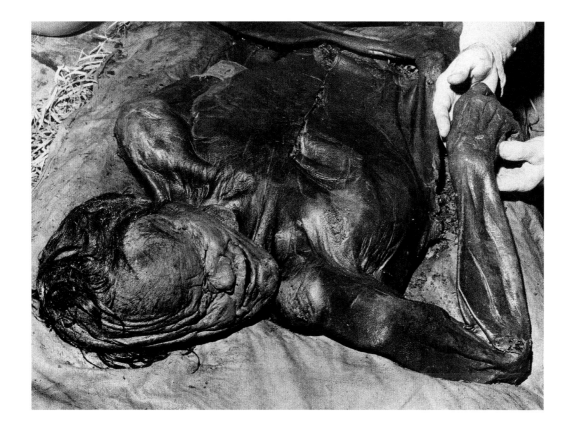

The public were impatient to see the result; would he, after two years absence, be still the same? Lange-Kornbak promised this would be the case by way of encouraging reports each time he changed the bath and press photographers confirmed his words with photo reports. While the body still lay in the oak-bark bath, the First Regiment's Soldiers' Association paraded with drums beating and flags flying in front of the museum in honour of both Grauballe Man and the museum. The bog body had sparked an historical consciousness in the citizens of Århus. The museum had now come into contact with sectors of the population who previously walked past in disinterest. Glob exploited this development as a gentle form of propaganda for a new larger museum, as the existing one was about to burst at the seams.

Exploitation and publicity

An interesting offer from Hother Hellenberg, a Copenhagen director in the perfume industry who also earned a living in show business, caused a terrible rumpus in the Jutish provincial town. For the goodly sum of 50,000 *kroner*, Hellenberg offered Grauballe Man a world tour. In return, the director wanted total control over the Iron Age man for a period of two years, for a scientific tour of Europe and the United States.

The director would, of course, also pay the insurance costs and for a travelling companion. The income from this rental agreement could then be used by the museum for scholarly purposes and the desired expansion of the museum. This written approach ended with an invitation to a meeting between Glob, Hellenberg and his lawyer, advocate to the Supreme Court, Karsten Meyer. When Glob failed to answer promptly, the director sent a reminder and a comment to the effect that the insurance arrangements were now in place.

"Absolutely no," said Glob. "Big city arrogance!" snorted the town's citizens. And the written press displayed its outrage, column after column: "We have to agree with the Copenhagener – people would probably come flooding in and a fortune in good hard dollars would be guaranteed. But in all other respects we disagree violently and we gladly confess that we are deeply outraged, really refreshingly outraged, something it is very difficult to be these days, when indignation is only associated with events concerning the Sixth Commandment, and in that respect not much remains to be invented. But this suggestion, this is one of the most disrespectful propositions seen for a very long time. It shows a completely bland and warped perception of what life is all about, a complete lack of respect for the most elementary concepts relating to humankind, namely life and death. The macabre in travelling around the world with a corpse, and displaying it for money, has apparently not been appreciated by the smart businessman – Grauballe Man died more than 2000 years ago and this circumstance apparently dilutes that which people understand by the term "The Horror of Death". But "The Majesty of Death" demands respect under any circumstances, and it is also this feeling that instinctively grips any person who, at our museums, quietly encounters the earthly remains of this country's former inhabitants. If one does not possess this feeling oneself, it will be spontaneously forced upon one when, in dignified surroundings, one is faced with these finds. But to use them as a means of earning easy money from the curiosity of the mob, this is simply the same as to violate the sanctity of the grave," *Aarhus Stiftstidende*, 5th November 1953.

Shares in Grauballe Man were sold to raise money for his glass "coffin". They went like hot cakes.

That same year an enterprising businessman had acquired the corpse of a Norwegian great whale, which he pumped full of preserving agents, christened "Miss Harøy" and travelled around the world with, becoming a multi-millionaire in the process. An inflated whale in a tent in the *Place des Invalides* in Paris that summer was easily able to out-compete Napoleon's grave as a tourist attraction. This was before *Animal Planet* and cheap airline tickets were within the reach of everyone. At that time, the cultures and animal life of foreign parts were still exotic and wonderfully strange. It was also that year that adventurer Jørgen Bitsch travelled around to packed village halls with the mummy Petra, which he had excavated with his own hands during an expedition to Peru. Of course, it was immoral and tastelessly commercial for the director of a perfume company to travel around the globe with a dead Iron Age man. But the boundaries of the term decency were fluid – also at that time.

In Århus, the West Town Civic Association sold shares in Grauballe Man in order to raise the 1000 *kroner* needed for his new glass coffin. The sum of 1 *krone* secured a share in the man and a certificate, the text of which stated that the sum would go in full towards payment for the world famous Grauballe Man's glass display case. Furthermore, and to avoid any possible confusion: "This share certificate is valid solely as a receipt for your contribution. Accordingly, a dividend can never be paid and the nominal value cannot be refunded, but for the help you have given in support of our work we would ask you to accept our best thanks." The shares sold like hot cakes under the auspices of grocer Østergaard Nielsen in Thorvaldsensgade.

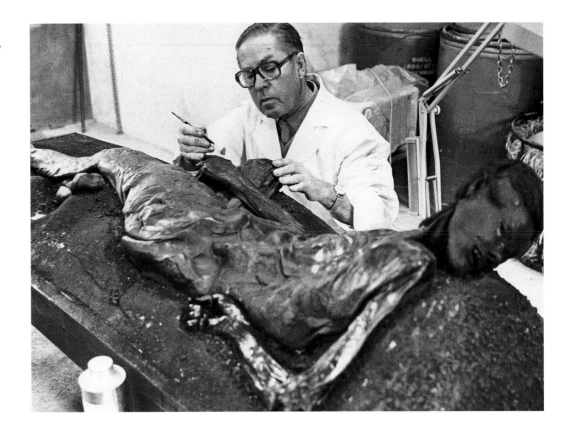

Following conservation, Lange-Kornbak spent many weeks alone with Grauballe Man. His profession as a sculptor attained its full expression.

Local publicity peaked on Århus Sightseeing Day in 1954, when the annual award went to Grauballe Man. On the town hall balcony, and under great festivities, the mayor, Unmach Larsen, handed over the prize of 1000 *kroner* to Professor Glob in the presence of 10,000 ecstatic spectators. Six contestants in the Miss Århus competition also accompanied the mayor and the professor on the balcony. The prize, the mayor said, was awarded to an old gentleman who had contributed to making Århus famous all over the globe. Mayor Unmach Larsen had himself also had a hand in Glob's transfer from the National Museum to the museum in Århus.

After-care – a good-looking corpse

After 18 months and 900 kilograms of oak bark, the tanning process was declared complete. "Grauballe Man is now leather," proclaimed a satisfied conservator. "The outer form and colour are completely the same as before the process," he added with great relief. Lange-Kornbak was, however, worried about what could happen now that the bog body had, so to say, emerged from the bog again. Would the corpse now shrink when the moisture left it? Grauballe Man's composition was now virtually that of shoe leather, and the choice of treatment agent therefore followed recommendations from

Even the black under his fingernails was removed.

the tanning industry for such material. This involved a thorough soaking in 10% Turkish-red oil followed by distilled water. After the oil bath, the bog body was laid out to dry, as it is termed when leather is allowed to dry slowly and at a not too low an atmospheric humidity. It was now make or break – would he retain his shape and volume as drying out gradually progressed? The conservator did not dare leave this entirely to chance. He was terrified that the body would loose its character and presence, and he began to inject those parts with the most natural form, especially the hands and feet, with a coagulating substance. This was an artificial resin that went under the German name of Cellodal. Conservator Brorson Christensen had successfully used it on wood found in bogs. Lange-Kornbak had also seen at the museum at Gottorp Castle how the form of a bog body's brain had been successfully stabilised by injecting it with Cellodal.

Anhydrous lanolin, cod-liver oil and glycerine are, in the correct proportions, known collectively as leather dressing, and the body was now rubbed with this several times. "So it could also last as long as was required," stated the conservator. Following a very successful conservation, Lange-Kornbak was proudly able to announce: "It could be, however, that with time the skin will become slightly dry and stiff, but then it just needs some dressing, exactly like an old boot". The public put pressure on the conservator to display the final result. For almost two years not even a glimpse had been had

*Conserved and durable
for posterity.*

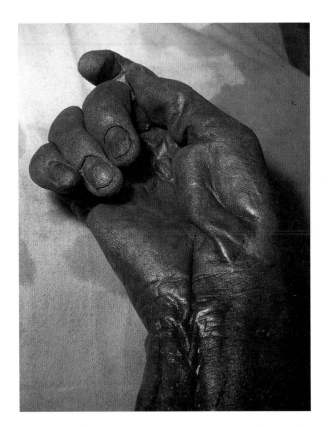

*During conservation his fractured
shinbone was bandaged. Later it
was carefully hidden beneath
artificial resin and wax.*

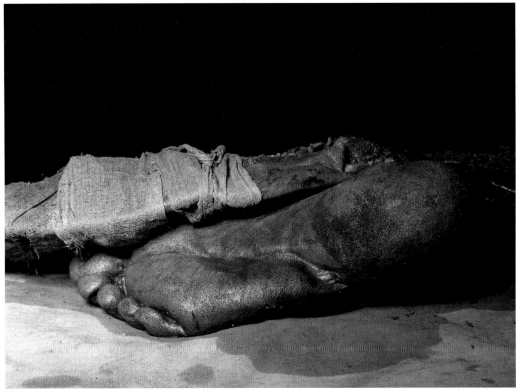

of Grauballe Man, and a further six months were yet to elapse. Lighter areas on the skin required interminable dressing.

The conservator spent the final months in his quiet laboratory, preparing a good-looking corpse so Grauballe Man could be exhibited to the public. The most stable parts of his body, in terms of form, were injected with Cellodal so the muscle tissue recovered its bulk and tone. The areas from which the internal organs had been removed during the autopsy were filled out with synthetic sponges. The head's collapse, resulting from the day of his discovery when a visitor to the bog unfortunately trod on him, was carefully reversed using copious injections of Cellodal. This restoration process did not have a conserving function, but was purely cosmetic, just like the small pieces of dyed modelling clay used to erase small cracks that formed in the skin. The wound to his shin was patched up with wax so that no-one could see that underneath lay hidden a fracture and skin lesion. Even the black substance under his nails was removed. There was not a mark or stain on the man that was not examined, cosmetically fiddled with and smoothed out. Even his hair was arranged under a hair net, like those worn by our grandmothers in the 1950s. This was to prevent it from detaching from the scalp.

This conservation work broke new ground and Lange-Kornbak received great recog-

It was very important to the conservator that the corpse should look good for exhibition to the public.

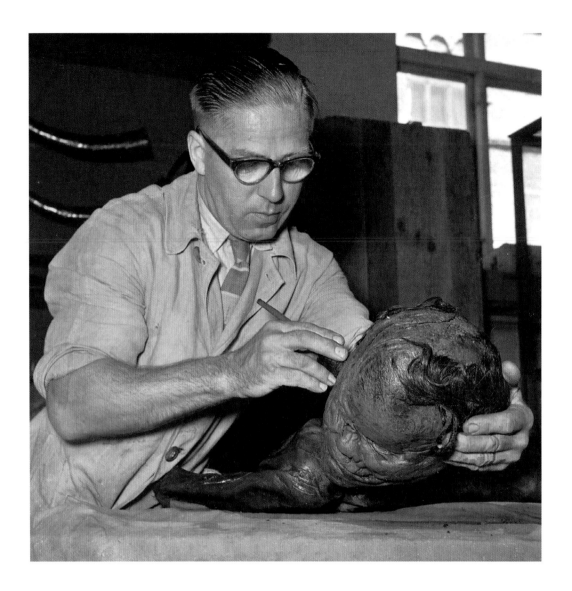

nition for his work. The news of the first conserved human body travelled around the world. Museum people from near and far journeyed to Århus to see the conserved Iron Age man and meet the wizard responsible. But there were not many expert tips to be picked up because, as Lange-Kornbak has subsequently expressed it, somewhat coquettishly: "Like all good craftsmen, I will take my secrets with me to the grave," – like all good Egyptian embalmers. This was probably not quite true. While enquiries flooded in from all over the world concerning the conservation, a detailed description of the tanning method was dispatched to the Chilean National Museum. Here, a more than 500-year-old Inca prince had just been found frozen in a mountain cave.

In May 1955, the Prehistoric Museum opened the doors of a permanent exhibition of Grauballe Man. He was given the place of honour in the museum's recently equipped galleries, where he shared a room with the great war booty find from Illerup Ådal. Later, he also gained the company of the mummy Petra.

It was professional integrity that motivated Lange-Kornbak to carry out his exquisite embellishment of the corpse, but it was also out of respect for the dead. As Grauballe Man's advocate, guardian and personal physician, he had spent more than two years in close contact with the Iron Age man and he considered him to be his life's work. Ethics, morals and professional ambition were very important to the conservator, who also had a well-developed sense of aesthetics.

In 1971, Lange-Kornbak was made Knight of Dannebrog for his efforts in the conservation of Grauballe Man. Where we today praise especially Lange-Kornbak's brilliant choice of conservation method, he himself highlighted the subsequent process of restoration. It was fortunate that he, as a sculptor, understood how to form Grauballe Man correctly, as he himself expressed it.

Despite the fact that the School of Conservation still shares an address with the Royal Danish Academy of Fine Arts, the profession today displays a strict reluctance concerning the forming of archaeological material. On the basis of a declared aim to display things as we find them, it would probably be the case today, 50 years on, that the decision would be to show reality, even though this can be brutal. On this point, ethics must today give way to authenticity.

In the scientific spotlight – again

*"The brain lies as an irregular mass lowermost at the base
of the cranium and continues down into the collapsed spinal cord."*

Since May 1955, Grauballe Man has been exhibited at the Prehistoric Museum in Århus which, in 1970, moved to the manor house of Moesgård, south of Århus. Again, he was accompanied by the magnificent Iron Age weapons from Illerup Ådal. In fact, he was located in a corner of the gallery, rather humbly, together with the briefest of information. If the museum staff had any ethical qualms about exhibiting the man from the bog, then the public approached him as the museum's crown jewel, the supreme discovery, the man from prehistory. He lies there with skin and hair and a life-like facial expression, and hands and feet one has the urge to caress. Like the bog he came from, neither land nor water but something in between, he is in limbo – between life and death.

Examinations from top to toe

With the approach of the 50th anniversary of Grauballe Man's discovery came the realisation that the time was ripe for an evaluation of his state of preservation and to secure him for posterity. The time had also come for a new, up-to-date exhibition, displaying him in full as the unique discovery he is. An exhibition in which the public could find answers to the many questions that unavoidably well up inside when standing alongside his display case. And – perhaps new, as yet still hidden information about his life could be documented.

In 1996, using the latest technique in radiocarbon dating, so-called AMS (Accelerator Mass Spectroscopy) dating, Grauballe Man was dated to the period 390-210 BC; this date can be narrowed down to around 290 BC. Modern radiocarbon dating is mostly carried out using mass spectroscopy, a method which enables the individual atoms in a sample to counted. This gives much greater precision than was previously possible and the technique requires only a few milligrams of material, in this case hair.

A quantum leap has taken place in science since Grauballe Man was first investigated in 1952. In the middle of the 1990s, research into mummies came sharply into focus. It had long been a favourite occupation of doctors who devoted their research and spare time to these kinds of activities. Initially, it was professional curiosity that motivated these studies. The situation changed with the discovery in 1972 of the uniquely preserved mummies of two children and six women, buried in the 15th century in a cave near the settlement of Qilakitsoq on the Nuussuaq peninsula, Greenland. Serious interest was aroused in what science can tell us about lives lived in the past. Doctors, with their professional approach to the human body, set up cross-disciplinary projects to investigate the mummy discoveries. A global network of experts was formed, meeting at regular intervals at mummy conferences around the world. The natural sciences were soon also invited to take part, for example in the fields of chemistry, botany and biology, together with archaeologists and conservators.

It was probably the discovery of the 5000-year old Stone Age man, Ötzi, in the Italian Alps in 1991 that prompted cross-disciplinary investigation of mummies in earnest. The invention of CT-scanning, by which an exact three-dimensional representation of the body can be created, providing precise images of the various tissues, bones, muscles, skin and sinews, has made it possible to study the body in detail without also having to make a single cut or puncture. The results of the investigations of Ötzi, better known as the Iceman, attracted great international attention. The mummy was a Stone Age man with skin, hair and muscles and he was, furthermore, a scientific object. No-one had the slightest ethical scruples when, immediately after his discovery, he was handed over into the custody of science. Not in the least - not when science was, into the bargain, able to construct a credible and detailed picture of a Stone Age life, lived 5000 years ago. The frozen mummy contained a wealth of information, which the natural sciences understood how to tap into. These analyses led to, for example, a characterisation of his appearance, his state of health, his profession, his age and the type of landscape in which he grew up. His clothing and accompanying equipment, comprising weapons and personal effects, provided surprising new information about Stone Age people's highly developed technology, craftwork and sense of design and aesthetics. Science took us up very close as his flight was mapped, his final 48 hours, up to the moment when, at an altitude of over 3000 metres in the Italian Alps, he was caught and shot - from behind, with a flint-tipped arrow - and subsequently died.

Since 1952, many new and advanced investigative methods have been developed which, collectively, can decipher a very great deal of information about a person's life. To date, however, no such targeted modern research initiatives had been directed at bog bodies. These were, after all, almost all "old" bodies kept in museum stores and museum staff did not attribute to them any great research potential. However, a phone call

in the autumn of 2000, to state forensic pathologist, Professor Markil Gregersen, Institute of Forensic Medicine, University of Århus, confirmed that it definitely is interesting and relevant to take "old skeletons" out of the cupboard and subject them to new investigations. This was the starting signal for a long and fruitful cross-disciplinary research project with Grauballe Man at its centre.

Besides his daily work as state forensic pathologist Markil Gregersen has, on several occasions, had the opportunity to pursue one of his great research interests, bog bodies. These included Haraldskær Woman who, in the meantime, had been grouped chronologically with the other Iron Age bodies found in bogs, and thereby finally cleared of rumours of her being the remains of a cunning Viking queen. For Gregersen, the enquiry concerning an opportunity to study Grauballe Man in detail, using modern investigative methods, came as no surprise. In the course of a short conversation, the professor had already sketched out in his mind a programme of investigation. This was despite the fact that there had been no detailed investigations of a bog body since the discovery of Grauballe Man. A similar enquiry to the head of the Anthropological Laboratory at the Panum Institute in Copenhagen, Professor Niels Lynnerup, prompted the same scientific enthusiasm and creativity in a forensic scientist who has mummies as his speciality.

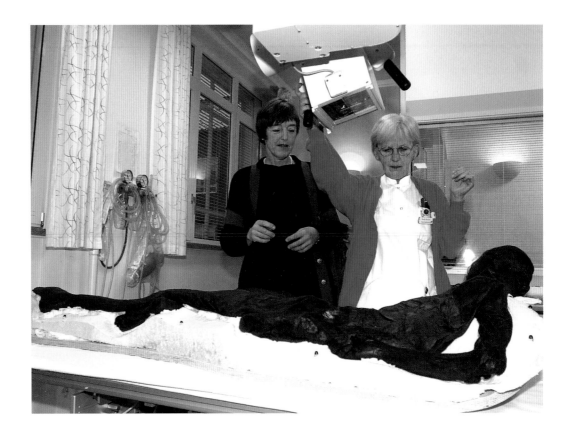

Radiography at Aarhus District Hospital. February 2001. Dr Anne Grethe Jurik and radiographer Sonja Sarauw.

Before long, support also came from chief radiologist, Dr Anne Grethe Jurik and lecturer in dentistry, Dr Dorthe Arenholdt-Bindslev of Aarhus University Hospitals. They constituted the core of a team of 26 experts: radiologists, forensic scientists, experts in 3D visualisation, dentists, archaeobotanists, geophysicists, archaeologists, conservators, and specialists in facial reconstruction and hair analysis. An intensive three-day programme of investigation, involving the admission of Grauballe Man to the Aarhus University Hospitals, was carried out in February 2001, with an effective series of investigations and visits to several of the hospitals' departments.

If we were not aware of the fact before, then it became abundantly clear on his admission to hospital that Grauballe Man is a national treasure. On the days prior to his departure for hospital, visitors flocked around his display case just to see him for a last time before his journey into the high-technological hospital environment.

Everywhere, doors were opened for this exceptional patient who was delivered into the hands of the greatest expertise in medical science. He did not, however, jump the queue on the hospital waiting lists, a possibility the press delighted in mentioning, perhaps in an attempt to arouse some righteous indignation. All those involved put their research time, and their free time, at the disposal of the project.

As was the case in 1952, Grauballe Man was, during his entire stay, guarded closely by conservators, who also had the pleasure of night duty. After the final investigation was complete, and all the others had fought their way home through the snow, it was a very unique experience to lie snowed in with Grauballe Man, in a two-bedded ward at Aarhus University Hospital in Skejby. All the fuss had died down and the hospital was again reserved for the ailments of the living. One couldn't help but smile wryly and sigh over the proximity of death and life, as the night nurse went her rounds out in the corridor, knowing he was lying alongside in the dark.

Questions for science

We asked the experts whether new technology could reveal any as yet unknown aspects of his life. Science had done a thorough job back in 1952, but had anything been overlooked that it would be easier to detect now? Conservation had left the body in a fixed state best compared with tanned boot leather. And there was, so to say, not very much man remaining. Only 15 kilograms was, in a collapsed state, lifted from his almost 50-year old support and placed in the arms of the waiting group of experts. Had conservation left him as "stable" as is required of such an undoubted treasure, and as the conservator had maintained at the time? Or would it be necessary to employ additional conservation measures? These were the questions asked of the conservators.

Radiography – taking the past up to revision

The investigations began with radiography. Using ordinary X-rays, images are produced showing the bones and the surrounding tissue. New images were to be compared with those taken in 1952, and the fractures and changes observed were to be re-examined with the aid of modern and more advanced equipment. Already in 1952, it was difficult to distinguish between the substantially de-calcified bones and the surrounding tissue in the body.

It was no easy task to examine a patient who could not co-operate and who, furthermore, required totally flexible equipment adapted to their own awkward posture. A satisfied group of experts could, however, after development of the first X-ray images, observe that the net-like internal structure of the bones was surprisingly well preserved. Even though there is, effectively, no calcium remaining in the bones, the skeleton still formed clear shadows on the images. The evaluation of the images quickly developed into a piece of detective work – modern doctors in plain clothes on the heels of their white-coated forbears from 1952, and archaeologists and conservators following in the tracks of the secretive conservator. It is true that doctors have, over the years, made many surprising and interesting discoveries inside the human body, but the finding of

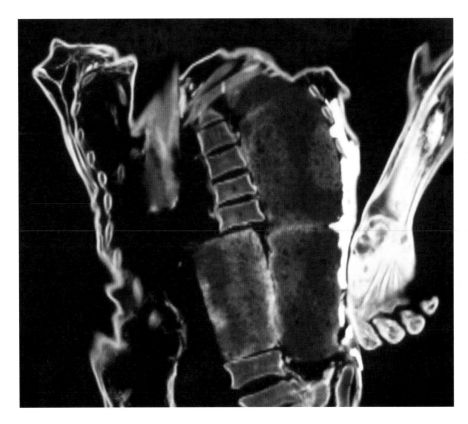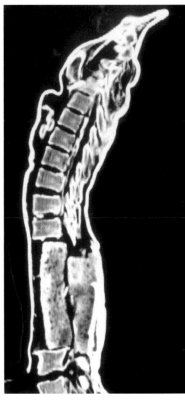

synthetic sponges is very much out of the ordinary, even for an experienced forensic pathologist. In the place where our four lowermost vertebrae normally keep our back straight, Grauballe Man had instead simply a sponge! There was no trace of his missing vertebrae anywhere, either in the museum's stores or by way of a note in the archives. We had to go to Greenland to pick up the trail. One autumn day in Nuuk in 2001, during a conference for specially invited participants with a particular passion for mummies, a young professor from the University of Wisconsin whispered to Grauballe Man's guardians that he knew the location of Grauballe Man's missing vertebrae: "In a jam jar in Alaska." Professor Bruno Frolich had seen them for himself as a young student under Professor William Laughlin. The jam jar could perhaps be found among Laughlin's estate, kept in Alaska. The lump of bone which, according to a newspaper article from 1956, was surgically removed from Grauballe Man for Laughlin's planned blood group determination was, in reality, four vertebrae and their removal must have involved a major operation.

The mystery was solved, and it showed the way forward to bringing Grauballe Man's "missing links" home to Århus. Furthermore, receipt of a now much sought-after sample of bone was to be anticipated – ideal for a new radiocarbon date and an analysis of where and what the man had eaten during his life. It was on the 9th September 2001

New radiographs and CT-scan images under professional evaluation by radiologists and forensic scientists. Aarhus District Hospital.

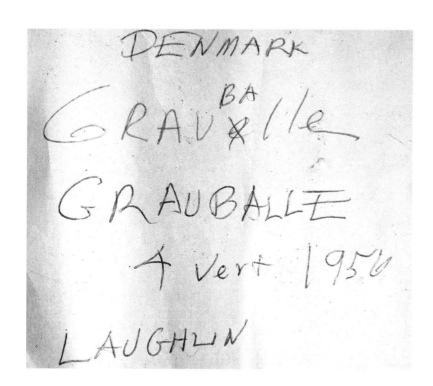

The four vertebrae lay in Alaska, in a jam jar bearing this label.

On his right foot, two toes were
modelled completely from
artificial resin. Radiograph.

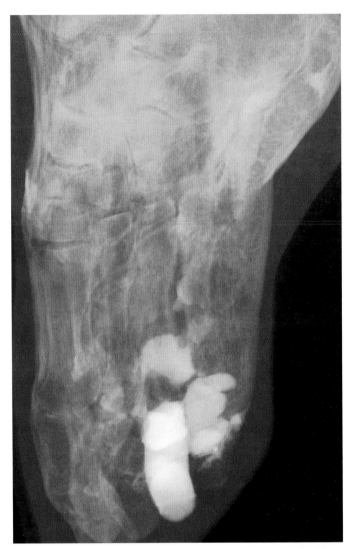

A total of 1363 CT-sections through
the bog body formed the basis for
three-dimensional reconstructions
of the Iron Age man. Section
through vertebral column, left leg
and silicone sponge.

CT-scan of the head. The rounding
of the head is reconstructed and
the form of the nose was created
solely with Cellodal.

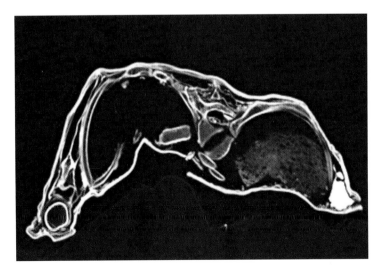

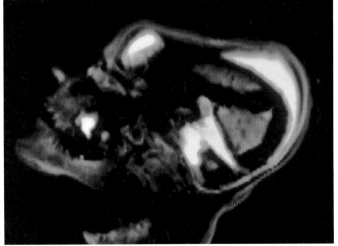

that we picked up the trail. Two days later, on the 11th September, when chaos struck the world and it again lost its innocence, the opportunity was lost for taking a jar containing some 2000-year-old vertebrae out of the American Continent. Although, by way of an inventive cargo declaration, the vertebrae eventually came to Århus in 2002.

Today, we know what lies behind the clear swelling of the skin over the vertebrae of Grauballe Man's lower back. The abdomen had also been stuffed with sponges, in place of removed internal organs. Furthermore, the radiographs revealed that the syringe filled with Cellodal had seen heavy use before the conservator could declare his work complete. In the places where the bones and muscles had collapsed, the "signs of ageing" were abundantly filled out with artificial resin. Two toes on Grauballe Man's right foot were also total reconstructions, ingeniously modelled in Cellodal and so well executed that it was impossible with the naked eye to distinguish them from the real thing.

CT-scanning

Computer tomography, CT-scanning, is a modern and augmented form of radiology providing clear images of all the body's tissues: skin, muscles, sinews, and bones.

During the investigative procedure images are taken of thin cross-sections of the body. The cross-sections are taken vertically, like slices of salami, 1-2 millimetres apart. Together, the images provide a detailed overview of the body, externally, internally, and from the front. The latter had not been possible for 50 years, as the conserved corpse is much too fragile for us to dare to turn it over. The CT-scanning method provides innumerable opportunities to isolate the individual parts of the body visually and evaluate them from all sides.

On the basis of 1363 cross-section images of Grauballe Man it was now possible to produce virtual reconstructions of his body. A brave new world in the form of two- and three-dimensional apparitions. There were no grounds for concern about the level of radiation – he had long since been declared a scientific specimen. Never-the-less, the man on the stretcher surrounded by the investigative equipment inspired great empathy.

An objective medical evaluation of Grauballe Man's head details the astonishing amount of human anatomy that has survived from the centuries just prior to the birth of Christ. Consultant radiologist Anne Grethe Jurik observes, on the basis of the X-ray examination and CT-scanning, that: "The brain lies as an irregular mass lowermost at the base of the cranium and continues down into the collapsed spinal cord. It is relatively well preserved with clear surface structure and division into right and left cerebral hemispheres as well as cerebrum and the cerebellum. The eyebrows are preserved, as are the optic nerves (up to the optic chiasm). On the lower jaw, there is a thickening of the

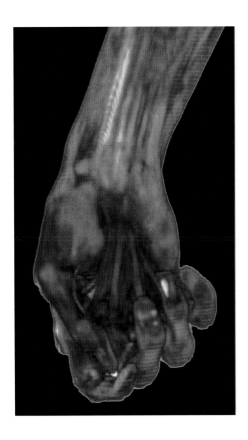

CT-scan of the right hand reproduced in two dimensions. Skin, muscles and sinews can be clearly seen.

bone of irregular structure in the molar area at both sides, most probably the consequence of infection. There is a 5 millimetre cyst formation at the root of the rear upper left molar. In the same area on the lower jaw, a *c.* 2 millimetre body of denser material can be seen lying on top of the bone, reminiscent of the small remains of a tooth." An evaluation of the cranium was, however, obstructed by the conservator's "X-ray dense" filler, used both externally and internally on the skull. "3D visualisation of the CT-data strongly suggests that there was not a vital fracture to the skull, but a possible break inflicted after death, either during his years in the bog or at the time of his discovery. Most of the facial bones have become detached from one another, resulting in Grauballe Man's "collapsed" facial expression," continues the radiologist with reference to Grauballe Man's squashed cranium. She continues concerning observations in the throat region: "The CT-scan shows that the gaping neck wound extends all the way into the vertebrae. Just beneath the defect on the throat there is, in front of the cervical vertebrae, a fillet of soft tissue containing the trachea. There is well-preserved cartilage corresponding to the trachea next to the thyroid gland, and there appears to be no fracture or other abnormality in the latter. The upper horns of the thyroid cartilage are relatively dark. A denser structure in front and above the cartilage may represent the hyoid bone, as the 3D reconstructions reveal two muscles attached to this structure, which extend up to the lower surface of the cranium. Based on the fact that both the hyoid bone and the larynx could be visualised and they have "avoided" the deep cut to the throat, it is thought that the cut was made with the head pulled backwards."

Anne Grethe Jarvik's detailed information continues throughout the whole body. The observations were hindered everywhere by the conservator's filler. There are no apparent changes in the bones to suggest osteoarthritis or articular rheumatism/ polyarthritis in the back or hip, as described in 1952. The lungs must have been removed during the autopsy and the windpipe, which is apparent as a ring to the left of the vertebral column, ends downwards in two threads that are the remains of the bronchi, after the lungs were removed. The thorax and clavicle are well preserved. The latter is fully developed, showing that Grauballe Man must have been at least 25 years of age when he died.

The CT-scanning also gave cause to re-evaluate the fracture to the left tibia. The fracture ran diagonally from above and behind the fracture lay several small pieces of bone. Around the fracture, the lower part of the bone has rotated slightly outwards, relative to the upper part. This is thought to have occurred in connection with the deposition of the body in the bog. The doctor is of the opinion that the fracture to the tibia probably occurred in connection with death. The diagonal fracture suggests a blow obliquely from above with a blunt instrument. A wooden stake could have caused the fracture. As the bone to the rear, the fibula, is still intact, it seems very likely that the

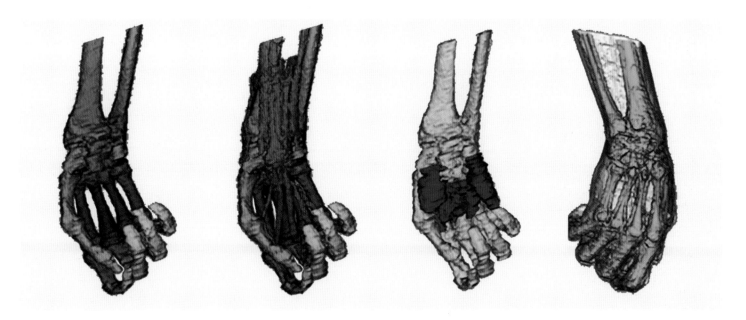

fracture was caused by a blow and not by pressure in the bog. In the right knee joint, a small cyst under the joint surface suggests slight osteoarthritis.

Apart from the two reconstructed toes on the right foot, the feet are well preserved, with bones, muscles, skin, sinews and nails. The well-formed pad of the heel is particularly fine. The delicate lines in the skin uppermost on the back of the heel are remarkably reminiscent of the "functional wrinkles" we today have in the same place just above the heel. The soles of the feet are smooth. The outer skin was dissolved in the bog, so the fine patterns of lines under the feet are clearly apparent. The soles of the feet bear no

Three-dimensional reproduction of right hand – bones, sinews, and muscles.

CT-scan of the cranium. The conservator's filler is marked in brown.

The CT-scan refutes previous claims of a fractured skull. The brain can be glimpsed as a small red spot.

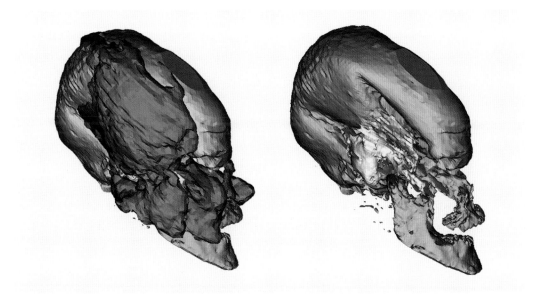

In the opinion of the doctors, the fracture to the left shinbone probably resulted from a blow.

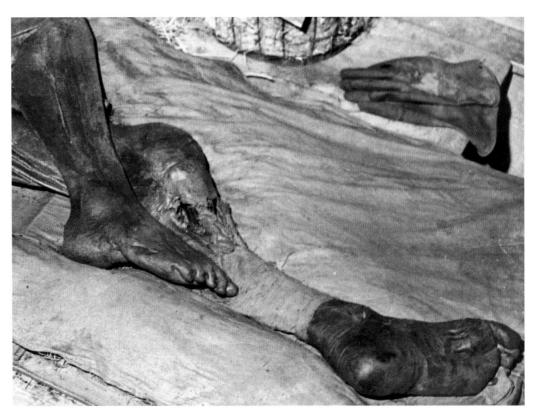

Small fragments of bone behind the fracture and the intact fibula are decisive for this interpretation. CT-scan.

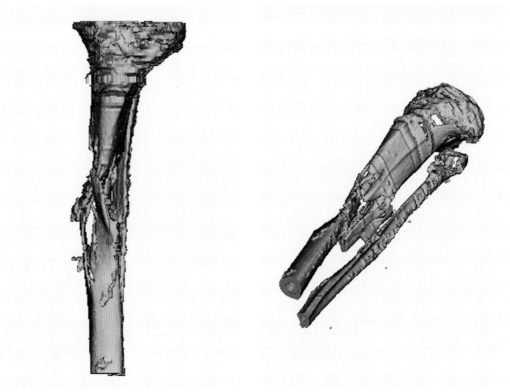

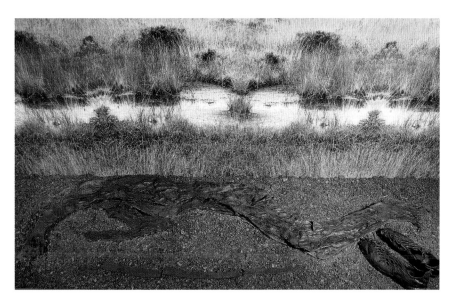

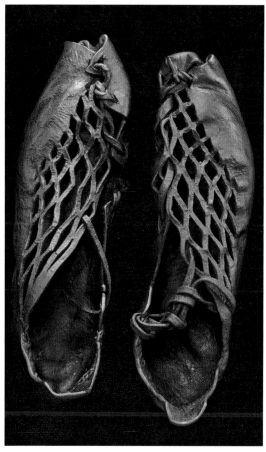

signs of scars or cuts, so we must presume that he wore shoes when he walked around on earth. Damendorf Man, an Iron Age bog body found during peat cutting in a bog in Schleswig in 1900, also wore shoes. He was deposited naked in the bog and by his side lay a pair of leg wrappings, a leather belt and a pair of beautifully made leather shoes wrapped in a pair of breeches. On the uppers of the shoes, open-work decoration of the leather forms a fine interlacing pattern.

Grauballe Man's hands are, like his feet, remarkably well preserved. This is due to the preservative properties of the bog having acted quickly and effectively on the small-er parts of the body. All the flexor tendons of the hands, as well as the bones of hands and fingers, resemble pictures of our hands when seen through the scanner.

Well knowing that *Homo sapiens* has looked much like us for millennia, it still gives cause for thought that an Iron Age man so completely resembles a modern person, down to the smallest anatomical detail. With one exception that is – an insignificant detail – a small fissure between left pubic bone and hipbone, which should be seen rather as a developmental variation. The radiologist notes that the bones of the legs have become a little "moth-eaten" during their stay in the bog.

Damendorf Man's beautifully made open-work leather shoes accompanied him into the bog. Schleswig, Germany.

"Overkill" of overkill

The presumed fracture to the skull which, in 1952, gave rise to the idea of there having been a violent blow with a club, fracturing the skull at the time of death, can no longer be supported by the evidence. There is no fracture whatsoever, but a gentle collapse of the bones of the cranium as a consequence of the pressure from the peat masses during his time in the bog. The foot which, by accident, trod on his head in the bog on 26th April 1952 probably also bears some of the blame for the collapse.

In the field of bog body research there is currently a debate in progress concerning the degree to which the bodies were subjected to so-called "overkill" in connection with their death. This is a bestial and, in our eyes, violent term which more than confers the idea that the victims, over and above the actual cause of their death, were stabbed and tormented to such an extent that bones were crushed and limbs severed. Every recorded mutilation of the bodies is most commonly interpreted as overkill. Modern investigations show, however, that the signs of exaggerated violence should probably be ascribed instead to the rather heavy-handed examination bodies were subjected to when they were dug up, and to their subsequent treatment in modern times. Bog bodies were most often encountered and excavated during peat extraction using rough tools. Furthermore, the bodies were often thrown to one side by the peat cutting until a decision had been reached as to their immediate fate.

When, in the latter half of the 20th century, people began to take a scientific interest in bog bodies, they were interpreted exactly as they lay in a miserable condition in museums. Not a great deal of attention was paid to the circumstances of their actual discovery. This was often just referred to in a few lines in a register. As a consequence, fractured bones and severed limbs were interpreted as part and parcel of a raw Iron Age reality. It was thought that bog bodies were punished traitors and lawbreakers. The idea came from the Roman historian Tacitus' account of the Germanic peoples who, according to his descriptions, had the habit of killing homosexuals and cowards and then securing them to posts in bogs. When Tacitus wrote his accounts the bog bodies had already rested in mires for centuries, and his account of the Teutonic tribes must be seen as one of the good stories of the time, containing an uncertain grain of truth. Overkill is a controversial matter that, to a certain extent, has won resonance in the media. Reputed brutal violence is good front-page material, especially if there is not much else to report. The term overkill comes from a time when people were more interested in death and how people met their end. At that time, methods were not available, as they are today, to reveal and narrate stories about the lives they lived.

In new research, involving the re-evaluation of bog bodies, evidence for overkill cannot be securely verified. One of the more brutal examples of overkill is Huldremose

Woman, who was found in a bog near Ramten on Djursland in 1879. Her right arm had been ripped off when the experts were handed her corpse. Since then, there has been a conviction that her arm was cut off in connection with her death, the cause of which is unknown. New medical evaluations of the fracture suggest it more likely that the arm was ripped off as she was discovered, probably because it was so fragile after the time spent in the bog. Borremose Woman from Himmerland who, since her discovery in 1948, has lain immersed in formalin at the National Museum, also probably did not have her face crushed in connection with her death. This was always thought to be the case, and it was tempting to believe so when she was exhibited in all her horror for a short period in 2005.

Bodies from the Early Iron Age have been discovered in recent years in bogs in Ireland. Old Croghan Man turned up during peat cutting in 2003. Whereas the peat spade previously was the cause of rough treatment of the bodies, today it is the modern mechanised peat industry that bears the blame for the fragmentary state of the three Irish corpses. Old Croghan Man was 178 cm tall in life, but only his arms and torso were found in the bog. On one upper arm he had a woven band of leather carrying a bronze amulet, bearing Celtic patterns. Small holes in the skin of his arms are interpreted as having been made by sticks which, according to the observer, were stuck through his

Huldremose Woman, Djursland.

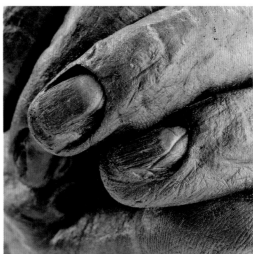

arms after death. The skin around his nipples is also frayed and is thought to have been intentionally lacerated.

The patterns on Old Croghan Man's amulet are interpreted as an indication of high rank in the wearer. In the Iron Age, prehistoric Ireland is thought to have been organised into small kingdoms. Within these kingdoms, the king's subjects demonstrated their subservience symbolically by sucking on the ruler's nipples. This practice has been highlighted by archaeologists, with reference to sources handed down through time. The latter were, however, were first written down several centuries after the Iron Age.

Irish archaeologists interpret Old Croghan Man and the other Irish bog bodies as deposed rulers. There are, however, conflicting opinions on this matter. The opponents maintain, for example, that the disfigured nipples are due the very thin skin found in this area of the body becoming dissolved. And the holes in the arms are thought to have been caused by the roots of wild plants growing in the bog. As long as the term overkill is accepted, doctors and other specialists will, with all desirable clarity, be able to find evidence for the phenomenon on the over 2000-year-old skin and bones of the bog bodies. The thought of a violent death is fascinating and makes us want to know more about the distant past when the swampy bogs were perceived as the entrance to another world. The story is a powerful one and fits so neatly with the theory of the bog bodies as punished outcasts or, as in Ireland, deposed rulers, sacrificed to the gods.

The concept of violence will probably cling to bog bodies for a long time to come, even though we believe today that the intention of the killings was not vindictive torture but sacrificial death in the service of a higher cause. Death can, however, be more-or-less violent in its expression and difficult to decipher. Ritual offerings may well contain a destructive or directly violent element, as we know from ethnographic accounts of societies elsewhere around the world. This form of ritual destruction comprises aspects other than those we normally associate with the signs of overkill seen in bog bodies and which we today have a tendency to interpret as agonising punishment. This will be dealt with further below.

A man past his prime – and hardly a giant

In 1952, Grauballe Man was described in the media as well-built and of the height required of a guardsman. In the 1950s, it was quite remarkable, and incited the ill-disguised envy of the mass of men of sub-standard height, when a young man exceeded the 175 cm required if one was to serve king and country beneath the bearskin helmet of a guardsman. Today, 50 years on, the average height of young men in Denmark is 189 cm.

A qualified estimate, based on the length of Grauballe Man's femur, puts his height at 165-170 cm. Tollund Man was about 168 cm tall and other male bog bodies have been estimated at 169-171 cm. Borremose Man, conversely, was relatively short, only 155 cm in height. On the basis of the skeletons from Iron Age burial sites, the average height for men is calculated to have been about 174 cm. The Iron Age diet of cereals and meat of, for example, cattle and sheep, copiously supplemented with the contents of nature's overflowing larder, was healthy and nutritious. The bones of prehistoric people are generally healthy and rarely show traces of deficiency diseases. It is first with the porridge- and bread-eating farming communities of the Middle Ages that we become shorter of stature and the skeletons bear witness to a greater prevalence of these diseases. With regard to nutrition, the latter situation persisted, by and large, until the middle of the 19th century.

Our age can be counted in the growth areas of our bones, almost like the annual rings of a tree. In Grauballe Man's bones it is possible to count ten pairs of double lamellae, here coloured red and green, and shown at high magnification. Ten pairs corresponds in men to an age of 34 years.

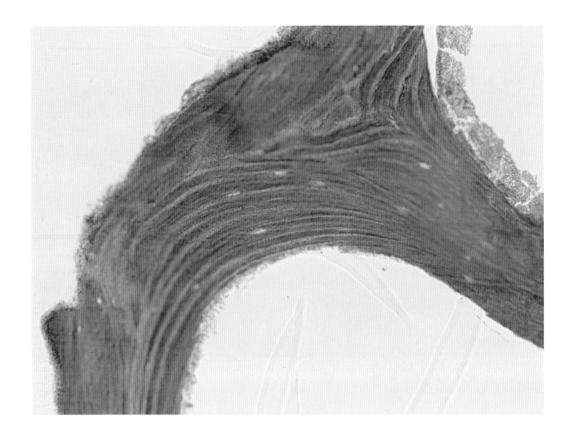

Grauballe Man had not suffered from arthritis, as was originally thought on the basis of the X-ray images in 1952, and his skeleton bears no trace of illness. An insignificant small cyst on his knee did not cause him any problems. The slight changes to his vertebrae are also completely normal, even for a young man who was not occupied in hard physical labour. He was apparently in good health when he died and had not toiled and laboured such that it had left its mark on his body.

Despite the fact that he is preserved complete with skin, hair and a facial expression and the natural wrinkles in his skin are apparent, the soft tissues of the body cannot reveal much about his age. On the skeleton, on the other hand, age-related changes or, more correctly, changes the skeleton undergoes as it grows and develops, are clearly apparent. The bones have growing points near their ends and these can be used to determine the age of a person, just as age-related changes in other bones are used to determine a person's age. The pelvis, in particular, is well-suited to assessing the age of an adult, as the bones in this area continue to alter – progressively fusing together – until around the age of 26-30. The frontal pelvic joint also undergoes a very characteristic development throughout adult life. The fusing of the sutures of the cranium are similarly diagnostic of age, but Grauballe Man's skull, as already mentioned, has collapsed. It was also filled with wax during conservation and is therefore less suited to age determination. Another age criterion is the wisdom teeth, their eruption and wear. Here too there is some uncertainty concerning an absolute age. We are not, of course, able to determine exactly how many years the teeth have chewed and wear depends to a very great extent on what has been eaten. The dentist estimates Grauballe Man's age to be at least 25 years, as suggested by the wear on his wisdom teeth, although with the same reservations concerning the composition of his diet.

A completely new method of age determination for bog bodies was discovered and developed during the reinvestigation of Grauballe Man's bones. Three small pieces of bone, of only a few millimetres in size, were carefully drilled out of his hip socket, through the gaping autopsy wound from 1952. These samples were intended to tell the history of the bog's influence on his bone tissue over the millennia. Surprisingly, the bones proved to be just as well preserved as if they had been drilled out of a young person today. True, there was not much calcium remaining, and they were peaty brown in colour, but the net-like structure, the cross-struts in the spongy tissue, the lattice that gives our bones strength and flexibility, was completely intact. The doctors noted that, given this rigid bone structure, he had clearly not suffered from vitamin-D deficiency. The perspicacious researcher, whose usual concern is the calcium content of our bones and keeping a watchful eye on incipient osteoporosis, then invented a new, alternative and much more precise method for age determination of Grauballe Man – and also of other bog bodies for that matter.

Seen in an electron microscope, a thin slice of our bone, one micron thick, resembles most of all tree rings on a tree stump. The secret is that our bones are, throughout life, renewed in small steps. Special cells create a hole in the surface of the bone, after which, the hole is filled in again by other cells, replacing part of the bone. At the same time, some lamellar structures are formed in the bone tissue. Younger people create much new tissue on top of the old but, not surprisingly, this process of renewal declines with age. The number of lamellae reveals how old we are. In Grauballe Man's bones there are 10 double pairs of lamellae which, when a little staining agent is added, can be counted like the rings of a tree. The process is, however, a little more complicated in us mortals where a conversion factor dictates that 10 double pairs correspond in a man to an age of 34.

This breakthrough in age-determination methodology is still so new that science has yet to accustom itself to accepting such a precise shot from the hip. So, out of respect for both old and new methods, we must say that Grauballe Man's true age lies between 28 and 34.

A young man in the prime of life we would say today, but human life was more fragile in the Iron Age. Even though prehistoric farmers and hunters apparently lived healthy lives and were well-fed, life expectancy was low and child mortality high. Every third, or perhaps even every second death struck a child, and half of adult males died before they reached the age of 35. Disease, hunger following failed harvests, incurable infections and war held the average lifespan down as low as 35.6 years, and men rarely exceeded 50 years of age.

Even though Grauballe Man, by our standards, died young and in the prime of life, it must be emphasised that, despite his unnatural death, he did not die earlier than was the norm at that time.

Toothache – a national scourge

Grauballe Man had, as already mentioned previously, 21 teeth in his mouth when he died, but one tooth disappeared during his long time in the bog. The teeth remaining in his mouth were pulled out and X-rayed in 1952 and then they subsequently lay forgotten on a shelf at the Dental College. At that time, there was a more lenient attitude towards such spare parts which were hastily removed and sent elsewhere for analysis without a second thought. But today, when the teeth have become relevant again and researchers stand ready with rubber gloves and advanced equipment, and Glob's clouds of pipe smoke are replaced by sterile environments, it is totally reprehensible that the teeth have, in the intervening years, shrunk or desiccated by 30%. These small brown stumps had to be placed under a large microscope before they could tell the story of a time, long ago, when they put the bite into Grauballe Man's welfare.

The teeth were well used during the almost 30 years they chewed Iron Age food. The tooth crowns are so worn that fear of the dentist is not necessarily a prerequisite for experiencing chilling sensations in the oral cavity on discovering that many of the teeth are absolutely flat and polished on their upper surfaces and completely worn down to the roots. He had lost four teeth while alive. Fortunately, the dentists in 1952 were wise enough to take casts of his jaws so we are able to reveal today the reason why. Periodontitis caused the loss of two teeth from his lower jaw. The infection was due to tooth wear so extreme that a cavity extended down into the nerve, after which both the teeth and the jaw became infected. Finally, the teeth became loose and fell out. It would have been very painful. At the age of about five, he lost an incisor from his lower mouth, probably as the result of a blow that also struck a chip off the neighbouring tooth. He had an infection in his jaw when he died. An upper molar was worn right down to the roots. The crown of the tooth was completely worn away, and he must have suffered severe pain in his jaw. At the age of around 34, Grauballe Man's teeth were no longer well suited for food requiring biting and tearing, but this was not uncommon at that time.

Prehistoric people generally had heavily worn teeth. The cause must be attributed to the coarse diet people lived on back then. It was not uncommon to find impurities in

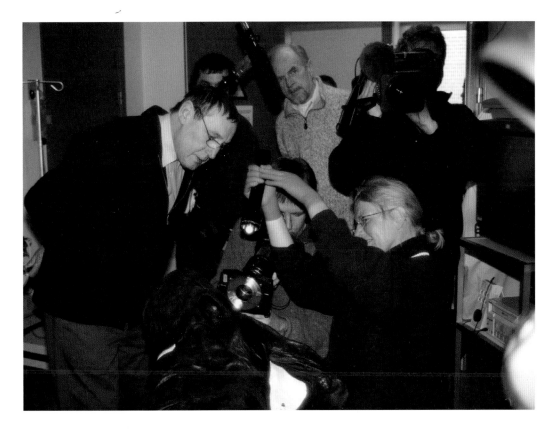

Dr Dorthe Ahrenholdt Bindslev
and Professor Markil Gregersen
consider that shrinkage of the
teeth, and the coating of conservation oils on the gums, make it
impossible to refit them.

the cooking pot or the bread, and there would be a terrible crunching and grating during an Iron Age meal in the smoke-filled rooms. The teeth were probably also often used as a "third hand" when making tools and carrying out other everyday tasks. As a consequence, toothache was very widespread among our prehistoric ancestors. The pain was solely due to excessive wear, whereas caries, "dental cavities", were a rare occurrence. The prehistoric diet did not promote caries and dental plaque had difficulty in adhering to the smooth, worn teeth. Only one slight incidence of caries was found on one of Grauballe Man's teeth.

It was first around the 15th century, when the diet became more refined, that teeth were spared this excessive wear. Conversely, there was then a rich substrate for caries on the uneven tooth crowns, which were rarely exposed to excessive dental hygiene. We know this from excavations of medieval cemeteries, from where analyses of skeletons reveal terrible cavities in the teeth.

As a small boy, Grauballe Man suffered from a serious, perhaps life-threatening illness. He carried traces of the illness for the rest of his life. The new investigations revealed ring-shaped developmental disturbances to his teeth, in a part of the tooth formed at the age of 2-3 years. With milk teeth in his mouth, suckling from his mother and chewing on his daily bread, his permanent teeth were, as is the case with us today,

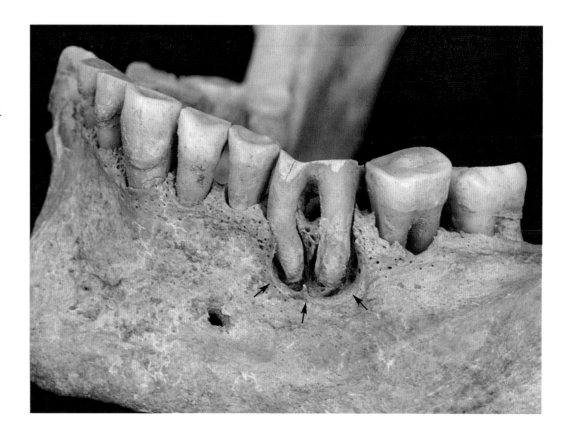

developing in the jaw below his milk teeth. Teeth are formed even before we are born and their developmental stages are fairly well-known. At this precise point in their development, when he was between two and three years of age, all the teeth show these changes, discernible as ring-like beads or ridges running all the way round each tooth. Only the dentine remains of Grauballe Man's teeth; the enamel has been dissolved away by the acidic bog water. Conversely, in skulls from burials found on sandy or clayey soils, the kind archaeologists are usually involved with, the enamel of the teeth is often all that survives. At present, we do not know enough about growth perturbation in teeth and how possible developmental disturbances are expressed in the enamel of the teeth – and whether it is at all possible to trace them there.

A period of malnutrition could be one cause of poor health, or simply some common disease or other. Infant mortality was, as already mentioned, very high in prehistory. Famine and disease were life-threatening for the young. Their parents were naturally aware of the healing and soothing powers of herbs, but were not able turn to the wonders of modern medicine. Neither was there a capacity for excessive care of the seriously ill in an Iron Age family. Only the strong survived

The life crisis that can be traced in Grauballe Man's teeth could also have arisen at another point in his life, after he had been weaned. The transition to solid food did not

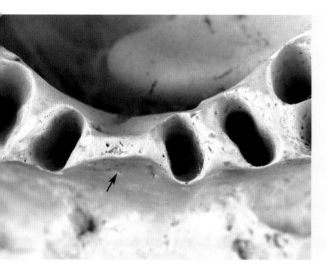 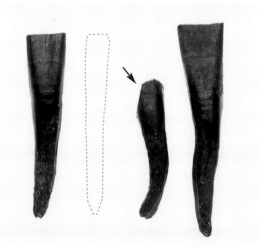 

Long before his death, presumably in his childhood, Grauballe Man lost an incisor from his lower jaw, and for the rest of his life he had a gap in his lower teeth. Perhaps he lost it due to the blow which also chipped a neighbouring tooth. However, the dentist cannot exclude the possibility that he never had the missing tooth.

Molar. The worn crowns were not so susceptible to caries attacks which, for the same reason, are rarely seen in prehistoric people.

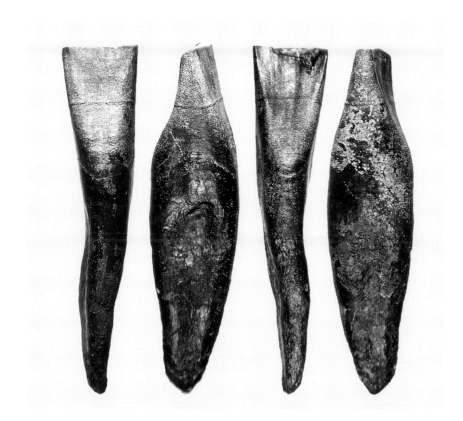

At the age of 2-3, Grauballe Man suffered a serious, probably life-threatening illness, evidence of which can still be seen in the ring-shaped marks on his teeth.

take place as easily and gently as in today's families with young children. The whole family ate the same food whether it was in the fields or at home around the cooking pot. In the past, weaning was commonly a critical stage for small children in many cultures around the world, even in fairly recent times.

The hunt for DNA

As with other modern research into molecular biological topics, a genetic analysis had to be attempted. This was not to verify the degree to which Grauballe Man and Tollund Man were related. It was in order to add Grauballe Man's DNA to the data bank of prehistoric material presently being built up and which, in the long term, should provide some exciting research perspectives in the future. Research in this field has made great advances and DNA profiles have been obtained for many Iron Age people.

Tissue from the inside of our teeth is among the best protected in the body and is therefore well-suited to a DNA analysis. The root tip of a tooth from Grauballe Man was therefore sent for analysis to the Institute of Anthropology in Mainz, Germany, where DNA research on prehistoric material is well advanced. Unfortunately, it did not prove possible to extract DNA from the sample due to penetration by bog water. However, research is advancing rapidly at the present time and before long a method will probably be developed that is able to draw out even a bog man's bar-code.

The last meal – Last Supper or famine food?

Emmer, spelt, bread wheat, rye, naked barley, hulled barley, cultivated oat, wild oat, green bristle grass, cockspur, timothy, Yorkshire fog, tufted hair grass, common reed, heath grass, wood bluegrass, lop grass, common rye grass, flaxfield rye grass, couch grass, oval sedge, field wood-rush, curled dock, sheep's sorrel, pale persicaria, redshank, common knotgrass, fat hen, goosefoot, common mouse-ear chickweed, lesser stitchwort, common chickweed, annual knawel, corn spurrey, meadow buttercup, creeping buttercup, common fumitory, field pennycress, shepherd's purse, wallflower, cow parsley, field mustard, parsley piert, silver cinquefoil, tormentil, field clover, lesser hop trefoil, flax, field pansy, field forget-me-not, self-heal, common hemp nettle, black nightshade, thyme-leaved speedwell, rattle, greater plantain, ribwort plantain, clustered bellflower, yarrow, scentless mayweed, nipplewort, autumn hawkbit, spiny sow-thistle, narrow-leaved hawkbit, smooth hawkbit.

This is the list of plant species included in Grauballe Man's last meal. In addition to these, there were fragments of pig bone. There were also spores of various fungi that attack mostly cereals and other grasses, as well as eggs of the intestinal parasite whip-

Hans Helbæk received great international recognition for his studies of prehistoric grain and other plant remains, including the gut contents of bog bodies.

Iron Age barley field. Historical-Archaeological Experimental Centre, Lejre.

worm, which is of no surprise in an Iron Age gut. When Hans Helbæk, following the autopsy in 1952, received Grauballe Man's stomach and intestines into his custody, he immediately judged the content to be uniform throughout "the system" and that no chronological studies were possible from stomach to small intestine. He therefore washed all the contents out in one go. The 610 ml of gut contents which resulted probably occupied a considerably greater volume in the form of food before it was digested. Furthermore, it probably did not arise from one single meal – his last meal, but from that which Grauballe Man had consumed during the last 24 hours of his life.

The interpretation of Grauballe Man's last meal as being ritual in character, comprised of seeds and fruits from a great diversity of grasses, herbs, and cereals, fitted well with Glob's interpretation of the man as a ritual sacrifice. It was Glob's opinion that his Last Supper was a step in the offering to the gods and that the seeds and fruits were gathered intentionally here and there especially for the purpose. The meticulous conservator and botanical expert Hans Helbæk, who had identified, counted, and listed the species in the meal, wrote, however, categorically that he did not see anything magical about its composition. He interpreted it rather as "simple food", possibly some kind of "prison fare", corresponding closely to the mixture of grasses and cereals he had already encountered in other finds from the Iron Age. There were, however, a couple of species that belonged elsewhere and were not from arable fields. They were more probably gathered from fallow fields or in woodland. The actual status of the meal was not established definitively in the 1950s. No unequivocal evidence was found to support its interpretation as a ritual offering.

Old gut contents under a new microscope

Since 1952, the gut contents, which most of all resemble old coffee grounds, had been allowed to settle out in jars in Moesgård Museum's stores, leaving a brown substance below an aqueous solution. It was now a question of whether, approaching from a new angle, the gut contents should be put under the microscope once more in order to arrive at a more precise interpretation of Grauballe Man's last meals.

There were good reasons again to find a researcher who would not just guess, but would also carefully unravel the truth about the gut contents. During the last 50 years, great developments have taken place in the field of archaeobotany. The method is the same, identification and counting, but the identification criteria have become more comprehensive and detailed and the analytical equipment much improved. Today, we also know much more about Iron Age agriculture and cultivation practices. This knowledge can be used as a basis for comparison for the meals eaten by bog bodies. There is also a continuing debate concerning the nature of Iron Age cultivation, to which the gut contents could perhaps make a clarifying contribution. Furthermore, in the 1950s there was limited interest in the actual amount of the various species present in the material, that is the proportion made up by cereals, persicaria, corn spurrey, *etc.*

For this task it was necessary to find an archaeobotanist who was uncommonly able at identifying seeds and fruits and who possessed a degree of patience that it can be difficult to find in present-day researchers. Only very few have the abilities to carry out this kind of tedious work, involving the identification, counting and listing of species from an ancient meal which has been chewed and passed through the digestive tract. Jan Andreas Harild was the man for the job – and he locked himself away in his laboratory for three months with his microscope, forceps, and fine-meshed sieves.

Helbæk measured the volume of the gut contents to be 610 ml. However, there was not this much in the jars at Moesgård Museum. After thorough searches of the stores here, there and everywhere, a small amount was found at the National Museum in Copenhagen and another in Scotland which, for inexplicable reasons, had been sent there from a laboratory in London.

Helbæk chose to investigate the whole of the gut contents, Jan Harild decided to select a specific amount that was, however, to be examined in minute detail. It quickly became apparent that the gut contents contained species that had not been identified

Portion of Grauballe Man's gut contents resulting from his last meals. The fineness of the material is not solely due to chewing, but that the grain and seeds were ground before cooking.

in the 1950s. We cannot criticise Helbæk for missing things when we know today that it can take several days to analyse just one teaspoonful of material containing several hundred plant remains.

The greatest challenge for the young archaeobotanist was quantification of the cereal remains and weed seeds – what were the relative proportions of the various species? It was here that the key to the interpretation of the gut contents would prove to lie hidden. A comparison with coffee grounds is not far from the truth. The gut contents contain millions of individual fragments, and there is no doubt that some elements of the food were ground before it was eaten. Furthermore, there were a number of "impurities" which, under normal circumstances, one would not expect to find in food. These included small pieces of charcoal, up to 7 millimetres in length, and small stones, of which some were as large as 8.5 x 5 millimetres, as well as a quantity of fine quartz sand of rather large grain size – about a dessertspoonful in all. There does not seem to be much tenderness and ritual associated with such a careless assemblage of ingredients, and apparently no great amount of love was invested in its preparation. It also contained a quantity of small flakes of charred and fused glumes and bran. It is these black flakes which, under good preservation conditions, are found on the inner surface of prehistoric pots. The porridge had burnt! Or the gruel, as Helbæk suggests, "the food

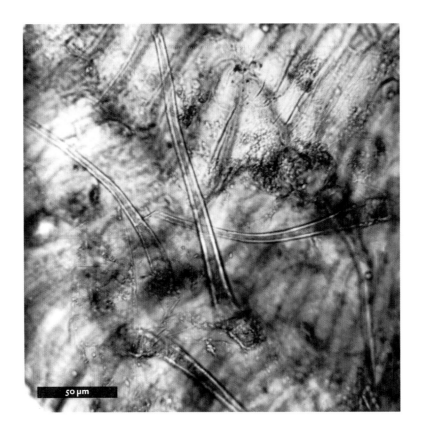

50 μm

was swallowed without any conscious attempts at chewing." We can concur with this assumption today, "as it is difficult to imagine that the man intentionally chewed the large and unwelcome ingredients – small stones, charcoal, sand – without subsequently spitting them out."

In the course of three solid months of work, 10 samples, each of 1 millilitre, were analysed. It took seven long working days to identify and count all the components of the gut contents in just one millilitre of sample. The reward was, however, a comprehensive picture of the species represented, and we also know now that marsh foxtail, toad rush, mousetail, field poppy, and wild radish were also present in Grauballe Man's last meal. The first-mentioned plants are associated with damp habitats. The latter three must be seen clearly as arable weeds. They were all introduced to Denmark in prehistory, possibly by way of contaminated seed corn. We will have to live in blissful ignorance of any further possible new species. If a researcher were to analyse all the components making up the entire the gut contents, Grauballe Man's last meal would become his of her life's work. It would take 35 years to identify, count, and list everything. And no researcher wants to be remembered for having spent the greater part of their working life analysing a meal which, at most, was swallowed in the course of a few minutes.

Prehistoric grain

Barley was the most common cereal in Grauballe Man's time. Next came oats and bread wheat, and finally rye and the two prehistoric wheat species, emmer and spelt, of which the latter has recently found resonance as a re-launched and reputedly healthy and tasty cereal type.

The role of rye in the material has been the subject of some discussion. Helbæk recorded a few hairs from the tip of a rye grain. At that time in the 1950s, it was thought that rye first appeared in Denmark about AD 200. This fitted in well with the first radio-carbon dates for Grauballe Man, which fell some time after the birth of Christ.

Since Helbæk's investigations, we have become better able to distinguish between the cereals, especially on the basis of small fragments of cereal bran. Some of the fragments that Helbæk identified as wheat and barley now proved to be of rye. It is, therefore, quite a sensation, knowing there definitely was rye in Denmark already in Grauballe Man's time, around 290 BC.

As mentioned above, the finding of rye in the material during the first investigation was limited to a few hairs from the tips of grains. Now attention was focussed on identifying fragments of rye bran. To do this it is necessary to examine the bran at cell level using a high-powered microscope. A magnification of a least 50 times is required in order to identify rye on the basis of its bran fragments.

Rye is a hardy cereal, and we know that it gained a really solid footing in Denmark in the Early Middle Ages. Then it was grown as a winter cereal using the so-called ridge-and-furrow system of arable cultivation, which came with the introduction of the wheel plough. Rye had its beginnings in small Iron Age fields. Stones, and various other rubbish, were laid around the edges of the small rectangular fields, eventually becoming heaped up to form banks. We can still see these "framed" fields of the Iron Age by way of aerial reconnaissance. The banks or dikes are apparent as a light-coloured mesh-work against the dark ploughed fields of winter. It is first around AD 200-300 that we are sure that rye had the status of a full cereal crop and possibly even a winter cereal in Denmark.

Arable farmers with a taste for weed seeds

The laborious analysis of the gut contents revealed, astonishingly, that cereal grains only make up a relatively small part. Until now, it has always been thought that cereals were the main component. Following the new investigations, the total weight of all the cereal grains in the gut contents – wheat, barley and rye – has been estimated at about 25-35 grams, corresponding to about 500-700 grains. The main component of the gut contents was weed seeds, of which persicaria (pale persicaria and redshank) and corn spurrey head the species list. The number of corn spurrey seeds is clearly the greatest, but the seeds are small and their collective weight in the gut contents is estimated at only 90-102 grams. The number of persicaria seeds is considerably less, but these are both larger and heavier and must be seen as being the main component with a weight of 315-367 grams. Seeds of these species together comprise 400-470 grams. In comparison, sheep sorrel comprises less than one gram and the other species on the list even less.

Weed seeds cleaned from the crops were apparently used for food in the last centuries BC and as this sorting was intentional, it is, in this context, probably wrong to speak of weeds in a negative sense. The seeds were, based on evidence from several finds, a resource and some of the plants may even have been cultivated. Many of the species represented in the gut contents, including corn spurrey, persicaria and goosefoot, produce large numbers of seeds, are very competitive and are superbly adapted to the environment of an arable field. It was probably hardly necessary to cultivate these species; they thrived perfectly well in a cereal field.

Weeds in the arable fields may also have presented some problems, as they would have ably competed with the cereals. The bog body gut contents demonstrate a great diversity of species that must have appeared as weeds in and around Iron Age fields.

Thin gruel made from seeds of persicaria and corn spurrey, some crop-processing waste in the form of spelt and emmer chaff, straw and grass stalks and a little compensatory grain, primarily wheat. This was what Grauballe Man ate or swallowed in his last hours, together with sand and small stones from the threshing floor, which scored and ground against his worn and painful teeth, if he as much as chewed a little at the food. In good modern Christian terms, it is difficult to see anything in the least holy in this "Last Supper." Neither is it any longer tenable to suggest that the seeds and fruits were intentionally collected for a religious meal. It seems more likely that the meal was a by-product of an Iron Age farmer's cereal processing. After threshing, the cleansing process probably continued by casting the grain across the threshing floor. This caused the harvest to be distributed in rough heaps according to weight. The large heavy grains travelled further than the smaller lighter grains, the light chaff and most of the small weed seeds. The grain would then be sieved to remove any remaining weed seeds, or sand from the threshing floor and other impurities. Ethnographic studies from other parts of the world have shown that the composition of the material cleaned from the grain closely resembles the composition of Grauballe Man's gut contents. His gruel was made from by-products from the last stages in the cleaning of the grain, the so-called tailings. This also explains why there is so much sand and so many other impurities in the food.

Spelt chaff.
The gut contents.

Measured by modern standards, this was a meal of very poor quality, but the nutrient content was fine. There are contemporary Iron Age finds of stored seeds and grain of a very similar composition. At the Iron Age village of Overbygård in Vendsyssel, a burnt granary was discovered, which provided a fabulous snap-shot image of a wealthy Iron Age farmer's household one fateful day around the birth of Christ. Charred wooden vessels, boxes and baskets together with 60 pottery vessels and a total of 100 litres of charred grain and seeds had stood stacked on shelves and the floor. These ample winter provisions, which all too quickly became engulfed by the flames, were sorted according to crop – grain and weed seeds were kept separate. Pots containing pure weed seeds, in particular persicaria and corn spurrey, were among the farmer's winter provisions. Some of the grain may have been next year's seed corn.

It is impossible to discover whether Grauballe Man's last meal represented the everyday diet of the time. There is no doubt that it was a poor diet which can be characterised as famine food. The food was probably nutritious enough, but according to our taste buds it would have been no great pleasure to eat. At the time of Grauballe Man's death, cereals had been cultivated in Denmark for almost 4000 years. Agricultural techniques were very well developed and people were able to produce excellent (cleaned) cereal products, of which we have many surviving examples. In other words, Grauballe Man's last meal was probably not the best an Iron Age chef could serve up.

Field of emmer wheat.
Historical-Archaeological
Experimental Centre, Lejre.

Persicaria and corn spurrey were tolerated among the crops. Perhaps these plants were intentionally not weeded from the arable fields because they were useful despite the modest size and weight of their seeds. Perhaps people even developed a taste for the seeds of these two species. Today, we eat millet, sesame, and sunflower seeds with great relish as tasty and flavour-enhancing additions to many dishes. Seeds of persicaria and corn spurrey could perhaps have stimulated an Iron Age palate in much the same positive way. Neither should the significance of the small pieces of bone, probably from a pig, be diminished. The porridge or gruel may have had pig meat at its heart, and even a good-sized lump of tasty wild boar would not necessarily leave many traces in the gut, but could have provided a wonderful taste experience, in combination with the healthy selection of seeds.

Despite the fact that the composition of the meals does not seem in the least sacred, especially seen in the light of the new investigations, it fits in well with the interpretation of Grauballe Man as a sacrifice. A winter offering, the ultimate sacrifice, in intercession to the gods concerning next year's subsistence. A mid-winter sacrifice, in which the last reserves are hazarded in hope of the return of the sun, and with it, the return of life itself. The last meals bore not the slightest trace of spring, summer, or autumn – there were neither shoots, fresh herbs, or berries. There is no doubt that this was a win-

Persicaria and corn spurrey.

ter meal, consistent with its character as the last reserves of winter. This conclusion is also confirmed by the state of preservation of the corpse. Stomach and gut, which are some of the most readily putrefying parts of the human body, were completely intact. This could only be due to Grauballe Man having been submerged in the cold, wintry bog water immediately after his death.

The last meals of bog bodies

Several of Grauballe Man's contemporaries from the bogs have also had their last meals subjected to the analytical apparatus. There is great interest in, and focus on, these meals and the stories they can tell about life in Iron Age society and the deceased's final hours. Tollund Man's last meal was also analysed by archaeobotanist, Hans Helbæk, in 1950, shortly after discovery of the body. Tollund Man died about 375 BC, apparently on an empty stomach. His last meal was found in the lower parts of the gut and must have been eaten 12-24 hours before he was hung and placed in the bog. The meal had been greatly altered by the effect of digestive juices after passage through almost the entire alimentary system. It was, according to Helbæk, "impossible to count the myriads of particles and even less possible to establish how many whole seeds or grains they corre-

Seeds of persicaria from a modern experimental plot. To the right, a spoonful of Grauballe Man's gut contents in which the seeds of persicaria can still be recognised.

sponded to." The precise composition of the meal and the quantities of the individual species could not be ascertained. His porridge/gruel was made primarily from barley, with seeds of persicaria, gold of pleasure, and flax. Further to these were corn spurrey, black bindweed, fat hen, field mustard, field pansy, and hemp nettle together with a little oats, sheep's sorrel, common sorrel, chickweed, field pennycress, shepherd's purse, treacle mustard, and ribwort plantain. There was also a quantity of cereal chaff and bran.

Tollund Man's meal has not been re-analysed using new methods, but its composition corresponds to the range of species that could be found in any Iron Age arable field. There is nothing in the meal to suggest that it had been intentionally composed with a sacred purpose. It seems more reasonable to characterise it as average Iron Age porridge/gruel of a low standard. The discovery of fresh sphagnum leaves in the gut contents could suggest that it was made completely, or partially, using bog water, or that Tollund Man had drunk water from a stream associated with a bog. The degree to which the seeds were added for the sake of taste or bulk is unknown, but not many of the poor souls who have tasted a reconstructed Tollund meal were seen to turn up their noses in disgust. There were no animal bones in the gut contents and the meal could have been of purely vegetable origin. Conversely, a good stock bone or a steak would not leave any trace, so we do not actually know whether the meal contained meat or not.

The very well preserved body of a man was discovered in 1946 during peat cutting in the bog Borremose near Års in Himmerland. His days were probably brought to an end by hanging, judging from the thick three-stranded bast rope that still sat around his neck. A radiocarbon date revealed that he died around 650 BC, corresponding to the

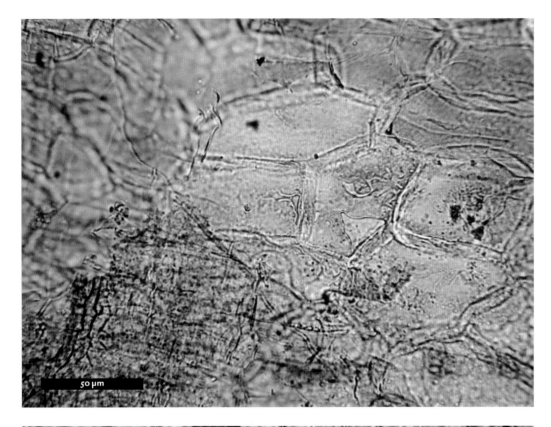

Fragments of bran of barley and rye, identified by archaeobotanists Jan Harild and Dr David Earle Robinson. At a magnification of x 400, the individual cells of the bran layers can be seen, revealing special characteristics of each species that enable identification.

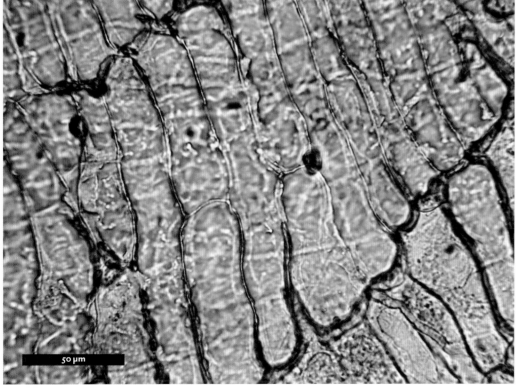

end of the Bronze Age, and over 300 years earlier than Grauballe Man. By way of an autopsy, his large intestine, containing the remains of his last meal, could be localised. Botanist Inger Brandt was given the task of identifying the components of his meal. She established that it consisted of weed seeds, persicaria, and corn spurrey, as well as grasses, sheep sorrel, soft grass, rye grass, and fat hen – accordingly, purely herbs, no cereals.

Seeds of persicaria and corn spurrey are such common finds throughout the entire Iron Age, and the latter part of the Bronze Age, that one is tempted to believe that these plants were of economic significance. Archaeologist and human geographer Gudmund Hatt who, throughout his long working life dedicated his studies to the fields and settlements of the Iron Age, raised this possibility as early as the 1930s. He found supporting evidence in, for example, the discovery of a concentrated find of charred persicaria seeds on a house floor in a settlement at Alrum in Western Jutland. More than 5 kg of pure charred corn spurrey seeds was also discovered on a house floor at Ginnerup in Thy. Iron Age potsherds with impressions of persicaria and corn spurrey turn up all over the place, as if the seeds were lying about everywhere on settlements. We do not know as yet whether these two very common plants in the Iron Age were cultivated independently or were just allowed to grow among the cereals. In any case, they are found as pure seeds on settlements and must have had an economic function by virtue of their taste or the bulk they provided.

Up until the end of the 19th century, seeds of persicaria were used for porridge in Germany, in particular because of their high starch content. Seeds of corn spurrey have a correspondingly high content of starch and are also very rich in oil. Persicaria seeds have a caloric value, exceeding that of wheat, barley, rye, oats and buckwheat. So the seeds were probably not just eaten to fill stomachs. They taste something like buckwheat, a crop which many people are so enthusiastic about nowadays, boiled like rice, coarsely ground in porridge or finely ground as flour. In poor areas during the 19th century, seeds of persicaria were cleaned from the grain and crushed to provide fodder for pigs and hens; two *skæpper* (measures) could fatten as well as one *skæppe* (measure) of buckwheat. According to V.J. Brøndegaard's great compendium *Folk og Flora* (People and Plants), persicaria has had many uses as food. Care should, however, be taken with plants of persicaria as they are also excellent medicinal herbs. A decoction of the leaves could be used as a laxative, while the crushed stems could purify the blood, heal fractured bones and wounds, and "drive out maggots from therein." Today, these plants have almost been eradicated from arable fields due to the widespread use of herbicides in agriculture, but are still very common plants in other parts of the landscape – towns, farmyards, waste places, wet hollows, etc.

As mentioned above seeds, of corn spurrey also have a high starch content and contain 30% oil, a similar value to linseed. According to Brøndegaard, however, the plant is unpleasant in smell and taste. A source from 1907 states that it imparts a bad taste to rye bread. Even so, it has found its way into the kitchen, also in recent times. Well into the 20th century, corn spurrey was grown on the sandy soils of Western Jutland and used as green fodder for cattle and for chicken feed.

A well known bog body has, in recent years, served up yet another Iron Age meal for science. This was in 1990, when the remains of a meal were ingeniously "excavated" from Huldemose Woman, who was discovered in 1879 during peat cutting in the bog of the same name on Djursland. Her meal, probably in the form of gruel or porridge, was quite simply made from three parts rye to one part corn spurrey. This was very coarse fare that had not been put through a fine quern, and even parts of the corn spurrey stems had also slipped down her throat. The presence of animal connective tissue suggests that she had eaten meat too. The woman has been radiocarbon dated to AD 65 and is, therefore, several hundred years later than Grauballe Man and Tollund Man.

Information provided by the four Danish bog bodies gives a rather uniform picture of Iron Age diet. The many finds of stored Iron Age provisions from settlements that have come to our attention over time, give an impression that porridge and gruel, porridge and gruel and more porridge and gruel formed a significant part of the daily winter diet of an Iron Age farmer. Other provisions would have run out and the fresh herbs of spring and the tasty berries and fruit of summer were still a distant prospect.

The point can, however, be made that the excellent state of preservation of the gut contents is due precisely to the fact that they lay within bodies that were deposited in bogs in the cold depths of winter. At this time of year there would be no trace of fresh delicacies to be picked or gathered from nature. Of the several hundred bog bodies, whose earthly remains are now to be found in the museums of Northwestern Europe, we have knowledge of the gut contents of about twenty. And there is nothing here to suggest that the diet was more colourful further south at that time. Dätgen Man is the name given to a bog body found in Grossener Moor in Northern Germany in 1959. As a new variation on a well-known theme, he had eaten porridge/gruel of wheat and millet and, in smaller quantities, corn spurrey, persicaria, and fat hen. In the Netherlands, Zweeloo Woman ate blackberries in addition to her porridge/gruel. The large number of pips suggests that she ate blackberries before or after the meal – or enjoyed her porridge complete with the sweet taste of fruit.

Neither do bog bodies discovered in England, Lindow Man II from 1984, and two other men, Lindow I and III, found in 1983 and 1987, reveal any new eating habits. Although Lindow Man III had eaten a quantity of hazelnuts in or with his usual porridge/gruel made of cereals and other ingredients that included persicaria seeds. Lindow Man II, who can be seen at the British Museum, ate primarily barley, wheat, rye, and oats together with a small quantity of weed seeds such as fat hen and corn spurrey.

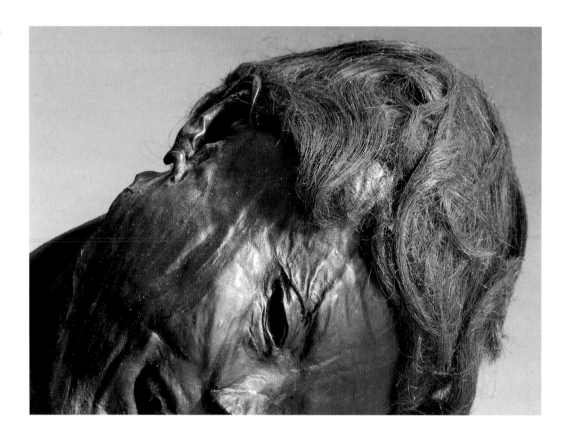

Through a complicated analysis of the wheat glumes, it could be established that they had been exposed to temperatures of 200-250 degrees C. As porridge or gruel is hardly likely to exceed 100 degrees C when it is boiled, Lindow Man's meal must have been in the form of bread. There was also pollen of mistletoe in his meal. In folk medicine, this plant is used as a sedative and to treat cramps. The individual properties of plants were undoubtedly also known in the Iron Age, when people lived off and with nature to a much greater extent than today.

The composition of the bog bodies' meals leaves an impression that people lived a puritanical, unimaginative and vegetarian existence in the Iron Age. This is misleading, not least because demonstration of the presence of animal tissue under these circumstances can be difficult. Of course people ate meat from game, fish, and domesticated animals, supplemented with anything from nature's vegetable larder they thought worthy of putting in their mouths. The interpretation of the gut contents from the Danish bog bodies as representing famine food, the last reserves of winter, is an obvious one. The other gut contents mentioned above comprised, to a greater degree, cereals with an element of weed seeds from plants occurring naturally in arable fields. Apart from Zweeloo Woman, who ate blackberries just prior to her death in August or September, the other bog bodies were apparently deposited in winter.

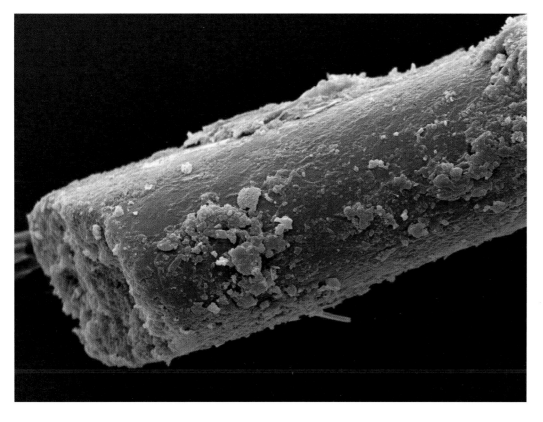

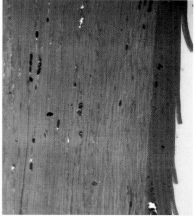

Details of our diet lie hidden like chronologically stored codes in each one of our hairs. Three hairs were sent to Bradford University where Grauballe Man's diet was revealed. At the same time, it was established that his hair had been cut with a knife or clipped with scissors, cf. the straight, cut-off ends of the hair.

The black areas are remains of pigment, but it has not proved possible to determine their original colour.

Hair as a witness

We do not really think about how much forensic information is present in our hair. Each single fine strand can reveal everything, and the longer the hair, the longer the story it tells about our otherwise private lifestyle; our consumption of alcohol, tobacco, medicine, steaks, or vegetables. Hair can, to an increasing extent, be used to map a person's life. And if the task has a criminological element, hair supplies excellent DNA.

In the hands of archaeological science, hair provides a unique opportunity to gather information about the last months of someone's life. At Bradford University in England, there are specialists in this kind of refined detective work and the hirsute Grauballe Man was well able to spare three hairs in order to provide a biography of his final nine months, corresponding to a hair length of 9 centimetres. Series of measurements of the hair's content of, respectively, the carbon and nitrogen isotopes ^{13}C and ^{15}N, for every 15 millimetres reveal that he lived a 100% terrestrial existence. That is to say, he lived inland, away from the coast, and ate food from forests, fields, and lakes. No fish soup or other culinary delights from the marine larder had satisfied his taste buds during the last months of his life. Minor fluctuations in the values just reflect the changing seasons. With his gruel or porridge fresh in our memory, we would not expect a propensity for sea food in an Iron Age man who was submerged in a bog in the highlands of Jutland, 60 kilometres from the coast. The hair's content of ^{15}N clearly refutes, however, any perception of a gruel- and porridge-dominated Iron Age. It shows that he lived to a much greater extent on animal products such as meat and milk rather than on grain and other plant food. Also, the menu was remarkably stable throughout. Meat, eggs, and milk were not just supplements, but were probably an important part of his diet, even though no evidence of this could be found in his 2000-year-old gut.

Analyses of hair from Clonycavan Man, who was discovered in 2003 during peat cutting in Ballvor bog in Ireland, read almost like a diary of his diet. For eight months of the year he ate meat, but for the rest of the year he lived on food of vegetable origin. Until the final results relating to Clonycavan Man become available, we can only guess as to whether his meat-eating was restricted to the colder months, with plant food providing the green kitchen of summer. Or whether the plant food represented four months on winter porridge or gruel. Old Croghan Man, who was found in the same area in 2003, ate a last meal of cereal products and buttermilk. But analyses of his hair and nails show that otherwise he lived primarily on meat.

The importance of meat in the Iron Age diet should probably not be underestimated, even though it can be difficult to demonstrate this 2000 years after the event. Analyses of bones preserved in Iron Age burials also give indications of a very uniform diet, primarily comprising meat. Perhaps particular rules and motives were in force when a sacrifice to the gods ate his or her last meal, made up of cereal and milk products as physical symbols of fertility.

The reddish-brown hair that characterises all bog bodies does not mean that red-haired people ran a greater risk of ending their days in an unnatural way before being submerged in a bog. This is, as mentioned previously, due to a special chemical process, the Maillard reaction, named after its French discoverer. It is a natural aspect of the chemistry of bog water. The presumed brown pigment in Grauballe Man's hair, thought to have been observed in 1952, is no longer considered a definite characteristic of his hair colour. A simple experiment involving museum staff, a blonde, a red-head and a brunette, who each sacrificed a lock of hair to be placed in bog water for a month, confirmed that we all become red-heads once we have lain in a bog for a sufficient length of time!

Ergot

One particular component of Grauballe Man's gut contents has given rise to much discussion and many long-winded interpretations, namely the harmful fungus, ergot. Ergot is a parasitic fungus that infects rye, barley, and certain wild grasses. Grains and seeds of infected plants are replaced by large fungal fruiting bodies containing alkaloids, substances that are closely related to LSD. A large consumption of ergot affects the central nervous system and induces hallucinations, cramps and headaches and can result in the painful condition, St Anthony's Fire, so feared in the Middle Ages and also well into recent times. In the worst case scenario, the condition results in gangrene of the extremities, which eventually wither and fall off.

Helbæk states that Grauballe Man's gut material contains a quantity of whole or fragmented ergot sclerotia. This has lead subsequently to a flurry of imaginative rumours to the effect that, in the Iron Age, ergot was intentionally gathered and used as an intoxicant and narcotic. Was Grauballe Man happily intoxicated with ergot when he was led to the bog and given that fateful and deadly cut to his throat? It is an obvious thought and easily reconcilable with the consciousness that there was, at least, a humane thought behind the action, *i.e.* an offering to the gods, intercession for the survival and continuation of the family line. A shot of ergot would perhaps also have soothed his aching teeth considerably. The theory caught the attention of an American TV company which then produced a programme on prehistoric intoxicants, according to which Grauballe Man, Tollund Man, and all the other North European bog bodies were said to have been led to their place of sacrifice intoxicated by ergot.

When all was said and done, and science had laid the decisive evidence on the table, the rug was firmly pulled from beneath the feet of Grauballe Man's LSD trip. "A quantity", as stated by Helbæk, has subsequently been interpreted as "many". The new analyses and counts of ergot in the gut contents shows that the estimated 0.23-2.64 mg of ergot present in his last meal does not even exceed the permitted levels for grain in present-day EU stores. There was no form of anaesthetising witchcraft or divine LSD trip contained in that meal.

Seeds of Yorkshire fog from the gut contents. Infected with ergot (right).

An Iron Age man of flesh and blood

"Grauballe Man had an intellectual expression,"
concludes the expert who, in her daily work,
also considers such mental characteristics
of the silent souls she brings to life between her hands.

While the various fragments of objective scientific data begin to adopt the form of a life lived in a distant past, the contours of Grauballe Man and his landscape begin gradually to take shape in the mind's eye. But what did he actually look like when he wandered around on the earth more than 2000 years ago – the man in the bog, the poor creature in the exhibition, who looks like us and with whom we can so readily identify?

A changing face

When he stuck his head up from the bog with that rebellious red shock of hair, the skin of his face lay in authentic folds around his full lips. His face seemed almost alive with visible pores on the skin, a flattened nose and red stubble on his chin. Today, more than 50 years later, his features have tightened around his open, toothless mouth. Otherwise he is still recognisable as the man produced by the hands of the conservator. But what did he look like when he was alive? Dr Caroline Wilkinson, of the University of Manchester, provided the answer after two days of concentrated work.

At the University of Manchester's Institute of Forensic Medicine lies the Unit of Art in Medicine, a studio complete with modern computer screens, plaster of Paris, clay, spatulas, and other hand tools for sculpting work. The walls are populated with life-like faces in plaster and clay, Stone Age hunters, Bronze Age farmers, Egyptian beauties from the time of the Pharaohs, Mycenaean aristocrats, King Midas and other deceased royal and historical celebrities, bog bodies, and present-day victims of crime and other fatalities. An absurd gallery of characters which has been conjured forth in earnest between the hands of the founder of the laboratory, Dr Richard Neave, and his successor, Dr Caroline Wilkinson. Dr Wilkinson leaves no-one in any doubt as to her artistic

Grauballe Man in the bog, 1952.

*– and exhibited
at Moesgård Museum, 2006.*

Dr Caroline Wilkinson in her studio, reconstructing Grauballe Man's face. Manchester University, 2002.

spirit, but alongside the title of sculptor she also has an academic degree in anatomy. In this small oasis within the otherwise death-obsessed institute, skulls are brought to life – given skin, hair and facial expressions.

The staff of the institute plays an important role in the solving of criminal cases, catastrophic fires, and deaths over the whole of Europe. The skull is an important source of information in the identification of deceased persons. Reconstruction is both an objectively scientific and a sensitive task, by which the deceased's cranium is gradually and systematically given life and identity. The declared aim of facial reconstruction is, on the basis of the details of the skull, to recreate a picture of the person "in life" that someone relatively close to them would be able to recognise. The method has been employed in more than 30 forensic cases over the past 25 years. A 75% success rate identifies the institute as a world leader.

Just as we all have unique and individual faces, our skulls are also correspondingly unique. Even all though all skulls may, superficially, look the same, the proportions of the cranium, the details of the skeleton and the morphological features of the face are, in reality, all very variable. Small variations during development and growth of the skull are the reason for the great variation seen in our faces. The appearance of the skull also determines small details of our facial expression.

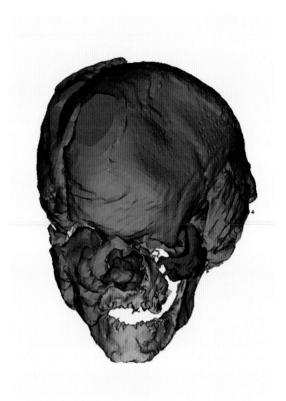

CT-scan of Grauballe Man's cranium. The conservator's filler is shown in blue.

Plastic copy of the cranium. Danish Technological Institute, Århus.

The method was developed within forensic science, but attempts have been made to employ it in archaeology for over a century. The first attempts were in the reconstruction of a Stone Age woman in Switzerland in 1889 and in experiments with mummies. Serious scientific use of the technique was first made in the 1940s by the American Wilton M. Krogman. He modelled the face solely on the basis of the known thickness of the soft tissues at various points, taking into account age, sex, and ethnic origin. Data on the thickness of soft tissues covering the skull is available thanks to investigations of present-day populations and statistical evidence from investigations of prehistoric skulls. Information on facial tissue within the various populations around the globe is carefully listed according to sex and age. An equivalent set-up was established in the Soviet Union in the 1950s by the Russian Mikail Gerasimov who, in the German edition of his book *Ich suchte Geschichte*, presented reconstructions of prehistoric faces. Gerasimov worked strictly anatomically, building faces up muscle by muscle, and subsequently completing the work with a layer of skin. The Manchester method, which for the last 30 years has been the world leader in the field, combines the Russian and American methods – in a convincing cross-disciplinary fusion between anatomic insight and approaches taken from medical science and the art of sculpture.

If blood was again to flow in Grauballe Man's veins, his skull was the essential starting point. The many cross-sectional images produced by the CT-scan of his head could be "cleaned" of soft tissue, leaving only data relevant to the cranium. All these cranial data were then transformed into a three-dimensional image on a single computer screen. The cranial reconstruction could not, however, proceed digitally but was possible solely on the basis of an actual tangible skull.

One of the functions of the Technological Institute in Århus is helping inventive souls and commercial companies who turn up with a good idea for a new product in industrial design. They have the necessary equipment and facilities to transfer a high-flying idea into a real product, for example a new mobile phone, a component for a digital apparatus or whatever. Even an Iron Age skull can, using Rapid Prototyping, be manufactured precisely 1:1, despite this being in the non-profitable part of the sector. The method is called stereo-lithography, and it has made redundant the production of hand-made prototypes in wood. With the aid of advanced equipment, a precise copy can now be produced of a computer model – using an artificial resin-like material. Data transferred from one computer to another activates a bath of liquid artificial material, in which a laser beam, at intervals of a few seconds, causes the liquid to set corresponding to the shape of the object. In this way, the skull was built up, starting from top of the head and proceeding down to the neck, through hundreds of set layers corresponding to the CT-scans. Grauballe Man's skull was programmed to start production late one afternoon and next morning it was complete. The push of a button, and the skull was raised up out of the liquid, causing the superfluous liquid to pour out of the eye sockets and nostrils as it emerged from the bath. Marvellous how cold data can be transformed to light, tangible reality!

It was necessary to "correct" the skull at the anatomical institute in Manchester. This was to relieve it of the distortions caused by the mechanical pressure of the bog and that exerted by the objectionable person who had trodden on Grauballe Man's head on the day of his discovery. To do this, the cranium was sawn up into its anatomical component parts. These were then re-assembled and built up in clay. The back of the head was modelled on the basis of measurements of contemporary male Iron Age skulls. A plaster copy then came to form the basis for the facial reconstruction. The compression of the cranium and the subsequent adjustments meant that some of his finer features were lost. Conversely, close-up photographs from the time of his discovery revealed clear details of the soft tissue of his face which contributed greatly to achieving a very precise result in areas where the details of the skull were less clear.

The anatomical features of the cranium were precisely deciphered. The cheekbones are high and broad. The eyebrows are large, low and relatively straight. There is also a prominent protrusion between the bridge of the nose and the forehead. The distance between the eyes is described as moderate and the eyelids formed a small inward fold of

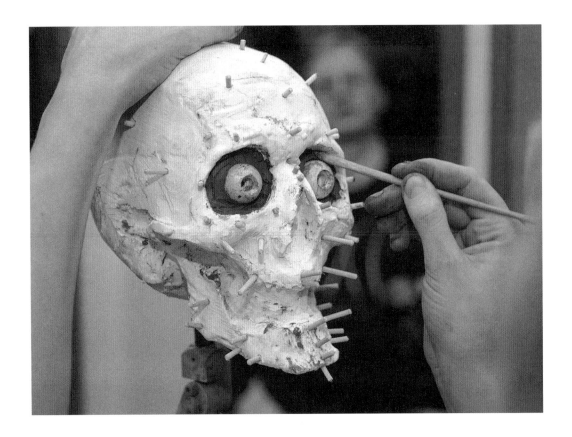

Copy of Grauballe Man's cranium. The white pegs denote the thickness of the muscles and skin of the face.

skin. The nasal bones reveal a moderately broad nose with a correspondingly broad root. The positions of the upper and lower jaws suggest a normal bite. The chin was angular and came to a distinct point.

The photographs from the time of his discovery supported the image of a man with a relatively high forehead. His nose has a rounded tip and wings and below it runs a broad philtrum. Under the eyes there are horizontal lines and small bags. The corners of the mouth are upturned and the lips are narrow with a marked Cupid's bow. He had light creases on his cheeks leading in towards his nose and there are fine mimic lines on his face, most prominent on his forehead and over the root of his nose. "Grauballe Man had an intellectual expression," concludes the expert who, in her daily work, also considers such mental characteristics of the silent souls she brings to life between her hands.

The form of the cranium left no doubt that reference material for the soft tissue of the face should be taken from the database for white European adult males of an age between 40 and 49. Small wooden pins were drilled into the skull at 32 anatomical points. The length of the pegs corresponded exactly to the known tissue thickness dictated by the database for these particular points. This gave 32 fix points for the thickness or depth of the facial tissue over the skull.

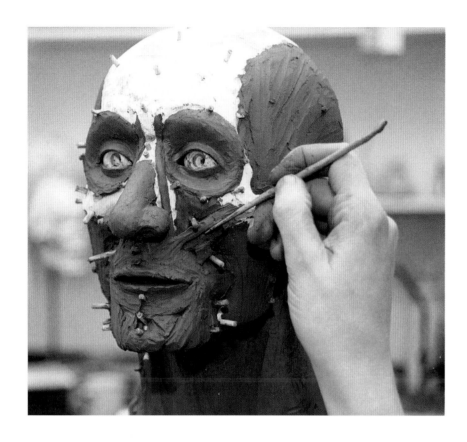

There was a free choice in the drawer of eyeballs – irises in green, grey, brown and blue – and there were also neutral coloured ones, in plaster alone. As we do not know the colour of Grauballe Man's eyes, a pair of the latter was affixed with clay in his eye sockets. The face was built up in clay, muscle by muscle, first the neck, then the area around the nose and the cheeks, all in anatomically correct dimensions and order. Thoughts of Frankenstein's laboratory were awakened as the man's facial musculature and sinews took shape and the exhibition *"Körperwelten"* with skinned corpses and "transparent" bodies filed past the mind's eye. Meanwhile, Caroline Wilkinson, with greatest accuracy, laid yet another facial muscle in place. Small, rounded ears without detached lobes, exactly as dictated by the cranium, were modelled and attached to the correct muscles. The skin was carefully rolled out using a rolling pin, cut into appropriate strips and laid over muscles and sinews until the outer tip of the wooden peg was just covered.

Then the sculptor got to work in earnest with details of the facial features, the nose, the lips, the eyebrows, and wrinkles on the skin. These were now modelled according to observations of the cranium and the soft tissue shown on the photographs from the bog. The surface of the skin was smoothed out and the work completed with a final sculptural finish. Grauballe Man from 290 BC was reborn!

How his hair, that unruly shock of unknown colour, was arranged on his beautiful-

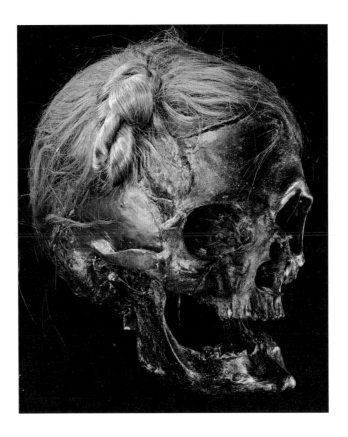

The man from Obenaltendorf with his hair set up in a so-called Swabian knot. Niedersachsen, Germany.

ly rounded head, we can only guess. Today, a hairnet protects it, but when he was discovered it stuck up in all directions. Most of his hair is about 15 cm long, but some at the front is slightly shorter, though only a little and this cannot be taken as evidence that he had a short fringe. Some of hairs are broken, but all in all it is thought that his hair was cut or clipped straight across just below the ears. He now has rather a strange hairstyle that is, as already mentioned, contained within a fine-meshed hairnet in the interests of its preservation.

So he was no Prince Valiant with a short-clipped fringe. But was the fringe held back from the face with a hair-band? Did he have a side or a centre parting? Or was his hair swept back *à la* Marlon Brando? There is not much inspiration to be gained from what we know about Iron Age male hair fashion. The length of Tollund Man's hair under his cap was about three centimetres, the British Lindow Man II had a short, trimmed man's hairstyle and a beard, just like the man from Obenaltendorf in Niedersachsen, Germany. The most striking male hairstyle is the so-called "Swabian Knot", also described by Tacitus in his work *Germania*. Despite the fact that Tacitus lived several hundred years later than the majority of our bog bodies, and that he is not a very reliable source as a historian, his account of the male fashion of the Teutons and Swabians is both entertaining and inspiring. Of the Swabians, who inhabited the largest part of

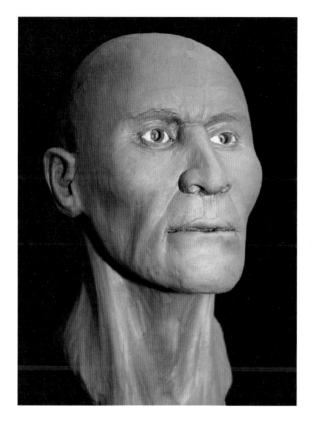 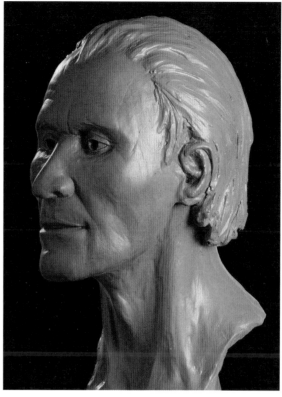

Germania, Tacitus writes: "A special characteristic of this people is that they sweep their hair to one side or put it up in a knot; in this way, the Swabians distinguish themselves from the other Teutons, and the free-born among the Swabians from slaves. Other peoples, either out of relationship to the Swabians or, as is often the case, in copying them, comb their spiky hair backwards and often tie it in a knot on the top of their head, but this is rare and only limited to their youth, whereas the Swabians retain their hairstyle into their grey old age. Their chiefs had an even more elaborate hairstyle. This is all the care they offer on their appearance and it is harmless. It is neither to love nor to be loved that they decorate themselves very carefully in this way, but in order to appear taller and more terrifying in the eyes of the enemy when they go to war."

Hair of the length of Grauballe Man's, which could be brushed backwards and gathered in a knot was, according to Tacitus, widespread among the warlike male Teutons. And it is thought-provoking that both bog bodies, Osterby Man and Dätgen Man, found in Schleswig-Holstein, respectively in 1948 and 1959, had their hair gathered into a knot, corresponding exactly to that described by Tacitus. Osterby Man has the knot at the right side of his head; that of Dätgen Man is at the back. There must have been a reason for the characteristic Swabian knot. Apart from this, hairstyles in the Iron Age appear to be just as diverse and individual as those of today, as is also inferred by Tacitus.

The completed reconstruction of Grauballe Man's face. An intellectual expression, in the view of the person who shaped him.

Caroline Wilkinson during the
development of the Iron Age man
behind the bog body.

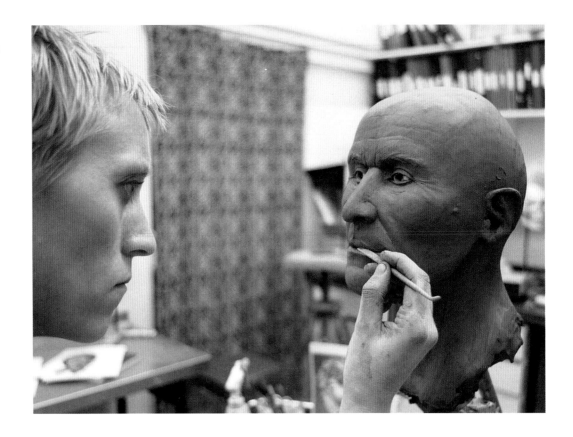

As for women, they often allowed their hair to grow. In the case of some, this was in order for it to be arranged in elaborate styles with complicated plaits such as seen on Elling Girl, found in 1938 in Bjældskovdal bog near Silkeborg, where Tollund Man was later to be discovered. Other women from the bogs are short-haired or have had their hair cut off. The 16-year-old Yde Girl, found in 1897 in Drenthe in the Netherlands, had her long, severed hair placed with her in the bog. It is possible that the hairstyles of some of the bog bodies should be seen in the context of the circumstances surrounding their death. They probably do not reveal very much about everyday hair fashion in the Iron Age.

The great silver vessel, the Gundestrup Cauldron, which was found in the bog of Rævemosen in Himmerland in 1891, has always been thought to be of Celtic origin, manufactured at the time when Grauballe Man was alive. The cauldron comes from the Balkan Peninsula – it is not possible to identify the place of origin more precisely for this impressive and totally unique vessel comprising eight densely decorated exterior plates. There are also decorated interior plates and a base plate – mentioned later. New investigations suggest, however, that the vessel may be several centuries later. Even so, it will be included here. The male heads depicted on the vessel reveal far from uniform fashions with regard to hair and beards. On the contrary, personal taste seems to be very individual, just like today (see p. 122).

Grauballe Man had his hair clipped with a pair of scissors. The ends of the hairs are cut more-or-less straight across, although they are now a little frayed due to wear and tear. Lindow Man II also had his hair cut with scissors. Iron Age scissors are like small shears. They have been found graves, where it is not uncommon for the deceased to be accompanied by tools and implements, including scissors, for use in the afterlife. Iron Age scissors looks like they would be no use for anything when they are excavated, covered in a thick layer of rust after a couple of millennia in the earth. But make no mistake! Behind the rust lies one of the finest examples of the blacksmith's art, with a razor-sharp edge. They closely resemble modern-day sheep shears and cut just as well.

Grauballe Man is unlikely to have walked around with his hair hanging down in front of his face. It must have been swept backwards and probably gathered in a knot or with a hair-band. The choice of hairstyle on the reconstructed head fell on the swept-back model. His "masculine" hairline was worthy of display and we have no suggestion of a knot or a hair-band. An interesting styling product from the Iron Age was revealed in connection with the discovery of Clonycavan Man in Ireland. Only his torso, arms and head escaped the modern highly mechanised peat extraction. Clonycavan Man was slender of build and 176 cm tall. Despite the damage to his body from the machine, the remains recovered were unusually well preserved, including partially intact internal organs. The approximately 25-year-old man had an extremely elaborate hairstyle. His hair was brushed up to form a pad on the top of his head, perhaps in order to add a few centimetres to his height. The hairstyle was fixed with a mixture of pine resin and vegetable oil. Analyses of the resin revealed that it came from France or Northern Spain. The view of the Irish archaeologists is that this hair gel was without doubt a very expensive and exclusive commodity, and definitely not a product available to all social classes of society. Just think! Our vain modern-day youngsters, with their addiction to designer styling products at sky high prices, have been outdone many times over by their Iron Age counterparts. There is no doubt that the resin-oil mixture was hair gel in the category "strong hold"! Not even 2000 years in bog water could disrupt this sophisticated, stacked-up hairstyle. We wonder what it was an expression of – fashion, social class, group affiliation, peace, war, profession or simply creativity? The Irish archaeologists believe it to be an indication of the highest social class. Tacitus' remark about the terrifying hairstyles of the chieftains was perhaps not too wide of the mark.

There is no evidence from Denmark of the use of hair gel by Iron Age bog bodies. It is true that we talk of the exchange of wares and trade during prehistory, but the idea of resin for this purpose as one of these possible wares is much more than even imaginative archaeologists can dream up. It is also rather superfluous to speculate how Grauballe Man kept his long fringe out of his face during a fierce battle or behind the plough.

For completion of Grauballe Man's face he needs a beard. When he was found, he had 15 millimetres of stubble on his chin and upper lip. However, almost all of this fell off during his extended immersion in the conservation fluid. Professor, state forensic pathologist Markil Gregersen has detailed knowledge of beard lengths before and after death: "After death, the skin contracts, which causes the beard to extend a further *c.* 4-5 millimetres out. As the beard was 15 millimetres long when he was found, it would have been 10 millimetres when he died. Beard hair grows 2.5-3.5 millimetres in a week, so he had a three-week growth at his death."

Men at that time were not scruffy, wearing beards down to their chests. It was actually the practice for most of prehistory to shave with a razor. At the beginning of the Iron Age, razors were crescent-shape, forged of iron and with a curved edge. Together with a knife, they were an essential part of men's personal equipment, carried in a leather belt-pouch. This is how we find them in graves from periods of the Iron Age when the dead were not cremated. In Grauballe Man's time, the dead, with the exception of those who ended their days in the bog, were burnt on a funeral pyre. Their remains, bones together with the burnt and fused grave goods, were buried in an urn or a small pit in the ground. In such cases, it can be difficult to identify razors, but they are often present. There is no doubt that Grauballe Man had shaved at regular intervals,

Yde Girl from Drenthe in The Netherlands. This bog body of a girl of about 16 years of age was transformed into a true Iron Age princess and the pride of the nation when a reconstruction of her face was created.

the last time was three weeks prior to his death. Some men kept their beards, for example Lindow Man II, who had a beautifully trimmed full beard.

When asked about Grauballe Man's body hair, the state forensic pathologist responded: "Professor Munck, who carried out the autopsy on Grauballe Man in 1952, was very interested in hair. He describes only the hair of the head and beard, but not hair in armpits and around the sexual organs. I also think it would be difficult to find traces of the latter, if it had become loose. Beard hair is often very coarse and very firmly attached to the skin. I do not believe this can be taken as an indication that pubic hair was shaved off in the Iron Age. Today, it is, for some reason or another, only women who do this kind of thing."

Scientific reflections on the landscape and that fateful moment by the bog

Just as the expert in facial reconstruction is totally focussed on recreating a portrait with a living expression, the forensic pathologist and radiologist work as persistently and unfailingly towards a characterisation of a person's physical state and how their life came to an end. In this way, the results of investigation upon investigation are drawn

On the outer plates of the Gundestrup cauldron there are pictorial compositions showing men and women, with gods in half-length portraits. Hairstyles, beards and hair length are very varied.

together producing a kaleidoscopic picture of the man who in the first centuries of the Iron Age ended his days on earth at the edge of Nebelgaard bog and who, in a soulless form, has experienced such a turbulent afterlife in the 20th century.

Pollen-analyst Svend Jørgensen visited Nebelgaard bog just a few days after Grauballe Man's discovery. He cleaned and surveyed the sections cut through the bog, and carefully collected numerous samples from the layers of peat. He took these with him back to the National Museum in test tubes along with section drawings by the metre. The peat's content of microscopic pollen was identified and quantified.

The vegetation of a complete landscape can be read from a peat layer just a few millimetres thick. After having identified and counted a million pollen grains, this wizard lets the ancient landscape of the time when Grauballe Man ended his days by the bog unfold like pictures before our very eyes: "The greater part of the area had been cleared, and there was woodland only in ravines and on the slopes and margins alongside these. Oak was by far the dominant tree in the woodland. Commonest of the rarer trees was lime but this, together with ash, elm, and pine, had only a scattered occurrence, while alder lined the stream banks. Beech was yet still sparse, but it had a foothold and was the most common tree after lime. Here and there stood a hornbeam or a maple, while hazel and hawthorn formed the woodland edge."

With a broad and convincing brush, page after page, Svend Jørgensen paints a magnificent landscape of a golden age around the year 290 BC. Hopbines were abundant and on the woodland floor "wood anemone, dog's mercury, and herb paris found a place to grow, and in clearings there were stands of bracken." A luxuriant summer landscape, perhaps the summer that turned to autumn and winter when everything withered away and people came with their ultimate sacrifice.

Dressed up against the cold weather, a flock of people moved down towards the bog. Small fields, framed within low banks carpeted the hilly landscape. In early autumn they had stood here, bent over the meagre harvest of barley, wheat, oats, and perhaps rye – and all manner of weeds. A large part of the landscape lay as open common. The soil was exhausted after many years of cultivation and had now been given over to grazing cattle. If there was not enough grass, the cattle turned to sprigs of the heather that was in rapid advance across the commons.

The little boggy hollow lay in a depression surrounded by naked birch trees, willows, and rowan. On the damp ground around the bog were rushes and the withered leaves of summer meadowsweet. The path to the bog had been trodden by the summer's crowds and during peat cutting. The surface of the bog was still pockmarked by peat cuttings, old and new, filled with water black as night. Marsh cinquefoil and cranberry spread withered stems like cobwebs over the mossy hummocks on this special winter's day.

Nebelgaard bog is today surrounded by willows and alder and gently rolling hills. 2002.

It is difficult to imagine what was said and thought – that would be to go too far. But the purpose of this little event was that one from the flock would end their days here, at the entrance to another world. "A good-looking man," and with his 34 years well into adult life. Perhaps he walked naked to the bog under a cape of wool or hide. Maybe he had removed his shoes beforehand. On that day, he had eaten pig meat and gruel made from the last remnants of the year's harvest. And there was a reason. He had not touched his beard for three weeks. He was healthy and strong and not remotely on his way towards a natural death. The throbbing toothache on the left side of his upper jaw was nothing compared to what now followed. At the edge of the bog, he was forced to his knees. It could be that he, despite acceptance of his fate, at the very moment of death tried to ward off his executioner. A sharp blow with a stick to his right shinbone focussed his attention on that pain. What happened next had been planned in advance. Someone from the crowd, a special person, grabbed the man's hair, forced his head back and held him close in towards their body. They drew a knife with their right hand and cut the man's throat from left ear to right, in one stroke, and so deeply that the knife grazed the vertebrae of the neck. A cry of terror rang out briefly around the hills, but

only for a moment, then it changed to a horrible, throaty gurgle. The man became unconscious while the blood continued to pump from his severed carotid artery. But there was an purpose behind it all. Perhaps the blood was caught in a vessel. On this special occasion, perhaps a meal was jointly prepared and eaten down by the bog in service of fertility. Dancing, singing, and prayers, perhaps?

One thing is certain. Part of the event involved carrying the dead and naked body 30 metres out into the bog and submerging it in a peat cutting, where the surface of water breached the boundary to the other world. The ritual was complete. The intention of it all was to gather consciousness for a common experience of the offering. But before they left the bog, they ensured for the deceased a proper afterlife deep in the bog and placed peat or branches over the corpse. For there, down in the cold dark water, nature only marks time. All natural laws about decay of the perishable are, by miraculous means, annulled – cancelled out by the special botanical and chemical alchemy of the bog.

The bog – a landscape between land and water

Millennium after millennium is lived and acted out on earth,
while the traces of earthly life
are folded away into the peat layers of bogs.

Contrary to all common sense and learning concerning decomposition of the decomposable, bogs maintain the earthly remains of everything living in a suspended state, in which the biological clock comes practically to a halt. Millennium after millennium is lived and acted out on earth, while the traces of earthly life are folded away into bogs. Microscopic pollen and seeds from various landscapes through time, extending right back to the last Ice Age, lie carefully incorporated into metre-thick layers of peat, narrating the history of people and nature through 10,000 years. Within the great layers of peat lie the remains of mummified plants and animals and the offerings prehistoric people brought to the bogs. Changing landscapes through time, and people's activities in and around the bog, can be read today from the compacted layers of dead bog moss. Year after year, bogs have archived everything that landed on their surface. Layer after layer lies hidden away, as if entered into a meticulously organised file-card system holding data on millennia of natural and cultural history. In order to understand this wonder of nature, it is necessary to become acquainted with the anatomy and biology of bogs.

Raised bogs and mosses

The term bog is used popularly to refer to all kinds of wetland areas and "poor fens", as they are also known due to their low content of nutrients. Biologically speaking, there is only one kind of true bog, a raised bog, the existence of which is dependent solely on climate. Raised bogs are special because they accumulate peat up to many metres in depth, exclusively on the basis of the nutrition and moisture the bog plants receive directly from rainwater and the air. Topogenous bogs, on the other hand, are various kinds of wet meadows, fens, or marshes. They are not as dependent on the climate, but

are bound to their wet hollows and formed under the influence of the groundwater. Topogenous bogs can be more or less nutrient rich, according to the nature of the geology through which the groundwater passes. Plants growing at the edge of, or in the open water, die and disappear below the surface. As there is very little oxygen in the water, the plant remains do not fully decay. Gradually, the dead plants accumulate and the layers of plant remains grow so that open water is, with time, replaced by peat. Topogenous bogs are often calcareous and provide a habitat for a large number of plants, including rare species such as blue sedge, bird's eye primrose, butterwort, and fairy flax.

A raised bog, in contrast, is a dead, water-saturated mass of peat that can be several metres deep. On the surface grows sphagnum, other bog mosses, heather, and cottongrass, interspersed with hollows containing shallow blackish-brown water and exposed peat. The edge of the bog is occupied by wet scrubby woodland comprising alder, ash, willow, and birch as well as plants of marshy and damp meadow habitats. Here, at the edge, the plants obtain nutrients from the groundwater and from the surrounding landscape. Conditions out in the bog are much more frugal.

Raised bogs originated in a period of wet, cool climate, when the water table rose and damp woodland and swamps became considerably wetter. Waterlogging suppresses growth and development therefore begins later in spring. A light and open woodland

floor provides particularly favourable growing conditions for various bog and peat mosses, all of which belong to the moss genus *Sphagnum*. Thousands of moss plants become interwoven and form domed cushions in shades of green, yellow, and red. Each has a main shoot and numerous thin branches out to all sides. On its own, the plant is limp, but woven together in thousands the plants quickly conquer the damp environment and are the bogs' supreme contributor to peat formation.

Sphagnum has a special ability to produce and tolerate acid. This transforms the wetlands into a habitat that satisfies all the mosses' own requirements. It does this by exchanging hydrogen ions, produced in its metabolism, for metal ions, causing the habitat to become progressively more acidic and poor in nutrients. Trees and reeds are unable to tolerate the acidic water and they gradually die in the increasingly acid environment, finally falling dead on the soft mossy carpet. Mosses, and a few other plants that can thrive in acid environments, then dominate the area – and a raised bog is created. Every year, a new layer of moss is formed. Dead plant remains pack down below the living surface and all the while the bog grows and grows – upwards. The connection to the groundwater is severed and the bog vegetation lives exclusively on rainwater, air, and minerals from the atmosphere. Sphagnum's branches are covered in small, scale-like leaves that comprise 90% empty cells. These absorb and store rainwater, which

Sphagnum spreads as domed cushions in shades of green, yellow, and red across the blackish-brown water. This hardy plant lives solely on rainwater, which it absorbs and stores in its scale-like leaves.

explains how sphagnum manages to grow in raised bogs where there is no contact with the groundwater. The ability to absorb and bind water just as effectively as a piece of cotton wool is crucial to the bog's ability to grow.

Lille Vildmose in Himmerland, Jutland, originated during the damp climate of the Iron Age.

This is how bogs arose in cool, wet times and, like great water bubbles held together by plant remains, they spread out across many square kilometres of the landscape. Peat formation takes place slowly, up to a maximum of about 15 millimetres a year. With time, the peat becomes compacted to a third. The growth of a thousand years leaves only five metres of compacted peat and often considerably less.

The oldest bogs were formed almost 10.000 years ago and they have stood their ground for millennia. Even through the change in climate that took place in the latter part of the Mesolithic, during the Ertebølle period about 6000 years ago, when the temperature was a couple of degrees warmer than it is today. Towards the end of the Bronze Age, about 2600 years ago, the climate declined steeply and the subsequent Iron Age became both wetter and cooler. Existing bogs grew, new ones were formed. From the beginning, in the Pre-Roman Iron Age, starting around 500 BC, the climate curve continued downwards in a step-like decent until around AD 200, the period we call the Roman Iron Age. Several hundred bogs were created and these spread out over large parts of the Northwest European lowlands: The Netherlands, Germany, England,

In the depths of the bog, decay comes almost to a standstill. Insects and plants from the Iron Age landscape lie preserved in the bog archives. Fuglsøgård bog, Himmerland, Jutland. 2002.

a. Birch trunk
b. Sphagnum
c. Knot in an oak trunk
d. Bulrush
e. Cereal leaf beetle
f. Willow leaf
g. Hazelnuts

Ireland, and Denmark. The raised bog Store Vildmose formed as early as the end of the Stone Age, about 3600 years ago, and extended rapidly to cover an expanse of 50 square kilometres in the course of the Iron Age. Lille Vildmose which, with its 20 square kilometres, is today Northern Europe's largest raised bog, arose late in the Iron Age around AD 400 and has subsequently accumulated peat six metres deep.

If one is fortunate enough to study a section through a bog in detail it is possible to observe the nature of millennia with the naked eye. This takes the form of completely preserved seeds, leaves, nuts, flies' wings, and beetles of all colours among the dead bog peat, all in meticulous chronological order. In the course of a few seconds, one can allow one's gaze to sweep six metres down through 1600 years of natural history. Pollen analysts can go even further and can very precisely expand the repertoire. They can read off the changing vegetation through time by studying the peat's content of wind-born pollen grains from the surrounding landscape. Using a lens and a microscope, the well-preserved pollen grains can be clearly identified on basis of their unique characteristics.

The secret behind the magic

Fed by nutrient-poor rainwater and a minimal scatter of nutrient salts carried by the wind, the peat grew in the bog layer by layer, in compressed form an average of 5 millimetres per year. Accumulation took place without any significant oxidation. It is well known that the lack of oxygen and, in particular, the acid bog water provide the explanation for the conserving properties of bogs. Sphagnum produces small quantities of sulphuric acid which, together with the formation of humic acid in the uppermost peat layers, is the reason for the acidic and virtually antibacterial environment prevailing in the bog, with its pH of 3.6-4.0. It was this very knowledge which was exploited when the decision was made to complete Grauballe Man's natural bog tanning process by placing him in an aqueous solutions of tannin, extracted from fresh oak bark.

The discovery of Lindow Man II in 1983 in Lindow Moss near Manchester, England, gave rise to yet another ambitious cross-disciplinary project, whereby, with the aid of modern analytical methods, answers were obtained to new questions concerning our enigmatic bog bodies. As Lindow Man was, furthermore, to be exhibited at the British Museum in London, it was necessary to carry out research in the bog's preservative properties and chemistry and into Lindow Man's continued conservation. Biochemist Terence J. Painter established that the bog bodies are superbly preserved, retaining both skin and hair, in raised bogs with a pH of 3.2-4.5. This was surprising in light of the fact that wine and cider production involves fermentation by active micro-organisms in anoxic environments at a correspondingly low pH. It could, therefore, not be the lack of oxygen and the low pH alone which are responsible for conservation of bog bodies. The

Ireland is known as "The Green Island" with its many lakes and bogs. For millennia, bogs have been the foundation of Irish life, for better and for worse.

secret lay in the plant sphagnum, a major component of bogs – the reason behind their preserved histories and extended afterlife. When sphagnum dies and becomes at one with the peat masses, this small rootless plant, comprising mostly empty cells which it draws full of rainwater, releases a substance called sphagnan.

Sphagnan is a natural sugar compound and is the explanation for all the magic. Sphagnan neutralises any nutrient-rich nitrogen coming from the surroundings, thereby starving and neutralising any bacteria, causing any decay to come to a halt. The investigations in Lindow Moss revealed that at a depth of only 40 centimetres in the raised bog, the bacterial flora was only one millionth of that present at the bog surface. Sphagnan preserves bog bodies by tanning skin, cartilage, and sinew, but at the same time it also de-calcifies bone. Collagen in the soft tissue becomes transformed into leather. Keratin in horn, nails and hair becomes more resistant to biological decay. The chemistry involved is referred to as the Maillard reaction and is a process in which sugars and amino acids combine to form dark brown polymers (humus) which have an anti-bacterial effect. It is the same reaction that colours the skins of bog bodies brown. It is also the reason that, regardless of original hair and beard colour when the bodies were laid in the bog, they are all, without exception, red-haired when they re-emerge.

A plant of great potential

Terence Painter's ground-breaking discovery has had an interesting sequel at Trondheim University in Norway, where research into sphagnan continues. As evidence for the excellent preservative properties of sphagnan, the staff of the Institute of Biotechnology display test tubes containing dead zebra fish which are kept in bog water at a temperature of about 20 degrees C, with free access to oxygen. After two years under these conditions, the fish still look good. They show no signs of decay and have retained their striped appearance. The only change is a brown colouration developed in the fishes' skin – just like in bog bodies.

Research, legend, and folk medicine are, in general, full of information about the excellent preservative properties of sphagnum. It is even maintained by a fairly reliable source that the Vikings preferred to carry bog water rather than spring water onboard their long voyages. The water from the bog contains no nitrogenous compounds that algae and bacteria can live on and retains its "freshness" for many months at sea.

It is said that bog water flows like blood in the veins of the Irish people. Throughout the millennia, the Irish have inhabited endless landscapes of peat, peat, and more peat. The bogs offered cold, hard toil, poverty, and famine, but they also embrace the Irish national soul and collective consciousness in a basic and fundamental way. Out of a desperate lack of sterile bandages, Irish soldiers, who fought at the front during World War I, laid sphagnum in bullet wounds and used it for field dressings. This prompted research into the antiseptic and healing phenol compounds in the moss which, long before the discovery of penicillin, saved innumerable human lives in the hospitals behind the front lines.

In prehistory, food, as well as many other things, was also deposited in bogs. From Scotland and Ireland we know of a special tradition of burying butter in bogs. A solid, well-made birch cask filled with butter, packed and ready to use, was found buried in a bog on the Isle of Skye in Scotland. Despite the barrel having lain in the bog since the early Iron Age, the butter still retained its original form and consistency when it was dug up 1,800 years later, although the smell was a touch rancid. Almost 300 finds of "bog butter" are known from Ireland and Scotland. Opinions are divided concerning how this tradition of placing butter packed in a barrel or a cloth in bogs should be understood. It is a practice that apparently existed for 2000 years, from the Bronze Age to the Middle Ages. Some see it being a preservative measure, because the bog, rather like an

Barrel containing butter, placed in a bog on the island of the Isle of Skye during the Iron Age, AD 125-340.

exceptionally well-functioning refrigerator, could preserve perishable foodstuffs for a long time. Other discoveries of food include a 300-year old suckling pig and a 100-year old piece of cheese, recently found in bogs in Scotland and England. Did someone just forget where the food was hidden or did something happen? Or is the reason more probably, as Irish researchers believe, linked with the offering of food to the deities in line with Danish bog pots from prehistory? The latter are, as we will discover later, not quite as boring as their name suggests! Archaeologists interested in these matters cannot always reach agreement as to what the deposition of food in bogs actually means, and perhaps there is no unequivocal answer. It is, however, a fact that people from the Stone Age to Viking times made offerings to the deities *via* the waters of bogs and lakes. It is a fact that sphagnum preserves food in an astonishingly fresh state for a very long time.

A special form of treatment of the dead, seen in Scotland's Bronze Age, gives yet another insight into the preserving role of the bog as temporary storage. On the island of South Uist, one of the Outer Hebrides, British archaeologists excavated in 2000 the remains of three buildings at a locality by the name of Cladh Hallan. These buildings are thought to be death-houses containing burials from the time around 1300 BC. Four well-preserved skeletons had been placed in narrow graves in a flexed position. The skeletons were completely folded up as if they had been tightly swathed at their burial, as seen in South American mummies. One of those buried, a woman, had two of her own teeth placed in her hands. These had clearly been removed from her jaw after death. These people were buried long after their death, apparently in a mummified state by which the soft tissues still maintained the integrity of skeleton. Analyses of the bones showed that the bodies had been kept in a bog, in sphagnum, for a couple of centuries prior to their final burial at Cladh Hallan.

"It is a plant of great vision," states Ebbe Kløvedal Reich, quite rightly, of sphagnum in his Danish chronicle *Fæ og Frænde* ("Cattle and Kinsman"). Botanically speaking, dog's flesh, as Kløvedal also refers to sphagnum, originated about 300 million years ago, when the little plant deviated as a side-shoot from the mainstream of evolution and specialised itself in taking up nutrition through its leaves rather than developing roots. In places where the sun rarely shone to disturb the process, bog grew alongside bog and dog's flesh out-competed all higher plants.

The bog as a biotope

Dog's flesh became a true creation and the immortalisation of millennia of Danish history. On the surface, in light of day, the bog's endless expanses of sphagnum lie in all shades of the seasons, and dog's flesh, cotton-grass and bulrush combine to form downy "foxtails" across its top. The soft landscape with its shivering, moving ground is

Insectivorous sundew and cranberry are among the few species that survive in the acid environment of the bog.

also a very hardy biotope, of which sphagnum has taken possession of the greater part. Almost as long as there have been bogs, cranberry and bog whortleberry have found their way out there, whereas various species of heather first became a major part of the Danish flora when Stone Age farmers, in the last millennia before Christ, got to grips in earnest with working the soil. In addition to sphagnum, only 13 other species tolerate the acid environment of the bog. These include the insectivorous sundew, white beak rush and, in rare cases, bog asphodel and cloudberry. Ling, bell heather, and bog rosemary take it in turns to impart to the bog's flat expanses their characteristic red and violet seasonal shades. In periods of wetter climate, such as in the Iron Age, sphagnum's penetrating, luscious and clear yellow-green colour formed a variegated patchwork of colour in all seasons. Common birch, the introduced mountain pine and crowberry are visitors to the bog surface, but often in a crippled and stunted form as they are not very able to tolerate the acidic conditions. Neither are there many animals fond of the bog's acid environment, where most are presented with a limited menu. Even butterflies are rare in this peaceful, sunny landscape due to the poverty of host plants. Out on the hummocks, in the great boggy expanses, many bird species do, however, find protection in the breeding season. And it is here that the heathfowl, as the black grouse is also known, has had its stand and playground as long as bogs have existed.

Cotton-grass. Lille Vildmose. Himmerland, Jutland.

The black grouse, bird of bog and heath, abandoned Denmark as a breeding ground in 2001 as habitats became too cramped.

The productive bog with endless landscapes of industrially extracted peat. Store Vildmose. Himmerland, Jutland, 2002.

The landscape of the bog

There were once several hundred bogs in Denmark, but most were drained or dug away during the 18th-20th centuries, when the last black grouse left the country and handed over the final remaining bogs to cranes and other waders. Surrounded by today's thoroughly drained and regulated landscape, where our knowledge and perception of bogs is limited to a yellow grow-bag by the name of *Pindstrup Plus* and the highly-prized scheduling of 1% of the country's wilderness, it is hard for us to imagine the diverse nature of former times. Back then the bog was the marginal zone between forests and people. Together with its closest environs, it was a morass of plants, wet and boggy ground, serene, blackish-brown waterholes with caterpillars and biting and stinging insects. A mysterious and desolate place between land and water, with no roads or paths or fixed reference points, but with the all-engulfing depths always lurking under the surface. A wrong step made in the leap from hummock to hummock and one was lost and gone forever. If we believe the folk traditions, bogs have through time engulfed a multitude of people and animals – anyone who dared to go out there, especially at night.

In the undulating landscapes of Ireland and Scotland, it was not just a question of taking care when going near the bog. It was here that the boggy masses dragged whole villages to a watery grave. With a rare sense of exaggerated evil, the Irish author Bram Stoker, in *The Snake's Pass* from 1890, gives an exceptionally hair-raising account of the fateful nature of the bog. It steps into cruel character as an evil carpet of death which, swathed in cold and fatal mists and fogs, engulfs everything and everyone in its path. Here lurks the snake as the cunning and gruesome being of the bog. This death-defying landscape is not Stoker's own destructive idea but nature's cruel creation of an all-consuming kind. When the law of gravity rules, and enormous reservoirs of water are displaced out over dramatic landscapes, a gigantic water bubble can, in the course of a few seconds, raise itself up and burst. Like the Great Flood it can take whole landscapes along with it, as has happened several times through history in the British Isles.

Our Danish wild bogs have never achieved such dramatic heights, despite the fact that Store Vildmose, at its peak, once covered an area of more than 50 square kilometres. Today, in terms of area, it can match most bogs in other countries, but it has, in agreement with our flat and phlegmatic landscape, always grown hesitantly and calmly, by a couple of paces a year – at the most.

In the flat nature of Denmark, the bog represents the boundary, the outskirts, the margin or the place where, for millennia, peat has been cut for fuel. Pollen analysts are able to read in the peat layers of the bog that, some time in the Bronze Age, around 1000-800 BC, people began to cut peat. And that is how we have continued, pragmatically exploiting the bog's resources well into the 20th century. The bog is more than a

Peat bog on Jæren. 1882. Kitty Lange Kielland.

resource we exploit to keep warm, it is also a mentally evocative landscape, serene and compelling. At dusk, when day meets night, things are afoot in the landscape of the bog. We know this from the prevalent view of nature of recent times, when bogs still existed. When the day and the peat cutting were over, the bog was transformed into a seductive landscape, inhabited by mysterious beings. The world of the living then played in the dark with this mythological landscape's unfathomable underworld of shadows and echoes from down the millennia, in a white, dreamlike veil drifting over the cold, black depths.

Elfin dance. 1866.
August Malmström.

The bog has been given its place both in a romantic view of nature, in art and in poetry, and in popular, traditional legends and ballads from the 19th century. Artists and authors maintained and worshipped the bog as a transcendental landscape, animated with spirits. Perhaps it was our own emotional projections that were allowed to unfold in the landscape, or more precisely the natural beings of popular belief and an insistence on a supernatural dimension.

A meeting between nature and culture

*Beneath the serene and unfathomable waters of lakes
and bogs ruled supernatural powers to which
not even myths of mighty ancestors could measure up.*

It is unlikely to have been just hay making and peat cutting or will-o-the-wisps and naughtily enticing elfin girls that drew prehistoric people to the bogs with their offerings. Back then, the bog as a landscape, also represented something much greater in people's consciousness, something detached from economic and romantic dependency. But in the beginning, bogs were just in the making and people focussed their attention elsewhere in nature.

Hunters migrating through the landscape

When the first bogs formed in Denmark about 10,000 years ago, Jutland, Zealand, Funen and all the other Danish islands formed a continuous body of land which, intersected by great rivers, extended all the way over to England. Remnants of the last Ice Age still lay as a colossal ice cap over Southern Norway and to the north of the great Swedish lakes. The post-glacial tundra landscape, with its great flocks of reindeer, was overtaken by light, open birch and pine forests. There were large shallow lakes where aurochs, bison, wild horse and later, when the forest grew denser, also red deer, wild boar and roe deer, foraged along the shore. The climate curve was in ascendance. The temperature in summer reached 18 degrees C and pine and hazel closed in around the great inland lakes and the developing bogs, where waterlilies and club rushes formed dense vegetation together with reed beds. Hunter-gatherer families exploited the seasons' changing resources of game, fish and plant foods along coasts, rivers, and inland lakes and bogs.

Over a land area of 300,000 square kilometres, people lived a nomadic existence, wandering between seasonal resources. Remarkably uniform cultural trends bear witness to the scattered population's extensive contact network throughout the endless tracts of forest and wetlands. Alongside the South Zealand bogs of Holmegård and

In the wake of the Ice Age's barren landscape followed open tundra with herds of reindeer.

Maglemose, which in the Stone Age were great lakes with just the beginnings of bog formation, are the remains of settlements of the Maglemosian people. Families comprising 6-8 members lived periodically on the edge of the lake in dwellings of about 20 square metres. From here, they exploited everything that nature offered by way of fishing, hunting game along the shore, and the rich bird life. Even though families lived from hand to mouth in a never-ending hunt for food, their tools, amulets and weapons, decorated with figurative and geometric art, bear witness to a society with an aesthetic, artistic, and even spiritual fellowship and energy. A belief in something greater and spiritual is seen expressed in their thanksgiving offerings to nature, comprising skeletal remains of game animals deposited in special places in the landscape. An example is seen at Skottemarke on Lolland, where the post-glacial hunters offered elk bones, after first having split them and perhaps eating the marrow at a ritual feast, or laying it out to be consumed by the deities.

6000-year-old art from Ertebølle times. Amber ornament. Holme, Djursland, Jutland.

Engraved figurative compositions of people and game animals, as well as symbols of fertility, are occasionally found at settlements from this time, and in bogs. We have no idea whether bogs and other wetland areas played a special role in their spiritual world. We are similarly ignorant of the situation in the subsequent Ertebølle period, when the climate curve continued to rise and rapid melting of the ice dramatically created the beginnings of a Danish island kingdom. It became warmer, the temperature was as much as a couple of degrees higher than today, and it was considerably wetter. After the melting of the ice masses and the drastic environmental changes that took place during the warm period, the Great Belt and Little Belt were formed by storm-surge-like events

The hunters of Ertebølle times
migrated between seasonal settle-
ments alongside lakes and bogs in
the dense primeval forest of the
interior and light, warm bays
close to the coast's abundant sup-
plies of oysters, fish, and marine
mammals.

in which the global sea level rose by 2.3 metres over the course of a century. Around 7000 BC, the area we today call Denmark was a landscape of innumerable islands and finely divided coastlines. With time, the land became covered by dense and almost impenetrable primeval forest comprising especially lime and elm with a dense understorey in which ivy twined and spiralled under optimal conditions. By lakes and bogs deep in the primeval forest, hunting families made camp on seasonal visits in their hunt for food and fur animals. With his bow and arrows over his shoulder, the hunter met pond tortoises by the bogs and the great lakes as he fought his way through the morass in search of red deer and wild boar. When the season was favourable, and resources available, they paddled down broad rivers out to the coast's bulging larder of fish, marine mammals, and pelicans, and oysters so large as hardly can be imagined possible today. People continued their nomadic existence and fell in with the natural order of things during their travels after food or raw materials for their tools and weapons. Spirit and art unfolded where people found themselves – expressed on hunting weapons, ornaments and

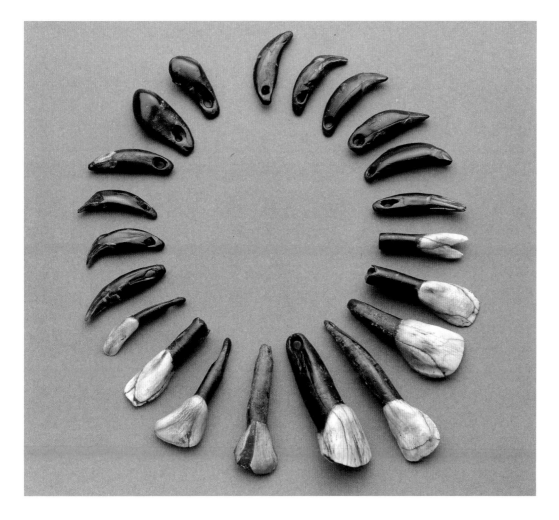

A collection of perforated animal teeth from the final part of the Mesolithic, found in Mosegårds Mose, Åmosen, Zealand. They could have been lost or arrived there by chance, but they could also be the beginnings of the tradition of depositing ritual offerings in water that came to play such a significant role for the farming communities of subsequent millennia.

amulets, and in their treatment of the dead. Contact between groups of hunters can be clearly seen in their art and in the common features of tools and weapons; exchanges of goods and gifts ensured friendship between tribes. Like ever-widening circles, contact between people spread out as the hunters paddled further away and crossed open waters, forging links with early farming cultures to the south in Continental Europe.

When we became farmers

Under the influence of these cultures to the south, with which there had long been contact, came a new occupation, farming. With it came a different way of life that also embraced a new view of nature in which offerings in open water played a central role. The practice of offering arrived in Denmark at the very end of the Mesolithic, rather more than 6000 years ago. It followed the distribution of a particularly prestigious type of axe, made from greenstone – a kind of stone that only occurs naturally in the Balkan

area and the Carpathians, more than 1.000 kilometres distant from Southern Scandinavia. From hand to hand and from tribe to tribe these axes were distributed northwards from farming communities in Central Germany, through Schleswig-Holstein and on to Denmark and Scania. As an important link in the formation and maintenance of friendship alliances and the creation of matrimonial pacts, whereby both artefacts and women were exchanged, the axes played an important role in relations between individual communities. These foreign axes were no better functionally than the local hunters' flint axes, but they brought with them status and a tradition from foreign cultures. Axes of jadite, mined by farming communities in the Italian Alps, also found their way by exchange to Scandinavia. A strong cultural network was under development, borne by an internal social battle for prestige in which exotic goods played a significant role.

The early farmers in Southern Scandinavia deposited these foreign and exotic axes as offerings in lakes and bogs. With this came the beginnings of an offering tradition that acquired great significance for the farming cultures of subsequent millennia. It was the reason Grauballe Man was laid in the bog. It may even have been the reason for his death. The bog continued as a place of offering until the introduction of Christianity. In pre-Christian farming communities, wetlands in general, and bogs in particular, played a special role in people's encounters with the supernatural, as the place for depositing gifts or offerings to the powers who had an influence over – or even controlled – human life.

In Scandinavia, neolithisation, as the transition from hunter-gatherer to farmer is termed, took place very consistently around 4000 BC. It began with exchanges of stone axes, special antler axes and fashions relating to both ornamentation and technology. The latter included weapons and the manufacture of pottery. Ceramics gradually became incorporated into the hunting cultures as a foreign and exotic element, although they had more a status-endowing rather than a strictly practical function. People became farmers at the same time across the whole of Denmark, but they did not abandon hunting and fishing as an occupation. It was a further 500 years before agriculture attained serious economic significance. Farming, as a way of life, was much more than cereal cultivation and the domestication of animals. It was a lifestyle that brought with it major ideological changes which, to a very great extent, involved the relationship with nature.

At the time when the first farmers took possession of the land, the temperature fell and the forest slowly became more open with an expansion in hazel, herbs and grasses. In the warm period, these plants had been suppressed by the dense, dark forest. Oak, birch, and ash also became more common and on the poorest soils heather flourished on the woodland floor. Pollen diagrams from bogs and old land surfaces, sealed under

The dolmen Poskær Stenhus on Mols, Jutland. The Mols land-scape lies close to the coast and is peppered with dolmens. Many offerings of axes have been found in the area's characteristic kettle holes, which were lakes and bogs during the Stone Age.

dolmens and passage graves, reveal that the first farmers created small clearances using slash-and-burn techniques and by grazing their cattle. Elsewhere, the gathering of leaf fodder created open areas. As sedentary farmers, people now settled at permanent sites, cultivated the soil, constructed burial mounds for their ancestors and generally developed a much more intimate relationship with their local landscape, including bogs, to which offerings were taken. Territorial division of the land was also about to begin.

Great megalithic graves lay close to rivers, lakes, and other wetlands that bound together the small hamlets. These graves lay some distance inland, up on the hillsides. In the wetland areas immediately below, the farmers gathered now and then to hold ritual feasts and celebrations and to make offerings. Valuable flint axes, together with pottery vessels used for the sacred meals were submerged close to the edge of the bog.

The term "bog pot" is used to describe hundreds of pottery vessels deposited on the edges of bogs and lakes during the Neolithic, the Bronze Age and, particularly, in the subsequent period - the time of Grauballe Man – the Iron Age. The bog pots were probably laid in the cold water filled with food. Whether their contents were intended for people or gods we will never really know for sure. We must just recognise that bogs played a major, but far from unequivocal, role in prehistoric society. The most beautiful bog pot of all – even if this is not a particularly flattering term for this absolute masterpiece – is the richly and beautifully decorated funnel beaker from Skarpsalling in Himmerland, from the time around 3200 BC.

In some cases, the pottery vessels stood singly. In others, they were deposited together with arrangements of woven branches and other forms of stabilisation for the quaking boggy ground. Here too, the remains of meals, comprising animal bones and other objects, were also deposited. In the bog Salpetermosen, south of Hillerød, are the remains of just such an offering place. At the tip of a small peninsula, which extended into the bog, the farmers had built a platform of branches and twigs in order to be able to walk out over the boggy ground. The platform followed the shore of the bog over an area measuring 22 metres in length by 10 metres in width, and was built of poles, sticks, and brushwood. On the platform lay charcoal and scattered, fist-sizes stones. These must be remnants of the farmers' visits to the site. In the bog, just by the platform, a tall funnel-shaped vessel had been deposited and there were two flint axes close by. A further pottery vessel had been placed by the platform. It stood surrounded by sticks pushed vertically down, securing it in the bog. Outside the layer of branches, a finely decorated bowl had been placed and, finally, there was a further flint axe, as well as the jawbones of a lamb and cattle limb bones.

Passage grave after restoration around 1980. Halskov Vænge, Falster.

The Skarpsalling vessel, Himmerland.

Pottery vessel with wooden spoon offered in Tømmerup bog, Zealand.

Bog offering of ten polished stone axes from Maglehøjs Vænge, Zealand. The axes were manufactured solely for ritual use. The largest measures 38 cm in length.

Places are known across the whole country where farmers, for ritual reasons, deposited pottery vessels. Alone from the islands east of the Great Belt there are 100 such sites where pottery vessels have been found in wetland areas: lakes, bogs and at the sources of watercourses. These sites lie close to prominent features in the landscape which were reference points or of cultic significance. At Alvastra in Östergötland, Sweden, a wooden platform was found measuring 45 metres in length by 20 metres in width. On this were preserved hearths, rough-outs for stone battle axes, flint axes, amber beads, and pottery vessels as well as the bones of animals and humans. Such platforms, located close to wetland areas, are known from the whole Denmark and the rest of Northern Europe, frequently in direct association with the farmers' settlements. Often food remains are found together with the pottery vessels, for example bones of cattle, sheep, pig, goat, red deer, and roe deer.

Even though these so-called bog offerings are not very conspicuous and they do not promote a spiritual understanding of society at that time, the numerous bog pots and, through time, also the overwhelming numbers of axes deposited – often several identical, newly manufactured examples laid in the same place – bear witness to the fact that wetland areas played an important role in acts of worship during the Neolithic. These communities were no longer a natural, integral part of their environment as had been the case with the hunter and fisher communities, whose rituals had the primary intention of reinforcing nature's given cycle. With the first farming communities came an ideological change by which the view of nature became much more progressive and had the aim of taming the mighty natural forces. At that time, people were organised into tribes or simple chieftainships. Ethnography tells us a little more about how early farming communities were organised and the relationships between people, nature and the spiritual universe. Society was at that time based on kinship and people saw themselves as direct descendants of a particular ancestor. In societies of this kind, religion encompasses god-like beings, for example the gods of the sky or the sun, but it is mostly focussed on spirits, fetishism, and witches. Spirits and witches could intervene in people's lives in many ways. They must be treated cannily *via* rituals performed by particularly powerful people with special abilities.

In these chieftainships, magic was a natural part of agriculture and was used in a very rational and practical way. The agricultural rites naturally followed the development of crops, with special rituals around sowing, growth and flowering, development of grains and fruits and, finally, harvest. The year was, in this way, divided up into a number of recurrent festivals and ceremonies.

In prehistory, the farming populations' offerings of pots were probably part of celebrations, prayers and tributes concerning the fertility of both nature and people. A pot and an insignificant collection of bones do not, however, immediately conjure up an

image of this type of life-confirming scenario. The apparently soul-less earthly remains arising from such seasonal celebrations are not in themselves interesting. It requires insight and empathy to understand their correct significance. Prehistory's societies and landscapes reside today behind a foggy veil, and educated, informed people find it hard to imagine prehistoric people's belief in, and subservience to, the supernatural. The material remains are just a fraction of the true story, which is endlessly complex. We will never uncover it completely, but ethnography and empathy do at least, all the same, make us a little wiser.

Prehistory's offering vessels were generally used pots, often bearing the remains of food that had burnt fast or had even boiled over and run down the outer surface of the vessel. After the ceremony the used vessels were left at the offering place. In ethnography, this phenomenon is called *mana*, and is seen in chieftainships as we believe they were organised during the Bronze Age and the Early Iron Age in Denmark. People or material objects possess a strong power, *mana*, which manifests both a fear and a blessing. This power can be transferred to objects touched by a person with *mana*. The objects, *via* this contact, or by participating in special rituals, become too powerful for earthly handling and must therefore be discarded, for example in a lake or a bog already included within the ritual.

Several similar theories are linked with the concept of purity. Objects can become either sacred or contaminated by having been part of a special ritual or having belonged to an ailing or weak person. They must therefore be disposed of. There may, of course, be many possible explanations for the offering vessels found in bogs, and the finds are not unequivocal, but there is no doubt that they formed part of something much greater.

Contact with the spirits played a particularly major role in the prevention of illness. Illnesses and accidents of any kind were bound up with hostile forces. These could be spirits who were offended by peoples' breaking of taboos, or spirits that were generally just evil and caused a person to become ill. This means that illness and accidents could be cured and avoided using the positive magic generated by an offering to the spirits.

In several of the wetland areas where offered vessels have been found there are also human bones of the same date. These bones are especially those of women and adolescents, the sex of whom cannot be determined. At the edge of the bog of Myrebjerg on Langeland, the menu at an offering celebration included all kinds of meat. Bones of domesticated cattle, wild horse, pig, sheep, duck, and pond tortoise lay at the water's edge under a small area of stone paving, together with the bones of at least five people: an adult woman, two adolescents of about 18 years of age as well as two children. There were not complete skeletons – just some parts of the deceased.

Neolithic religion involved human sacrifices. In burials in dolmens and passage graves, the bodies were laid to rest after the de-fleshed skeleton had been divided up

Facing page.
During the Battle Axe culture
large amounts of amber were
included in the offering rituals.
In Sortekær bog in Western
Jutland, this pottery vessel was
offered, filled with amber beads.

according to special rules and in particular locations. The actual bones then received caring and specific treatment and were deposited in various different places, for example in megalithic graves and at ritual places of assembly. Some of the bones from an individual skeleton could have been reserved for ceremonies during the bog offerings. Several of the animal bones at the offering sites had been split to extract the bone marrow; perhaps this was of ritual significance. Human bones were, conversely, never split in this way. We can therefore reject any suggestion that cannibalism played a part in the offering ceremonies.

Human sacrifices

In a little bog associated with Veksø bog at Sigersted in Northeastern Zealand, the skeletal remains of two young people, both probably women, and, respectively, 16 and 18 years of age, were found during peat cutting in 1948. Around the neck of the oldest were the remains of a cord made of plant fibre, suggesting she had been strangled. The skeletons lay about five metres apart, and close by was a large pottery vessel dated to around 3500 BC. The same date was indicated by radiocarbon dating of the skeletons. At Boelkilde on Als, human skeletons were found of the same date. These were of two men of 16 and 40 years of age, respectively. The oldest had a rope around his neck with which he had probably been strangled. The men were laid in the bog around 3400 BC. Something very terrible took place prior to offering of the ultimate sacrifice – human life.

Lakes and bogs were the scenes of ritual ceremonies and feasts for Early Neolithic society. The productivity of the fields and the continuation of the family line were matters between people and supernatural powers who controlled life and death. In this way, wetland areas have, through time, consumed enormous quantities of gifts brought by people in real earnest and with respect for life and death. Pottery vessels, beautifully worked flint axes, some of which – alone by virtue of their size – must have been manufactured exclusively for ritual use and offering, were deposited in bogs. Several hundred finds of axes – a single example from Haderslev had 99 axes neatly stacked in piles – were offered at ceremonies over a period of 2.000 years. Flint axes were deposited meticulously in the bogs, probably according to some particularly meaningful rule, for example arranged like the spokes of a wheel, in the form of a cross, stacked up or pressed down into the peat. Copious amounts of chisels, flint blades, and amber beads, the latter in quantities of up to 12.000 at a time, were offered by farmers in a bog at Mollerup in the western part of Salling.

In the later part of the Neolithic, the communal megalithic burials were succeeded around 2800 BC by individual burials. This period is called the Battle-axe culture. The tradition of offering continued steadily, but now it was axe types typical of this new period that were sacrificed. Amber and pottery vessels accompanied the dead to their graves instead.

Offerings in bogs and grave goods were two sides of the same coin: Wealth was taken out of circulation and deposited. Gifts and rituals at the funeral were for the benefit of the descendants and perhaps, in particular, the world at large, being used to demonstrate the wealth of the deceased and, in turn, that of his or her family. The ritualised offerings of wealth in bogs are an expression of the same idea. A group, part of a family, can possess wealth, but this wealth was borne and manifested by men of high rank. The aim of the offerings was probably to increase the prestige of the local community relative to other communities. It must be borne in mind that in a kinship-based society, like that of the Neolithic, the group was a finite and an indivisible unit. The individual existed on behalf of the group, which represented the highest authority. Personal equipment belonged to the individual whereas land, houses and other wealth were owned jointly by the group. Everyone had a kinship-determined position in the hierarchy of the group.

In ethnography, a similar kinship system is described in the Northwest Coastal Indians along the Pacific Ocean. Here, the term *potlatch* is used, which means that wealth must be expended in lavish consumption. In this way, personal wealth and power over others was displayed, conferring esteem and prestige on the kinship group. The extreme consequence of *potlatch* involved the giving away or destruction of valuable items. A person of high rank invited people to *potlatch* and gave away highly-prized gifts, dug-out canoes, rugs and other valuable objects, to the invited guests. The ceremony conferred prestige and respect on the giver. However, for the recipient the opposite was true. Therefore, in order to win greater prestige, the recipient must then also invite to *potlatch* and ideally give away gifts of even greater value. This phenomenon provided the opportunity for internal competition between groups and at the same time reinforced solidarity within them.

In the final centuries of the Neolithic, around 2000 BC, when the first bronze arrived in Denmark from the Bronze Age cultures of Southeastern Europe, the community's offerings accelerated in this internal competition within society. In a fashion trend acquired from the south, the dagger overtook the role as the male prestige weapon. Flint mining in Northern Jutland was in full swing and the highly developed domestic flint technology was sublime in its accuracy and design with respect to copying the exotic bronze daggers from the south.

Denmark has no natural occurrences of tin or copper, the two components of the alloy bronze. Despite this, local social structures and powerful networks that existed in the latter part of the Neolithic were geared up to participate in the demonstration of status in the Bronze Age, expressed *via* the possession of bronze. In Central Europe, cul-

Facing page.
Flint daggers in large numbers were deposited as offerings in lakes and bogs in the final part of the Stone Age.

"Burial mounds crown the green country", wrote Johannes V. Jensen in "Hvor smiler fagert den danske kyst" (How fairly smiles the Danish coast) in 1925. Skyum Bjerge, Thy.

tures had existed for a couple of centuries in which bronze was the medium conferring social prestige and power. In Scandinavia, a strong and independent Bronze Age culture developed from humble beginnings around 2000 BC. It was borne on the widely branched network formed by the leading clans or chieftainships with Central European cultures, and from where the raw materials for bronze, tin and copper, came to flow in copious quantities.

The time of the mound people

The Bronze Age became in all respects a period of expansion, not least with regard to exploitation of the landscape. The monumental, towering burial mounds that everywhere crowned Danish hills and ridges, speak their own clear language. There are still 20.000 burial mounds out on the hills; epitaphs to the great chieftains of a distant time when competition for prestige and power was a matter of life and death. Bronze Age farmers probably built somewhere in the region of 50,000 burial mounds, but grave robbers and mechanised agriculture destroyed a very great number before the act providing legal protection – *Fredningsloven* – put a stop to the vandalism in 1937.

Hohøj near Mariager, Jutland is, with its height of 12 metres, the largest Bronze Age burial mound in Denmark.

The building blocks in Bronze Age burial mounds were grass turves, cut from the surrounding area. The individual turves can still be seen with the naked eye. From the excavation of the Bronze Age burial mound Diverhøj on Djursland.

Bronze Age burial mounds are built solely of turf, cut by the farmers from the surrounding area. Raw material extraction on this scale must have left a significant mark on the productive agricultural landscape. Hohøj near Mariager is, with its height of 12 metres and diameter of 70 metres, absolutely one of the largest burial mounds from the Bronze Age. An area of 20 hectares was cleared of grass turf alone in its construction.

Otherwise it is pollen evidence from bogs that again helps us paint a picture of the landscape, admittedly with a broad brush. Pollen of beech appears for the first time and it is also the first time in prehistory that we can speak in earnest of an open cultural landscape. Cattle and people exploited the woodland intensively for grazing and harvesting of leaf hay for winter fodder, not to speak of firewood and timber for houses and fences. There was great social differentiation in Bronze Age society. The size of the farmsteads varied from humble long-houses to settlements with great halls, up to 50 metres in length, that perhaps housed several families. When the construction of burial mounds was at its peak, the few in possession of power built houses on the ridges, close to the burial mounds of their ancestors. Others built lower down and more modestly in the landscape, close to the wetland areas.

The Bronze Age was a turbulent period, full of contradictions, when rituals in the bogs and lakes came to play an increasingly important role in demonstrations of power by leading families. Beneath the serene and unfathomable waters of lakes and bogs, on whose surface the moon rhythmically reflected its fiery red orb and where white veils of mist played, ruled supernatural powers to which not even myths about mighty ancestors could measure up. The still mirror-like surface of bog water assembled people in intercession and the heavens provided answers and omens like the surface of a crystal ball. Treasures were lowered down to the gods residing within the bog's black depths. The Bronze Age was a veritable celebration of these solemn and essential offerings aimed at ensuring people's well-being. This period's extravagant treatment of valuables cannot be interpreted in any other way. Initially, when supplies of bronze were scarce, bronze axes were offered, first one, and then whole bundles, in honour of the gods and for personal social gain. The *potlatch* function was in full bloom and through the offering of items of great value, the system of power became altered. Already in the Early Bronze Age, the individual was not assigned any great influence by way of burial rituals. It was alone the power of the group or the family – the community – that was demonstrated through offerings. Grandiose procedures and rituals probably accompanied these offerings. The ceremonies would be remembered, commemorated, and recounted through generations with due reference to the burial monuments of the ancestors that towered proudly over the landscape, there where the fields meet the sky. With time, as bronze found its way to Scandinavia in more abundant quantities from new cultures, for example in Hungary, who controlled ore extraction, local core areas began to devel-

op. On Northern Funen, in Eastern Jutland and in Northern Zealand there were areas that, apparently *via* direct long-distance trade, had close contacts with the rich Bronze Age cultures to the south. Bronze flowed northwards along land routes, and amber, wax for bronze casting and furs undoubtedly flowed in the opposite direction as payment.

The ritual offerings made a yet greater contribution to reinforcing the power of local core areas. Even though the offerings manifested power and wealth through their abundance, the system was vulnerable, borne exclusively by supplies obtained *via* distant connections. Following displacements in the economic power balance of Europe, under the influence of the blossoming Greek and Mycenaean Bronze Age cultures, new, stronger cultures arose on the European Continent, centred on the Carpathian Basin. An extensive exchange network, transporting rich supplies of raw materials and finished products, permeated Europe. A new supra-regional structure arose, borne by a warrior aristocracy who buried their dead in burial mounds. Southern Scandinavia followed this trend and the old group fellowship fell apart in the early part of the Bronze Age. Burial mounds were now built which, by virtue of their size and the rich grave goods contained within them, signalled that it was smaller family groups and individuals, rather than the broader kinship, who made their mark in the hierarchy of society. The individual became more prominent in the battle for power and prestige.

The bog played a great role as an offering place for golden metal treasures in the Bronze Age.

The burial mounds of the Bronze Age were built over great men and women from leading families. A handful of these particularly well-preserved Bronze Age people, including the Egtved Girl, have become part of the Danish national identity. Not as well known, but just as well-preserved, is the Bronze Age family interred in Borum Eshøj, near Århus. The young man from Borum Eshøj was laid to rest wearing a loincloth and a woollen cloak and with a magnificent wooden sheath with a leather suspension, in which a bronze dagger had been placed for the occasion. A pious fraud, they said, when the burial was discovered at the end of the 1880s.

The bog played a central role as an offering place throughout the whole of the Bronze Age. We no longer find traces of platforms with the remains of offering ceremonies, and neither are there pottery vessels deposited in large numbers. Communities were focussed on prestige and power and the deposition or, more correctly, the destruction of status objects. While Europe boiled from the internal manifestations of powerful and affluent warrior aristocracies, while Greek culture expanded and Homer wrote both *The Iliad* and the account of Odysseus' fabulous journey and death, the Bronze Age cultures of Southern Scandinavia felt the influence of a supremely powerful European melting pot offering fluctuating supplies of metal.

Swords, axes, and brooches, together with more exotic wares, occasionally of gold, accompanied the men buried in mounds on their journey through death towards the afterlife. Women embarking on the same journey were given great necklaces, bracelets of gold and bronze, belt ornaments, dress- and hair-pins. Worship of the individual and the chieftain as the ultimate leader of the group, with its consequent lavishness of burial rituals, shifted the focus away from bog offerings. People probably still talked, sang and celebrated, said prayers and offered in the bogs in ample measure, but not with the same intense extravagance as was previously the case. Initially, it was men's status that was offered in the bogs in the form of axes and swords. Later, around 1400 BC, women stepped forward onto the powerful platform of society. This is apparent from communal offerings of magnificent belt ornaments and large neck- and arm-rings, often deposited in paired sets. Perhaps it was the tradition that two women acted together when offering. In general, women became much more prominent through the offerings, perhaps because they played an important role in alliances by entering into marriages within the elite. Around 1000 BC, the construction of the mighty burial mounds

ceased. Inspired by cultures to the south, cremation was introduced to Scandinavia at this time – completely and consistently. Small personal items of bronze, such as knives, razors, awls and tweezers, as well as miniature swords, accompanied the burnt bones. Conversely, precious objects were now sacrificed in bogs as never before.

People came into contact with the supernatural everywhere in the landscape. At every bog and damp meadow near their settlements they carried out ceremonies and offered treasures, ornaments of bronze and gold, axes and swords. Also cultic objects, far removed from the personal universe, such as gold bowls, horned bronze helmets, lures, and bronze figures were deposited in bogs. These offerings of bronze objects rarely left traces of the rituals that undoubtedly unfolded in the process of their deposition.

An offering well at Budsene on Møn did, however, reveal rather more, like offerings during the Neolithic. At the base of the well, formed of a hollowed-out tree trunk dug in at the edge of a bog, lay two so-called suspended vessels, in reality oversized belt ornaments that women probably wore during special ceremonies. There was also another belt ornament of a different voluminous design, as well as three long spiral arm-rings, all of bronze. Perhaps three women had, together, in fellowship, carried out this sacred

Facing page.
The role of women becomes apparent in offerings from the end of the second millennium BC, perhaps because women played a special role in the marital alliances of the elite. An offering found at Vognserup Enge on Zealand comprised two sets of female ornaments, collars, belt plates, and 41 small ornamental plates intended to be sewn onto costumes. There were also small bronze bosses, also intended to be sewn on, spirals and small cylindrical bronze tubes. In these tubes were the remains of woollen thread. They were probably attached to a string skirt like that in which Egtved Girl was buried.

offering. With the bronze artefacts in the well were also bones of cattle, sheep, pig, horse, and dog. These could be the remains of a sacred meal, or perhaps these bones bear another secret concerning the ritualised offering cult of the Bronze Age.

Towards the end of the 7th century BC the Bronze Age went into decline. Crises in ore supplies in Central Europe, linked with economic disruption arising from the rise and fall of various power centres, together with the increasing importance of iron, caused the strong supply network with Scandinavia to collapse. Bronze Age Scandinavia suffered a decline and became marginalised, uncoupled from the European power play. Offerings in bogs were still practised in continuation of a millennium-long and well-rooted tradition, but they represented only a pale afterglow of the pride and manifestation of previous times. Worn-out swords and jewellery continued to be offered to the supernatural powers and the family's prestige, but only in modest amounts, as supplies of bronze failed and finally came to a complete halt.

The Bronze Age in Southern Scandinavia was a powerful and contradictory period, lived on the basis of plentiful supply and prestige networks and filled with conflicts and battles for respect on a flimsy foundation, resting solely on contacts with well-consolidated cultures far away. It was also a time of broad horizons in spiritual and religious ethereal respects. True, there was much at stake in the battle for access to the status-conferring bronze. But the religious symbols of the time also leave an impression of the period as a brilliant time, with room for artistic and aesthetic expression in the working of exquisite bronze artefacts, produced by craftsmen of great technical skill. The masterpiece, the Sun Chariot from Trundholm bog in Odsherred, and the many rock carv-

In the cosmology of the Bronze Age, a fish, a horse, and a snake follow the daily cycle of the sun on its journey with the ships of the day and the night. In the morning, the fish helps the sun across from the night ship to the day ship. Razor from the Bronze Age.

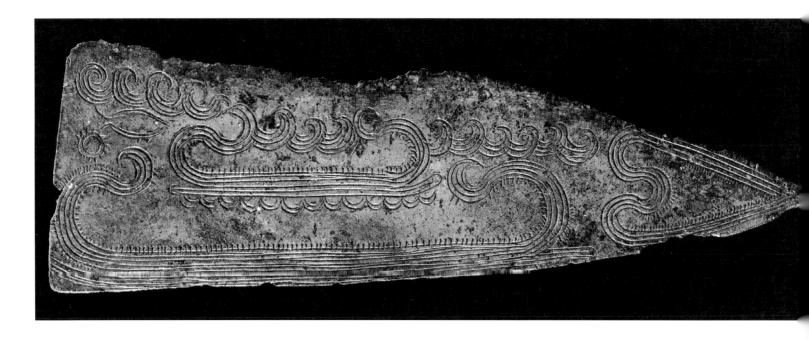

ing-related motifs seen on, for example, razors, show links with Norwegian and Swedish rock art which, loaded with cultic symbolism, gives the impression of a period of great spiritual richness and energy. If we are to believe the archaeological record, this was a time of sun and warmth. Climate researchers are even able to confirm the latter. The sun played a significant role in the ornamental and cultic expression of the period, and the rather revealing skirt worn by Egtved Girl, when she was buried on a summer's day in 1379 BC, conveys an impression of warmth and great sensuality. The sun has played a central role throughout all generations of farming society, ever since the Stone Age when it was the ultimate expression of light and with that of life itself. In the Bronze Age, the sun was exposed through a great iconic richness. In the case of Stone Age farmers, sun worship is not evident in their artefacts to the same degree. But the sun's transit across the heavens undoubtedly occupied an similarly major role for the early farming societies of the Neolithic as expressed, for example, in the orientation of the entrances of megalithic graves towards sun and moon.

The Sun Chariot from Trundholm bog on Zealand, 14th century BC. The divine sun is drawn by the horse across the firmament. The night side, conversely, has no gold-plated sun.

The time of Grauballe Man

"The rawness came sailing
with the clouds of the sky over the old summer people.
In the cold rain much was whipped away that,
for the Iron Age people, would be surplus,
but for their forefathers was life itself."

It was the founder of the National Museum, Christian Jürgensen Thomsen, who, in 1836, according to the basic principles of evolution and the relative chronology between artefacts, advanced his *Ledetraad til nordisk Oldkyndighed* (Guide to Nordic Antiquarianism). In this, he defined developments during prehistory in terms of Stone, Bronze, and Iron Ages, named after the dominant technology of the time or, more correctly, the material from which people manufactured their tools and weapons. After bronze came iron.

The decline of European Bronze Age cultures apparently left Southern Scandinavia in a vacuum as regards archaeological finds, stripped of status symbols in the form of prestigious metal artefacts deposited in graves and wetland areas. The subsequent Iron Age began as an anonymous time with no outstanding finds or events, or so it appears on the face of it. There are no indications that a new period's greatness marked the accepted transition to the age of iron, set at 500 BC. Seductive shiny yellow bronze and irresistible gold are attractive for demonstrating status and power, but quite, perhaps almost totally, fraudulent with regard to strength and functionality. As nothing in comparison to the cold, grey metal of the Iron Age that ages to ugly, rust-encrusted clumps after millennia in the soil, but which is much more suitable for tools and weapons.

Iron's strength and rawness was exactly what the peoples of Europe and Asia Minor came to feel now the Celts had overtaken the European arena. Herodot and other classical authors called the Celts, who probably originated from the Balkans, Gauls. This warrior people, who had taken power after the final Bronze Age elite had expired within their empire in Southern Germany and Eastern France, appeared to be invincible. The culture of the Celts arose out of trading links, and good business sense now moved as a mobile army on war chariots, southwards in all directions. They went out of lust for the fruits and women of the south, driven by overpopulation or simple imperial ambi-

The Dying Gaul marked for the Romans the end of the Celts' advance into Southeastern Europe and Asia Minor. The sculpture was included in the Athena temple in Pergamon, Asia Minor around 220 BC. The Gaul (the Celt) wears a torque around his neck – the characteristic Celtic neck-ring, also known from discoveries made in Danish bogs. The Capitol Museum, Rome, Italy.

tion and, with a complete disregard for danger, they struck down everything in their way. These fiercely advancing Celts who, in the 3rd and 2nd centuries BC, vandalised Mediterranean countries, feared no less than that the sky would fall down upon their heads, wrote Caesar from his battle camp after a meeting with the fearless and warlike strangers. In 225 BC the Celts were, however, forcefully defeated in Rome and retreated from Italy. From their Central European territories, they did, however, continue to influence European art and craftwork in subsequent centuries, right up into the first century B.C.

Events in Southern Europe during the first centuries of the Iron Age did not have any great effect on the farming communities of Southern Scandinavian. The ill-mannered Celts were busily occupied in expansion towards the south and initially there were not many cultural currents running in a northerly direction. As quiet and calm as it apparently appeared in Southern Scandinavia, at least quiet and calm in terms of archaeological finds, seen through the eyes of posterity, life continued in its own sweet way. There was no inkling of the fixing, precisely here, by talented archaeologists from a much later time, of the boundary between two of prehistory's great time periods, the Bronze Age and the Iron Age.

The millennium of mists

After the many magnificent finds of the Bronze Age's gleaming precious metal that bore witness to the farmers' worship of the sun and the cosmic universe, the relative poverty of archaeological finds from the Early Iron Age has shed a grey and sad light over this period.

A cold, wet time characterised by crisis. This is the way the Iron Age has been depicted by many authors, as is often the case when the archaeological record does not quite come up to scratch and fill out the whole of cultural history with stories of people who once lived here. The transition to the Iron Age also marks the boundary between two climatic periods, and it is true that the Iron Age was significantly wetter and cooler than preceding times. The climate curve broke around 700 BC and the subsequent damp, cool climate intensified further around 500 BC. "The millennium of mists," is Martin A. Hansen's name for the Iron Age in his chronicle *Orm og Tyr* from 1956. "The rawness came sailing with the clouds of the sky over the old summer people. In the cold rain much was whipped away that, for the Iron Age people, would be surplus, but for their forefathers was life itself. Culture lost its quality of beauty." With his never-failing storyteller's art, Martin A. Hansen elaborates the consequences of doom-laden climatological prophesies in a depressed cultural landscape as if it were present-day climate fears that raged. Misfortune and crop-failure flooded in over the farming communities,

The conqueror of Gaul, Gaius Julius Ceasar.

"the grain becomes lodged while still green, becomes overgrown by rampant wild herbs, will not ripen, becomes infected with black rust. Moss and lichen grow thick on the trunks of the forests, the trees become hose-clad. Cancer creeps up into the wood from the acid soil. Trees die and many places in the depths of the forest become a morass of rotting windfalls." The advance of beech is given the blame for the poverty of berry-bearing bushes and the lack of fertility. Everything goes wrong and climatic catastrophe penetrates right inside the houses, where the Iron Age people on winter-frozen mornings could find their "dead animals lying up against the house walls, stiff-legged, soaked by the dripping from the eaves."

There is no doubt that the climate changed markedly around this time. Observations in the bogs of Northern Europe paint an image of a very sudden shift in climate from relatively warm and dry to cool and wet conditions, beginning around 800 BC and reaching a maximum around 500 BC. The water table rose and many low-lying areas became transformed into bogs. Reduced solar activity and increased cosmic radiation are the probable cause of this change in climate. Increased cosmic radiation leads to a greater proportion of ^{14}C in the atmosphere, and this has an influence on cloud formation and precipitation. Changes in the solar wind became reinforced, leading to a sudden change in climate. In low-lying areas, for example in The Netherlands and in our own Lille Vildmose, Iron Age farmers were apparently forced to abandon their settlements. The elevated water table naturally had an influence on the location of settlements. Altered ocean currents in the North Atlantic also resulted in much windier weather with a prevailing westerly wind. The changes in cosmic radiation had the opposite consequence in the Southern Hemisphere, where the sun's activity was increased and precipitation failed to materialise.

Iron Age farmers

Today, the anonymous and find-poor transition from Bronze Age to Early Iron Age has been populated with new information from the excavated remains of villages and cemeteries. There are no signs of crisis, distress, or failure of crops as a consequence of the change in climate, and farmers continued to cultivate the soil in their small fields enclosed within low banks – accumulations of stones gathered up from the fields. The soil now became increasingly fertilised with manure from cattle housed in byres. In general, there are no great changes to be seen anywhere. On the other hand, we gain an insight into a time when the ancient occupation of agricultural was in the throes of an enormous expansion. The forests were rapidly opened up during the first five centuries of the Iron Age. An overall stability in the exploitation of the cultural landscape had its beginnings, at least in the more fertile areas. In several places these attained the charac-

ter of open plains. Beech conquered the woodland that still extended over large areas of the country. Cutting of wood for fuel and timber also opened up woodland areas to a significant extent. We can begin to speak in earnest of an open cultural landscape with commons, arable fields, meadows, and pastures. The farmers of the Bronze Age had, to a great extent, obtained their hay – leaf hay – in the woods. These had now been transformed into commons, and the farmers had to turn to grazing their animals and hay-making on damp meadows near the settlements. The settlements moved together forming clusters of farmsteads and, over the course of the following centuries, the farmers came to live in small hamlets that we can perceive as the beginnings of village communities. With regard to the basic agricultural way of life there was nothing much new to be picked up on, just an increase in population as seen in every millennium throughout the history of agriculture. There were an estimated 300,000 people in Denmark in the Early Iron Age, from 500 BC until the birth of Christ, also known as the Celtic Iron Age, from the influences which, even so, managed to reach the country from turbulent Central Europe.

Wetland landscapes

Agriculture apparently thrived during this period of great climatic change. The water table rose, and the farmers understood how to exploit damp meadows for cattle grazing in summer. The population became increasingly linked to one another through the beginnings of a village structure and to the landscape through continuity in settlement. Existing bogs grew and new ones arose, spreading out across the land. In the course of the first centuries of the Iron Age, a quarter of the country became covered by wetlands – wide rivers cutting through the landscape, lakes, meadows, and bogs. The bog was, as in the Stone Age, not just a marginal area. Many settlements now lay lower in the terrain in closer association with low-lying wetland areas. And offerings were again taken in great numbers to the still waters of the bog and sacred offering celebrations were held on the margins. Bogs could now also play a new and important role as an energy source. As early as the Bronze Age, farmers had begun to cut peat in bogs. Around 1.400 BC the inhabitants of the village at Bjerre in Thy heated their houses with peat. The region's extraordinarily dense and prosperous settlement had, in the course of the Bronze Age, left a virtually tree-less landscape, in which the farmers sought alternative sources of energy in bogs. It is known from historical times that peat is a significantly less resource-demanding heat source to obtain than wood. The Iron Age's new technology,

iron-making, also required enormous fuel resources for extraction and forging. The farmers' activities in the bogs were more than just simply sacral.

Grauballe Man's landscape

Out by the bog, back then when the blood flowed and a human life was gifted away, the panic-stricken birds of winter all flew away in the same direction, and silence reigned.

In the Iron Age, we can begin in earnest to speak of an open cultural landscape with commons, arable fields, and grazing areas. Historical-Archaeological Experimental Centre, Lejre.

Over the breaking sheets of ice, between hummocks of sphagnum, they carried the warm body thirty metres out into the bog and lowered it into the grave. This was no ordinary burial, but a water-filled peat cutting where, in previous summers, cold hands had taken out peat. With vessels and ladles of wood, they emptied the peat cutting of water, laid the body to rest and covered it with peat. Before long the cutting again became filled with water. Soon the lapwings would dance across the sky and spring would be on its way.

Ten thousand years previous, a mighty Ice Age glacier had lain only 15 kilometres distant and great melt-water rivers flowed under the ice close to the Grauballe area, standing as a plateau between the raging waters. Millennia of alternating frost and thaw caused the soil to flow from the hills and soften the sharp contours of the landscape. Long after the ice had melted and the first hunters had begun to roam the landscape, massive lumps of ice from the Ice Age glaciers still lay buried within the morainic masses. As the climate became milder, these great blocks of ice began to melt, the layers of soil around the holes collapsed and the ice became transformed into lakes with still, deep water.

In the wet time at the end of the Bronze Age, about 800 BC, the old kettle hole between the hills at Nebelgaard became transformed into a bog, a so-called kettle-hole bog, a mere 150 metres from one side to the other. The highlands of Central Jutland are, true enough, a rough, turbulent landscape of lakes formed by melting lumps of ice, hills and ridges created by the glaciers and the thaws of warmer times. Nebelgaard bog lies within this landscape. When Grauballe Man was alive, in the third century BC, the landscape was already open, bearing traces from centuries of agriculture. On steep slopes and ridges there was still woodland, where beech had now begun to dominate the scene. Otherwise, the area was characterised by cultivated areas, commons developed from former arable fields where cattle now grazed, low-lying meadows with juicy green grass and fields of barley, wheat, oats, and rye, inter-mixed with those of flax and other crops. On former fields, where the cattle now grazed, heather unfolded its light purple carpet and productivity had come almost to a standstill. Grauballe Man lived in a cultural landscape with an overall structure, back then, more than 2000 years ago.

There were clearances in the dense alder thicket around the bog where the wet climate nourished the soft, wet covering of sphagnum with its jumble of shades of green and yellowish brown. Over drowned and fallen trees, which had cleverly laid themselves over the springy surface of the bog, the farmers went out with their baskets and vessels and dug peat for fuel. They cut pits in the bog with wooden spades and gathered the peat masses in the containers they had taken with them. They had to be quick. Soon, the seeping, trickling water would refill the peat cutting. A cutting rarely reached more than a couple of metres across before it, so to say, drowned and a new one had to be dug

alongside. In drier periods of the year, and in winter, when ice formed a bridge, they could go further out into the bog to cut their peat.

The Roman author Plinius, who lived in the first century AD, saw or heard rumours about what happened at this time out in the peat bogs among the Teutonic peoples to the north: "With their hands, they dig mire, which they dry more by the wind than the sun, and with earth as fuel they warm their bodies, frozen by the north wind."

Out at Nebelgaard bog, the peat was, as in subsequent millennia, probably laid to dry in summer over on the hill above the bog, where the wind had free rein. The people who were responsible for the water-filled peat cuttings in Nebelgaard bog, where sphagnum now took possession of the blackish-brown water, surely lived in the vicinity. There are many stretches of boggy land in the area, and the farmers probably cut their peat as close to their villages as possible. In the vicinity of the bog, on dry even terrain close to damp grazing areas, we would expect to find remains of the Iron Age farmers' villages. These have not yet been located, but archaeologists are on the track of them. In several places within a radius of one and a half kilometres of Nebelgaard bog, potsherds have been found dating from the first centuries of the Iron Age, Grauballe Man's time. There are also so-called refuse pits, holes dug in the earth, then filled up with potsherds, ash from fires and other refuse from people and animals. Traces of the earth-set posts of

10,000 years ago, Nebelgaard bog was a mighty block of ice from the last ice-age glacier.

Peat spades from the Iron Age.

their houses are, on the other hand, much more vulnerable to the heavy-handed cultivation of recent times. They are rapidly ploughed down beyond all recognition, and are therefore much more difficult to trace. On the hilly plateau, only a few hundred metres to the north of the bog, lies a several thousand square metre system of Iron Age fields that may well have been cultivated in Grauballe Man's time. The fields were surveyed and recorded by aerial photography in the 1930s, and appeared then as a fine-meshed network of small arable plots enclosed within the remains of low banks.

There are traces of the Early Iron Age settlement around Nebelgaard bog, but we need to go much further away to find the well-preserved remains of villages from that time. Many contemporary villages have been located, and a number have been excavated, but not nearly as fully as those from subsequent centuries, the time following the birth of Christ. This is due, as already mentioned, neither to crisis nor migration, but is simply an expression of the settlement traces from this time being more difficult to recognise than those from later times. Although those villages that have been excavated do appear fairly uniform, sketching a picture of the first real village communities that arose precisely in Grauballe Man's time.

In the Early Iron Age, the farmers still lived in farmsteads standing singly or in small clusters, as seen, for example to the west, at Grøntoft near Grønbjerg on the high ground *(bakkeø)* of Omme Bakker, Western Jutland. Intensive archaeological investigations here have enabled the mapping of the development of an entire Iron Age community through the years. The remains of 250 houses from a period extending over several centuries draw a clear picture of a fascinating settlement structure. At the beginning of the fourth century BC, there were two clusters of farmsteads separated by a river valley. About a century later, these two settlements became united to form a cluster of seven farmsteads, each with a long-house and an outhouse. The long-houses, each of about 100 square metres, were living quarters for both people and animals. At the western end of the house, the family lived, ate, busied themselves with crafts and slept. The eastern end housed the cattle in winter. The architecture of the houses was completely uniform. The thatched or turf-covered roof was borne by two rows of posts within the house. The entrance to both living quarters and byre lay in the middle of the house. The walls were of wattle and daub. One particular farmstead stands out by virtue of its size. The house was 22.5 metres long and there was room in the byre for 22 cattle. By comparison, several of the other farmsteads only had room for about half this number. Approximately every 30 years the settlement was moved a couple of hundred metres. The houses were thoroughly worn out by this time and, furthermore, the farmers knew how to exploit the higher nutrient levels in the soil of the old settlement area. When the farmsteads had been moved the area where people and animals had lived for a generation, and had manured the soil in a natural way, was brought into cultivation. These wandering vil-

Peat cutting in the process of growing over. Lille Vildmose, Himmerland, Jutland.

lages, as they are known, in which people moved around within the same resource area for up to 1500 years, were common at that time.

Late in the third century BC, the farmsteads became gathered together in dense clusters and fences were built around them punctuated by several communal entrances. For the first time we see an organised village community, apparently with co-operation between the inhabitants. But this did not mean that there was equal access to all assets. The varying size of the farms, and therefore their ownership of cattle, now became even more apparent. Such a radical re-organisation of the village community and increasing inequality between the farmsteads suggests that the hierarchical social structure of the Bronze Age was still in force. In the Iron Age, we can now speak in earnest of actual farms. Houses, with living quarters in the west and a byre in the east and, with time, an entrance hall in the middle, as well as an outhouse for provisions or a workshop, are seen across the whole of the country. More and more small family units became gathered together within a community that saw its visual expression in the enclosed, fenced villages. In the Iron Age, communities changed to a form of agriculture based to a greater extent on family farming. This new way of farming involved the animals being housed in a byre and the use of manure became more widespread. The result was an altered and more intensive exploitation of the landscape, as can be read in the pollen

*Peat spade and part of a hoe
together with hand-kneaded peat.
From a peat cutting at Nørre
Smedeby, Southern Jutland.*

evidence preserved within the bogs. These beginnings of village communities involving family farming characterised Iron Age society right up until to the birth of Christ. There were fenced village areas of about 3,000 square metres, each comprising 10-20 farmsteads of varying size; some had 8-18 cattle, others only 3-4 and a few had no housed animals at all. A village such as Nørre Omme, located between Holstebro and Herning, had between 8-10 households with a total of rather more than 50 inhabitants. In addition to this, there were 70-80 cattle. The village fence marked the limits of the community and kept the cattle out of the houses in the months when they grazed the surrounding meadows. Some families had, of course, a higher position in the hierarchy than others. There was also a hierarchy among the individual villages. Some were more prosperous and played a more important role than others relative to their surroundings, both locally and in their contacts with more distant areas.

In Central Jutland, near Nebelgaard bog where Grauballe Man was found, there were also villages or collections of farmsteads on the edge of the ridges close to lakes and rivers. Even though no villages have been excavated in their entirety in the area, the traces left in the form of refuse pits and potsherds in the arable fields, as well as a few house remains, show that Iron Age farmers lived here. So far there is nothing to suggest that this was a particularly prosperous or "internationally orientated" area. Conversely, we now know a great deal about everyday life in an Iron Age village at that time. The farmers ploughed their small arable plots using an ard, a primitive plough, which did not turn the soil but just drew a furrow through it. They sowed, weeded and harvested the crops in the autumn. In the spring, the cattle were turned out to grass; sheep and goats also received their share. Around the farmsteads, the hens went around in flocks with geese and ducks and a couple of fat porkers, while the dogs munched rubbish from the refuse pits. All summer long, ox-carts rumbled in and out of the openings in the village fence, loaded with reeds and timber for repairing the houses. All kinds of household utensils, such as jars, bowls, pots and cups, were manufactured in clay and wood by the village inhabitants. Clay for the vessels was obtained from a clay pit in the autumn and matured by the winter frosts. The pottery kiln was a highly developed speciality of the Iron Age farmers. These kilns were large and domed and built of clay with room for the firing of about 50 vessels and jars. All summer long, stores of berries, fungi, and everything edible the forest and clearances could offer were plucked, gathered, and dried.

On a completely ordinary day, while the hens clucked, the cart rumbled, and the women wiped the clay from their fingers, the aroma of simmering soup of herbs and game birds mixed with that of the smoke from the fire. Perhaps children, in the calm noontide, were fishing by the river, and a group of men had gone off hunting in the forest from early morning. Others had gone to the bog to cut peat. Inside the houses, a couple of women were busy at their looms. Others sat outside and sewed hides together. Life was to be lived all year round. When the dark cold winter came, and the landscape froze, they had to manage on the summer's stored fruits and grain and the surplus afforded by the farm animals. Game from the forest and the lake could only supplement the gathered provisions to a limited extent. There is no doubt that supplies ran short in the late winter months and that human lives were lost through hunger, illness, disease, and cold, while everyone awaited the return of the sun and of life itself.

In death all souls are equal

Already in the Bronze Age people began to cremate their dead on funeral pyres. It was a tradition that, like so many other innovations, came to the country through the influence of cultures to the south. The bones of the dead were carefully cleaned and placed in an urn or a stone setting, and buried in the ancestors' great burial mounds. The practice of cremation was continued to extremes in the Celtic Iron Age and all the dead were now burnt on a funeral pyre. This was probably based on a formal perception of the soul or the spirit being released when the smoke rose from the funeral pyre and fire consumed the body. But there were others for which different rules applied after death – people like Grauballe Man, whose life ended in a bog.

Iron Age village with enclosing fence. Reconstruction of the village Grøntoft in Western Jutland. Historical-Archaeological Experimental Centre, Lejre.

In contrast to the Bronze Age's careful treatment of the burnt bones of the dead, handling of their bones in the Iron Age took place with a completely different level of casualness. Now only part of the burnt skeleton was placed in an urn and the bones, which were rarely cleaned, were crushed and broken up into small pieces. On the face of it, this appears to be rather an offhand way to treat the earthly remains of one's nearest and dearest, but there was obviously an idea behind it. It could be that the deceased were, prior to cremation, laid out for defleshing, and only some of the bones were burnt, while the remainder were included in rituals carried out elsewhere in landscape, for example by bogs, as outlined below.

Not only are the remains of bones of Iron Age farmers few and small, their graves are also very modest. Few of their graves have been discovered, as they are difficult to detect in the landscape. In Southern Jutland, however, whole cemeteries have been found, containing over a thousand burials from the first four centuries of the Iron Age. At these burial places, the urn was placed in the ground and covered by a small hillock, surrounded by a ditch. These hillock graves were laid out side by side and are remarkably uniform. The grave goods accompanying the bones in the urns are also modest: a pin, a belt hook, rarely a neck-ring, in bone, iron, or bronze. The universal cremation, the uniform construction of the graves, and the modesty of the grave goods must be an expres-

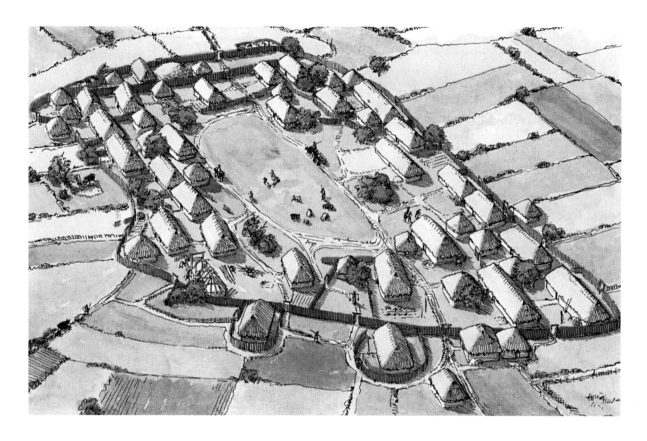

Iron Age village with fenced farm-steads surrounded by a common fence. From Grauballe Man's time. Hodde, Western Jutland.

sion, or manifestation, of the belief that all are equal in death. This is yet another aspect of the community also seen reflected in the villages. The social inequality, expressed by the ownership of cattle and in the varying sizes of the farmsteads, is no longer reflected in the deceased's sepulchral monument, as it was among Bronze Age families. Even though social differences between farming families gradually became greater during the first centuries of the Iron Age, the farming communities maintained, accordingly, equality in death. Iron Age cemeteries were often laid out with a point of departure in the burial mounds of the Bronze Age. With time, graves became increasingly simple in form, with the urn being placed in a small hole in the ground, which was then filled with pyre remnants, or the pyre remnants alone were placed in a small pit.

Warriors from the south

Through contacts with the Celts to the south, and later with the Roman Empire, social inequality gradually became more apparent in the gifts from their earthly life given to the dead for their afterlife. The Germanic peoples began to involve themselves in the witches' cauldron of European wars, either as mercenaries or in the form of actual armies from the north. In any case, warrior graves containing exotic Celtic riches turn

Urn burial from the Iron Age. The remains of the cremation pyre, together with the burnt bones, were placed in the large vessel which has another up-turned vessel as a lid. Several smaller vessels and cups have been placed beside the urn.

up in the cemeteries of otherwise like-minded souls. This was about the time of the legendary "Cimbrian Trek", which could also have forged new links between the peoples of the Continent. The beginnings of a warrior aristocracy, with an extensive network of contacts, again entered the villages of the farming communities. From about 250 BC, there are graves in the cemeteries containing weapons, spearheads, swords, and shield bosses of Celtic origin, with numerous pottery vessels containing food for the journey of death, side by side with anonymous graves. Magnificent bronze-mounted belts of Swedish origin apparently had an inherent social status for women, or there may have been cases of exogamy, whereby high-ranking men married women from distant areas; this in itself conferred status. Flamboyant swords, Celtic bronze vessels and bowls, magnificent dress ornaments of bronze and gold followed the members of the warrior aristocracy onto their funeral pyres and into their graves out in the village communities. A very few were dispatched to their cremation in a wagon. A cemetery at Langå on Southeastern Funen displays impressive wealth. The most magnificent of all was a man's burial: the urn was a great Celtic cauldron and among the ashes lay a couple of bronze vessels, one of Etruscan origin. There was also a pair of outstanding golden spiral finger-rings, four swords, two shield bosses and a spearhead – and harness mountings, parts of a bridle, bronze and iron fittings from a Celtic ceremonial wagon. The cauldron was manufactured in Northern Italy in the fourth century BC and had been in circulation for three centuries before it served as a burial urn for a powerful farmer on Southwestern Funen. All these remarkably rich graves found in the farmers' cemeteries at sites across the whole country are consistent with the growing social differentiation seen in the villages. These exotic objects seem, on the face of it, to be rare visitors to a farming community of cereal growers and cattle breeders. We do not know whether these warriors had returned home after successful military campaigns to the south, or whether people here in the north had learned the decadent habits of Central European peoples who buried their dead with similar wealth. Influenced by events to the south, a warrior aristocracy began to develop in earnest in Southern Scandinavia. The more they became involved with the warlike societies to the south, the more vulnerable they themselves became, and the greater became their need to defend themselves. Riches were apparently accumulated in the form of cattle. This was the scene out in the villages.

Iron – a new technology

The discovery of iron was a complicated process, invented by particularly creative minds in the Middle East already in the third millennium BC. By way of Greece and the Balkans, knowledge of iron reached Central Europe around 1500 BC. It was probably the first failing supplies of tin and copper, needed for the manufacture of bronze, in the eight century BC, that focussed attention in earnest on iron as a raw material. In Southern Scandinavia, people had known about iron for a long time, but it first became of significance here when a vacuum occurred in metal supplies. The social network of the Bronze Age functioned perfectly as long as supplies of bronze flowed freely. It was first when they failed, and bronze disappeared as a common unit of value and the structure of society collapsed, that iron was embraced. The new technology afforded completely new potential. Partly because people were no longer dependent on strong social contact networks, partly because iron was, as a material, completely differently suited to the manufacture of tools and weapons. And equal access to resources meant that everyone, in reality, was master of their own destiny.

In the beginning, however, iron was imported in limited quantities. In the Southern Alpine area, extensive iron production began in the seventh century BC. It was a technology that subsequently became of great significance for the metal adventures of the Romans. Several centuries elapsed before ironworking took hold here in earnest and blacksmiths, as specialised craftsmen, became fixtures as inhabitants of villages. As early as 500 BC, however, there were people in Denmark who were able to work iron.

In Denmark, we have deposits of bog iron ore at the edges of bogs and marshes and along the slopes of river valleys. A condition for the formation of this resource is that

the soil is acidic, *i.e.* with a high humus and a low chalk content. Acid rainwater dissolves and takes up iron molecules from iron-rich minerals in the earth. If there is oxygen available in the soil when the groundwater comes into contact with the surface, the iron molecules in the water will react with the oxygen and precipitate out as a solid substance, or bog iron ore as it is termed. In Western Jutland, there are a number of large continuous occurrences of bog iron ore. In Eastern Jutland and on the islands, the occurrences are more scattered. The highlands of Central Jutland are, on the other hand, relatively rich in iron.

When the ore had been dug up from the bogs, it was dried, roasted, and crushed. Then it was stacked, together with charcoal or peat coal, in a furnace built of clay. We have no idea of the appearance of the early furnaces, but later in the Iron Age, when the beginnings of an industrial-scale production of iron developed in Western Jutland, these were tall, conical, and shaft-like. The furnace was fired-up and, with the aid of bellows, the temperature was increased to the necessary 1300 degrees C. The carbon then caused the iron to be released from the charcoal or peat coal and the impurities were smelted from the iron. These impurities are called slag, and this is what we find at several settlements from this time as evidence of iron production. At Bruneborg, near Ejer Bavnehøj in Eastern Jutland, at the beginning of the Iron Age around 500 BC, there was a collection of farmsteads where people knew about smelting iron. Traces were found here of extraction in the form of large quantities of slag. An actual bellow plate from the forge was also found. This is a clay plate that protects the bellows from the extreme radiant heat of the forge. Iron slag lay in heaps near the forge. There was also finished, forged iron, raw, untreated bog iron ore and 50 kilograms of roasted, granulated ore. The whole process, from digging up the ore to working and production of the finished

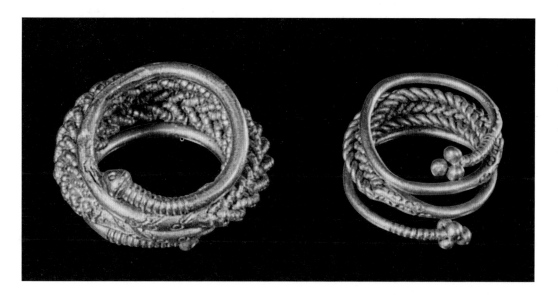

iron, took place at Bruneborg. About 500 metres from the blacksmith's workplace there were great deposits of bog iron ore. Even though a couple of centuries were to elapse before iron found widespread use in the production of weapons and tools, people were well on the way to developing the technology in Eastern Jutland already at the beginning of the Iron Age. The production of iron for, for example, knives, sickles, and axes was a resource-demanding process. Three kilograms of iron was the yield from each smelting process, and this required about 20 kilograms of charcoal or peat coal to produce. The slag, the waste from one furnace, weighed about 10 kilograms.

Alone felling, cutting up, gathering and transporting the wood to produce 20 kilograms of charcoal would have taken some considerable time, not to speak of its conversion to charcoal. It seems more likely that the Iron Age farmers used peat coal as an energy source for iron smelting. In the bogs from where the bog iron ore was extracted, peat was right at hand in unlimited quantities.

Peat coal

The production of peat coal is today a "forgotten" technology, and there are only few records of this kind of high-energy fuel. In the 19th century, when great expanses of forest were no longer a matter of course in Denmark, peat coal was used as fuel in certain areas of Jutland. Peat coal is produced in almost the same way as charcoal in a stack or clamp, where a minimal supply of oxygen prevents the turves or peats from burning completely. The peats must only be made to glow so the last remnants of water and impurities evaporate, or are deposited at the base of the stack. On the Orkney, Shetland and Faroe Islands, and on Norse settlements in Greenland, there is evidence for smith-

Peat coal is excellent high energy fuel. Experiments with the production of peat coal and subsequent forging. Historical-Archaeological Experimental Centre, Lejre.

ing activity from Viking times, around AD 800. Already at this time, wood was a scarce commodity on the North Atlantic islands. Peat coal was probably produced for use in ironworking on these treeless islands. J. Christian Svabo, in his reports from the Faroe Islands in the 1780s, wrote a long chapter on the various types of peat and their suitability as fuel. Of one type, which contains the roots of juniper bushes, he writes that "this type is used and by blacksmiths." On the Hebrides, a stack of 14 cut peats has been found which could be dated to the beginning of the Bronze Age. Modern experiments with iron smelting using both peat coal and charcoal have shown that the peat coal gives a significantly better yield than smelting using charcoal. After charring the resulting peat coal contains only pure carbon which is easy to ignite, burns evenly and does not contain substances that can contaminate the iron. As already mentioned, people began as early as the Bronze Age to cut peat for fuel to heat their houses, and in the Iron Age this peat cutting became dramatically intensified. Even though peat coal leaves no traces in the iron-smelting furnaces, the extensive peat extraction that was launched at the beginning of the Iron Age, and which can be traced in innumerable bogs large and small across the whole country, must be explained in terms of the beginnings of iron technology. The high-energy fuel necessary was manufactured from bog peat.

Iron Age peat cuttings could be up to a couple of metres in depth and four metres across. It was not possible to dig more than this before water seeped in, filling the cutting. In some places peat cuts were dug very close together, as in Nebelgaard bog.

In a peat bog in Nørre Smedeby, in Southern Jutland, traces were found in 1943 of extensive peat exploitation from the first century of the Iron Age. Peat cuttings the size of a bathtub lay very close together over the surface of the bog. At the base of the cuts, household items and tools had been deposited. In one there lay a 1.5 metre long, finely-carved wooden dish and in another was a deep wooden vessel. In a third were two troughs. Others held a plough, a pot, and a peat spade. There were even fist-sized peats, such as those described by Pliny. These had been kneaded and shaped with the bare hands and impressions of fingers still formed grooves on their surfaces. It seems very unlikely that the wooden objects were placed in Nørre-Smedeby bog for temporary storage. This was the practice in recent times when cracked or loose wooden items were left in wetland areas to swell and tighten, but the wooden artefacts here lay spread throughout cuttings over a large area. Despite the fact that the farmers now had another reason to go to the bog, to obtain peat and bog iron ore, bog water continued to play a major role as an offering site in the Iron Age. But now it was objects of a more everyday character that were deposited, such as those seen in the peat cuttings at Nørre Smedeby. A more recent find gives a very good impression of the situation and a key to an interpretation of the Iron Age farmers' practice of depositing offerings in old water-filled peat cuttings in bogs.

Offerings in bogs and peat cuttings

*The still, clear water, at the boundary to the other world,
reflected the clouds of the sky and the farmers themselves,
while their offerings were lowered down into the black-brown depths.*

At Fuglsøgård bog, south of Hadsund, there was in the Iron Age a small kettle-hole bog like that at Nebelgaard. Peat was extracted here in the Early Iron Age, about 500-300 BC. It was obtained from several hundred peat cuttings, each up to a couple of metres deep and up to four metres wide. The peat cuttings lay very densely, a few metres apart, along the edge of the 3000 square metre area of the bog. With time, these water-filled pools riddled the bog surface. For a couple of decades, the water-filled peat cuttings stood open, and sphagnum had already begun to thrive at the surface of the water. Leaves from willow scrub on the edge of the bog, together with sand from the adjacent arable fields, blew out across the bog and was deposited at the base of the cuttings. Dead, waterlogged trees had fallen out over the bog margin, and in some places their branches extended out over the peat cuttings. The farmers had lived in the area for generations, cultivated the soil, sent their cattle out to graze, and cut peat in the bogs. Now they returned to Fuglsøgård bog, but with another purpose in mind, commanded by tradition and belief. In the water-filled peat cuttings they placed pottery vessels filled with grain, slaughtered and butchered animals, puffballs, other crops and foodstuffs gathered from nature. Newly slaughtered and butchered animals, including the skulls of cattle and horses, were placed around the pottery vessels. Tethering stakes, used to secure the cattle in the fields in summer were deposited together with wooden clubs and finely crafted wooden items, down around the pots.

Where possible, the Iron Age people balanced out across the bog on fallen tree trunks to reach the water-filled peat cuttings. Precisely there where a trunk divided to form two thinner branches, they submerged pots full of grain. These scenes did not occur on just one day, but extended over months, perhaps years, as recurrent offering rituals were performed according to various events in the farmers' annual rhythm: the return of light at midwinter, the growth of spring and the germination of seeds in the

Fuglsøgård bog, Himmerland. In the Iron Age this 200 by 100 metre peat bog was riddled with bathtub-shaped peat cuttings in which offerings were placed – pots containg food, tools and slaughtered animals, especially horse skulls.

soil, the benevolence of sun and rain and the harvest, the fertility of animals and people. The still, clear water, at the boundary to the other world, reflected the clouds of the sky and the farmers themselves, while their offerings were lowered down into the blackish-brown depths. Between the pots and the newly butchered animals, they placed small pieces of white quartz that gleamed and twinkled through the surface of the water in sun- and moonlight. The bog was two organisms in one – a place where raw materials were obtained and a place where the supernatural reigned supreme. It was where offerings were taken in intercession for the continuation of the family line. The bog was a magical and solemn place intrinsically linked with the great mysteries of life. It was not one or the other, but both. Back then both spirit and belief were deeply embedded in people's everyday life.

The offerings deposited in Fuglsøgård bog show neither the influence of lavishness nor social prestige. For the village community, and each individual family, they reflect very much the basics of life that extended far into the family's daily welfare. Pottery vessels filled with grain, ploughshares and animal bones relate to the produce of the fields, and the fertility and survival of both people and animals. Manifestations of power between individual farmers and between villages were not issues on the minds of the people out there in the peat cuttings. It was contact with the spirits of life and fertility

Vertical section through a peat cutting with offering vessels. Fuglsøgård bog, Himmerland, Jutland.

on the other side, through the surface of the water and the firmament that was at stake.

It is rare that such everyday scenarios can be sensed through excavations in bogs. Many small boggy hollows have been heavy-handedly emptied of peat over the centuries. And the latest initiatives involving the digging out of kettle-hole bogs for the benefit of fire-bellied toads has almost robbed us of the possibility of seeing once again a scene such as that at Fuglsøgård. There is no doubt that many similar sacrificial bogs associated with Iron Age villages were lost at an early stage. The modesty of the finds do not attract much attention when great mechanical excavators and economic or biological considerations have highest priority. Museum stores bulge with finds of potsherds and bones from our bogs, but as the fragments they represent of their original greater context, they have not attracted much interest.

We know of offerings in peat cuttings best through the discoveries of bog bodies, as these people definitely attract attention when they emerge. In Hjortspring bog on Als, around 300 BC, a whole boat, complete with warriors' equipment, was offered in a large peat cutting. The same happened around AD 375 in Nydam bog in Southern Jutland where, after systematic and intensive peat cutting of the whole bog basin, a boat and the equipment from en entire army were taken from the battlefield after a mighty battle and were offered. People returned repeatedly to Nydam bog to offer to the spirits of war.

The Hjortspring Boat. Copy of the boat which, together with military equipment, was offered in Hjortspring bog, Als.

Through the extraction of bog iron ore and the cutting of peat, bogs took on a new role in people's lives. It was, however, still by way of the water in lakes and bogs that they came into contact with the powers that ruled over them. And now they went out more often to offer to the powers of nature. It is hardly a coincidence that offerings were deposited in the water-filled peat cuttings from which nature had made its contribution to the maintenance of human life.

But it was not only in peat cuttings that people offered in the Early Iron Age. Bronze Age offerings of sets of ornaments declined in line with failing bronze supplies to the paired neck-rings seen offered in the final part of the period. The tradition continued into the Iron Age, though at a reduced intensity; bronze was, of course, scarce. Twisted neck-rings, worn in pairs, were also offered in pairs and deposited in bogs, as were brooches and arm-rings. The tradition of sacrificing neck- and armrings was seen throughout most of Northern Europe at this time. It continued to be primarily the status of women that was marked by offerings in the bogs. Perhaps offerings took place in connection with the formation of friendships and alliances through the entering into of marriage, or they could have been an expression of the worshipping of women's fertility. A neck-ring can also be seen on several of the small bronze figures from the period, interpreted as ceremonial objects.

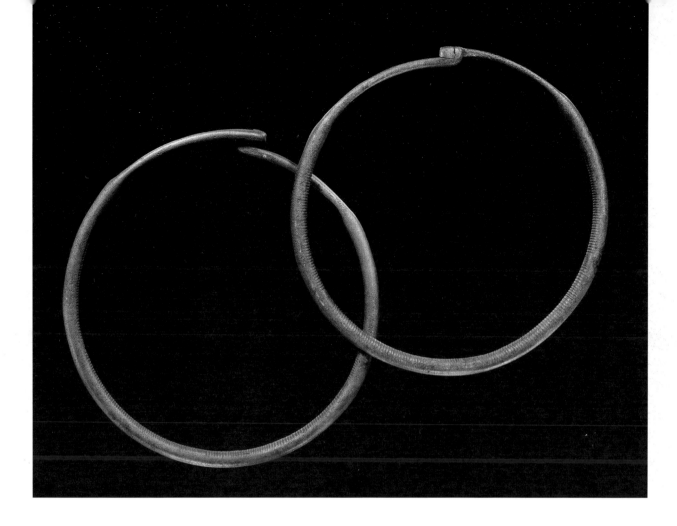

The scant amounts of bronze that were still available were apparently converted, in particular, into ornamental rings of all sizes. Neck-rings, arm-rings and ankle-rings, as well as medium-sized rings of a special form with a small eyelet, were all deposited in bogs and lakes. There was apparently a particular local tradition of offering the small eyelet rings in Eastern Central Jutland. During peat cutting in Smederup bog near Odder in 1942, bronze rings literally poured out of the peat. The story began at the end of the Bronze Age, around 600 BC, when a well was constructed of 14-15 oak planks in a little bog, probably around a natural spring. When the well was excavated, numerous pottery vessels dating from the end of the Bronze Age were found at its base, as well as a bucket carved from a piece of elm wood. The well was about a metre deep and had two handles. Its upper diameter was 77 centimetres. Theoretically, it could have functioned as a reservoir of drinking water for the inhabitants of a village in the vicinity. Many wells are known from the Iron Age, located at springs in wetland areas, and the cups and other pottery vessels found at the bottom of them once served as ladles and buckets. The Smederup well lay a good way out into the bog. Perhaps back then, before the climate changed, it was possible to walk out to obtain clear drinking water from the well without getting wet feet. Subsequent events in Smederup bog leave us in no doubt about the function of the well as an offering place in the Early Iron Age. In and around

A pair of identical Wendel rings were, in the Early Iron Age, deposited in a small bog near Årre in Southern Jutland.

it were found 360 rings of bronze – twisted rings, spiral rings and rings that were smooth, rings the size of neck-rings, arm-rings and ankle-rings, as well as small eyelet rings, which made up half the total. The rings were discovered during peat cutting and several were first found after they had been taken home in the peat and burnt on local kitchen ranges. It is unclear whether the rings were originally thrown into the well or had, by chance, fallen into the water beside it. In any case, not many decades could have elapsed between the construction of the well and the deposition of these ring offerings.

In a little bog at Falling, only a few kilometres distant from Smederup, peat cutters found identical eyelet rings when working by the conveyor belt that transported the saturated peat mass up from the bog to be pressed and dried. A total of 270 eyelet rings were, in several batches, sent to the National Museum in Copenhagen as peat extraction progressed, but there were probably many more that were just not seen by the peat workers.

Also in the vicinity, at Sattrup in Østbirk, 148 bronze artefacts, primarily spiral arm-rings and neck-rings, together with four eyelet rings were found in an elongated stretch of boggy land. Ring ornaments of bronze and eyelet rings, the function of which is uncertain, were also deposited at Sahl and Rødding near Viborg, and at Lyngå near Århus, as an element in the same tradition. These latter small rings, fitted with a little

Facing page.
In the Early Iron Age, more than
350 bronze rings were offered at
the well in Smederup bog in
Central Jutland.

Eyelet wheels with loosely fitting rings perhaps served as jingle-plates in the offering rituals at Smederup bog.

transverse eyelet, are interpreted as belt fasteners because, with a little imagination, they can be seen to resemble today's simple belt rings. But it is equally relevant to interpret their function relative to the offering ritual, *i.e.* as having had a ritual rather than a practical function. Decorated with feathers or other ritual adornment they could have performed a special role in the sacrifice. The ring offerings include bundles of rings and so-called eyelet wheels, fitted with rings that produce a clinking metallic sound when shaken. This kind of jingle-plate is known from Hindu offerings and ceremonies at Indian temples. Clinking, jingling metal may well have been heard beside the bogs of Jutland, back then, when ring offerings broke the surface of the water on their way towards "the other world".

The bronze that was still in circulation in the Early Iron Age apparently materialised in slender rings of various sizes and shapes, wed to the offering rituals in lakes and

bogs. Whether the offerings reflect one or several depositions, possibly with the participation of several women at particular times of year, none of the finds is able to resolve. They only show that there was a common tradition in Eastern Jutish farming societies of offering rings of remarkably uniform character.

The practice of offering rings continued almost up until the birth of Christ. New contacts with cultures lying to the north of the Greek world contributed to keeping the tradition alive. Heavily-cast so-called crown torques, weighing up to a couple of kilograms, found their way in abundant numbers to Southern Scandinavia at this time. It must have been no pleasure to wear these eccentrically-formed rings with their sharp edges which slotted into the local offering tradition, together with Celtic-inspired neck-rings of more restrained design.

New rituals arose in the Early Iron Age as an element in changes in people's religious perception. The farmers now visited their sacred places more often, and in some places permanent places were established for the deposition of pottery vessels. An example of this is seen at Fjaltring in Western Jutland. Here, on a pavement setting of flat stones, 20-50 pots had been deposited over a 3.5-metre stretch along the edge of a wetland area. The pots were each covered with a lid or a layer of flax. There are about 400 known localities with offerings of pots from the Iron Age. Just less than half date from the centuries immediately prior to the birth of Christ. The others are from subsequent centuries, when the practice reached its peak.

Offerings took place in both large and small bogs. A single vessel or almost a hundred could be sacrificed in a single bog. In many cases, the offering of a vessel formed part of celebrations, during which the consumption of food was an important part of the ritual. Joints of meat were also deposited, together with clay vessels filled with grain and other crops. Potsherds, ash and charcoal from the fire and scattered animal bones, incorporated into bog peat, are just the modest remains of the substantial celebrations held as part of the ritual on the edge of the bog.

Crown neck-rings or torques, of bronze were offered in large numbers during the Early Iron Age.

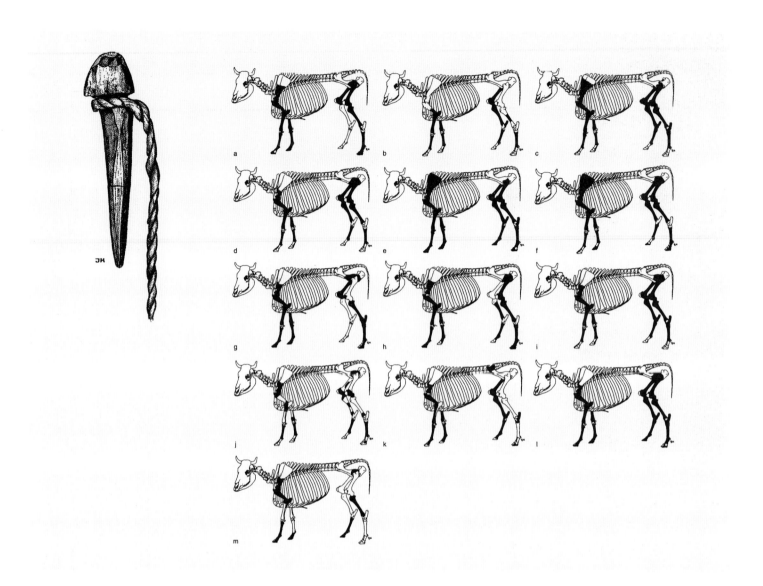

Offering of cattle in Bukkerup bog on Funen took place according to particular rituals, in which the front and rear parts of the animal were deposited in the bog. The rest of the slaughtered animal was probably eaten at the offering feast. Sacrificed animals were often deposited together with the tethering stake to which they had been bound during the offering ritual.

A bog at Bukkerup on Funen played a major role in the Iron Age farmers' contact with the spirits of nature. The farmers here went to the bog on special business. Under their arms they carried vessels full of food, and one of them led a cow to the offering place. At the edge of the bog, the cow was sacrificed according to the established rules: The fore- and hind legs, often together with the shoulder and the pelvic region, were cut from the animal and offered in the bog, together with the pots and the animal's tethering stake. The body of the beast was, on the other hand, prepared, cooked and eaten during the celebrations on the edge of the bog. The ritual was repeated at particular times of year, and/or on special occasions, year after year. A total of 13 cattle had been offered according to uniform rituals, together with 50 pots. The skulls of the cattle were not found when the site was excavated in the middle of the 20th century. They would

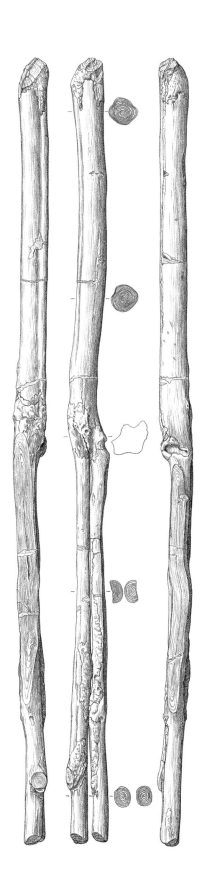

The almost three metre high goddess from Forlev Nymølle, erected where she was found in Central Jutland.

The sex of the idol is marked with simple cuts. Forlev Nymølle, Central Jutland.

surely have had their own precisely defined role in the ritual. Perhaps they were, in conclusion of the offering, mounted on stakes rammed down into the sacred bog as a visible sign of the celebration of a special event.

Offerings for life and fertility

The fertility cult had its clearest expression at this time. It was not just the fertility of animals and crops that life was all about. The fecundity of women and the continuation of the family line were deeply dependent on the fertility of nature. At several offering places, human fertility symbols were deposited together with the offerings. At Forlev Nymølle, in Eastern Jutland, excavations revealed nine small offering places in one area of bog. They all featured stones, including pieces of white quartz. Beneath one pile of stones was an almost three-metre long tree trunk that divided into two branches. Exactly at the bifurcation, where the legs began, the female sex had been marked with a few simple cuts. The idol had originally stood erect in the heap of stones, and the slight sway of her back could be glimpsed from far away. Pots, the contents of which are

unknown, were deposited at her feet, together with joints of goat meat. Two tufts of flax have prompted fantasies among modern archaeologists concerning their original location, perhaps somewhere on the woman. Flax was cultivated and used for textile production and also for food and oil at this time and was naturally included in the farmers' fertility rituals together with other crops. Other offerings at Forlev Nymølle comprised a varied range of pots and parts of cattle, goat, sheep, hare, and horse primarily young animals. There was also a human bone, as well as a large fragment of human scapula, showing cut marks. Tethering stakes and clubs accompanied the animals into the bog. The concentrated nature of the offerings suggests that they took place within peat cuttings of various sizes within the bog. There were also carefully carved ash rods at several of the offering places. These were up to two metres in length and one to two centimetres in diameter. They lay mainly in pairs in association with the offering sites. It has not been possible to arrive at a definite interpretation of these rods which must have formed part of the ritual in the bog, perhaps standing vertically like the idol. As at Fuglsøgård bog, people reached the offering places by way of fallen tree trunks.

Whereas the Forlev Nymølle idol would be perceived today as an insult to the female sex, Bråddenbjerg Man seems quite differently optimistic. It is true that he dates from the last century of the Bronze Age, but he is more reminiscent of the Iron Age's primitive figurative representations than images from the Bronze Age's cosmological universe. The exceptionally phallic Bråddenbjerg man was found in 1880 during peat cutting in a small kettle-hole bog, located at present-day Broddenbjerg, near Viborg. This was small woodland lake in the Bronze Age. The figure is 88 centimetres tall and coarsely carved from a tripartite branch. The face, which has a pointed chin possibly denoting a beard, is otherwise marked solely by a few axe cuts. The most dramatic feature is the figure's 30-centimetre-long erect phallus which showed traces of an applied resinous substance. Bråddenbjerg Man was found close to a small heap of stones and potsherds. A bronze neck-ring from the same period was also recovered from this sacrificial bog.

The figures of a man and a woman were found in an area of bog at Braak near Eutin in Holstein, in 1946. These are just less than three metres tall, and they were, so to say, created by nature. Use had been made of nature's own forms, to which were added carved faces and genitals. Together with this tall couple, who undoubtedly once stood upright in the bog, there were potsherds and a burnt layer, also containing pot fragments.

Similar human-like, so-called anthropomorphic, wooden figures are known from contemporary and later Iron Age cultures over large parts of Europe, especially in the northwestern lowland area: Ireland, Great Britain, The Netherlands, Scandinavia, and Northern and Central Germany. The area is characterised by cultures with related features, which existed under the same conditions of landscape and climate and for whom bogs and other wetland areas played a major role in their fertility cult. It has been suggested that these wooden figures are depictions of the gods to whom people made offerings, and that they are the forerunners of the deities of the Asa religion. In this respect, the furrow around the neck of Bråddenbjerg Man is interpreted as marking a noose. A hanging cult is linked to the Asa religion's Odin, "the god of the hanged". With respect to bog bodies, of which several show the remains of a noose, attempts have been made to fit them into this interpretative model, together with the wooden figures. Hanging and strangulation extend, however, much further back in time. An example is seen in the bodies from the Neolithic in Sigersted bog. Whether the gods of the Asa religion

The fertility symbol from Hedelisker, Central Jutland.

had such early antecedents, around 400 years prior to us otherwise having any evidence of this religion, is an interesting thought deserving of closer study and the location of new convincing finds.

The finding of a fertility symbol at Hedelisker, north of Århus, expresses in no uncertain terms the object of the Iron Age farmers' prayers. A phallus in wood, as large as any, formed a very central aspect of a sacred offering. It had been created from an S-shaped branch, 55 centimetres long and 5 centimetres in diameter. It was deposited in the bog on a small heap of un-burnt human bones, where it had completed a prayer for fertility. Close to this great stave was an extensive layer of charcoal containing burnt bones of both humans and sheep. On top of this lay crushed pots and a couple of iron knives. Immediately around the charcoal layer lay the articulated skeletons of 13 dogs, placed between large stones. Two of the dogs were bound with bast ropes to the stones. The finds from Hedelisker express so clearly the farmers' belief in the supernatural – the mighty powers of nature which, supremely, rule over the life and death of humans and animals.

It is not uncommon to find human bones at Early Iron Age offering sites together with the bones of sacrificed and/or consumed animals. At Hedelisker, some of the human bones had been burnt and sacrificed together with parts of a sheep. The iron knives were probably used in the jointing, perhaps even in the slaughtering of the animals, when the blood flowed. Subsequently, they were included as a natural part of the offering.

The primitive image world of the Early Iron Age is of a completely different character to the Bronze Age's cosmological and structured pictorial universe. There is no doubt that the fertility cult occupied a prominent position in the religion of Iron Age farmers, where cattle played an important role in the rituals. The horse was the ritual animal of the Bronze Age as is apparent, for example, from the horse-drawn Sun Chariot. This role had apparently not been fully played out in the Iron Age. In a sacrificial bog at Balmose-Rislev on Zealand, 11 sacrificed horses were found in the form of skulls and limb bones, in addition to bones of sheep, cattle, dog and three humans.

Human life has, in more than one respect, formed part of the offering rituals. Among the animal bones and layers of ash and charcoal from offerings at the edge of the bog there were human bones at both Hedelisker and Forlev Nymølle. These were not whole skeletons, just individual bones. There are similar finds of human bones associated with Iron Age offerings of pots and animals from several other sites. As mentioned above, cremation graves from this time contain only parts of the burnt skeleton. Perhaps the corpses, or some of them, were defleshed or cut up prior to cremation. At a cemetery at Møllegårdsmarken on Funen, dating from the first centuries AD, some of the corpses had been cut up prior to cremation. This is revealed by cut marks on the bones. There are examples from ethnography of corpses being laid out for defleshing or excarnation prior to burial. Something similar was also the case in the Neolithic. The cleaned defleshed bones of skeletons of the ancestors were scattered in various locations at ritual structures and in burial chambers. This tradition followed the agricultural way of life and was an element in the marking of kinship, an affiliation to the family, and ownership of the land. By sharing out the mortal remains of a person between several locations on the family's property, the spirit of community was reinforced, along with the demarcation of property rights.

Treatment of the dead in the Iron Age was clearly far more complex than previously believed. The underlying significance expressed by the individual human and animal bones is difficult to unravel. As in the Neolithic, animal bones seem to represent partly the remains of meals, partly sacrificed bones and whole, jointed animals. The human bones show no evidence of having been split to extract the marrow, so cannibalism can definitely be excluded. The Bukkerup site, where there were the limb bones of 13 cattle, and other similar offerings of particular parts of animals, or simply jointed animals, could express a perception of completion on delivery by the spirits, the supernatural powers. In many cultures around the world the understanding behind the offering ritual is that what is offered in a fragmented state in one world, becomes complete in "the

The Brå cauldron was hacked to pieces before being offered, probably using the axe that was buried together with the cauldron. The three great carrying rings were ornamented with the heads of owls and bulls. The cauldron was manufactured near Bavaria in Germany and was brought to Denmark in Grauballe Man's time, in the 3rd century BC. Århus Museum, 1950s.

One of six bulls' heads looked out from the rim of the Brå cauldron.

other world"– the world of the gods, *i.e.,* there is a complementary relationship between the worlds of people and of spirits. It could be one of the reasons that many of the offered objects were damaged or destroyed in connection with their deposition. It could also explain why only parts of the bodies were burnt, whereas other parts were offered unburnt out in nature, or were burnt during offerings in the bog. People who died a natural death could, hereby, be both buried and united with the spirits through offering. Perhaps it is an expression of the perception of a person's rebirth in another world.

Neither do the bones of jointed or whole animals included in the offerings ever show signs of having been crushed or split to extract the marrow. This leads thoughts in the direction of the legend of Thor, who slaughtered his billy goats and served them up for his friends, but expressly forbade them crack the bones. Next morning, he would swing his hammer and bring the animals to life again. Even though Thor belongs to a much later time, a corresponding set of perceptions and ideas could well have been in place long before the Asa religion became widespread. The perception concerning a juxtaposition between the worlds of the living and the supernatural is universal in societies with early religions. The animals sacrificed were also primarily young individuals. People gave the best, the most fertile, precisely in order to reinforce fertility.

From distant lands

In the centuries just prior to the birth of Christ, great riches were deposited as offerings in bogs, for example great bronze cauldrons. The Mosbæk cauldron is named after a

Facing page.

The Gundestrup cauldron from Rævemosen in Himmerland, Jutland. Nine kilograms of pure silver bearing a divine wealth of images from Celtic mythology.

bog of the same name in Himmerland. The cauldron weighs more than half a kilogram and is half a metre in diameter. It was a stranger to Scandinavia, decorated with images of the god Hercules, but apparently found a role in local offering rituals. It is a piece of Etruscan work, manufactured in Arretium, north of Rome, around 300 BC.

The Brå cauldron is the ultimate example of a foreign bronze cauldron. It was found buried in a pit on a hillside near Horsens and should probably be perceived as an offering. The cauldron had been chopped up into pieces, probably with the iron axe that lay beside it. With its height of 70 centimetres and a diameter of more than a metre, it had a volume of 600 litres. The upper and lower parts consist of hammered-out bronze plates, whereas the rim and the three large carrying rings are made of iron embellished with bronze. The inwardly facing part of the rim is decorated with owls' heads and foliage in Celtic style. On each side of the carrying rings sits the cast figure of a bull. The owls' heads can be compared with similar fittings from Bayern, where the cauldron was probably manufactured in the third century BC.

The bogs Illemosen at Rynkeby on Funen and Sofienborg in Northern Zealand have both produced finds of outstanding bronze cauldrons of Celtic manufacture. Most of the bronze cauldrons from this time bear bull motifs, and there are several finds from Danish bogs of bronze bull's heads. The bull played a prominent role in the Iron Age, economically, cosmologically and in offering rituals.

The masterpiece above all others, the Gundestrup cauldron, was manufactured completely in silver. Almost nine kilograms of pure metal was used in the making of this vessel. No other prehistoric find contains such a large quantity. The cauldron was found in 1891, during peat cutting near the village of Gundestrup in Himmerland. It lay about 50 metres out in the little kettle-hole bog of Rævemosen.

The base of the cauldron is rounded and the sides vertical. The sides comprise relief-ornamented inner and outer plates that were soldered together. However, in connection with being offered in the bog these plates had been dismantled and placed on the bottom of the cauldron. The rounded base has a depth of 21 centimetres, its diameter is 69 centimetres and the side plates are each 20 cm high. Originally, the cauldron had 14 relief plates mounted on the inner and outer surface, but one was missing. The plates are decorated with embossed reliefs. They show Celtic gods, including "the horned" Cernunnos, who was worshipped in the western Gallic area around the birth of Christ. Other interpretations indicate Greek mythology's Orpheus, depicted as the lord of the animals and as a god who reigned over nature and its mysteries. A bearded male figure surrounded by animals and with a wheel in one of his clenched fists is probably the Gallic equivalent of the Roman god Jupiter, who is sometimes depicted with a wheel. It is possibly an adapted version of the Celtic god Taranis, the god of the heavens and, especially, of thunder and war, to whom the Celts made human sacrifices. The god has

The Gundestrup cauldron, three inner plates:

Above left.
"The Horned One", Cernunnos or the Greek
Orpheus, ruler of animals, who had power
over nature and its mysteries.

Below left.
Relief plate showing the Celtic Taranis, the
god of all the heavens and of thunder and
war, and to whom the Celts made human
sacrifices.

Triple bull sacrifice.

an assistant on each side. One plate shows the sacrifice of a bull, repeated thrice. For every bull, there is a wolf and a hyena-like figure. The triple composition is Celtic. The battle between three heroes and three monsters is similarly known from Irish mythology. There is also a goddess surrounded by animals. Up from the base plate rises a powerful bull, the degree of detail on which is amazing. The outer plates show male or female figures in half-length portrait, presumably gods.

The cauldron displays Celtic features, but was more probably manufactured by a Thracian people who inhabited a large area centred on the Southern Balkans. It was made in the time around 100 BC and could have come to Denmark with refugees who fled northwards from turbulent Europe. It could also be war booty, or have been brought home following the Cimbrian Trek to the south. The remains of a village have been found close to Rævemosen of the same date as the cauldron. It is possible that the inhabitants of this village made this outstanding sacrifice.

The bog Præstegårdsmosen at Dejbjerg in Western Jutland played a major role in the lives of prominent Iron Age families in the time around the birth of Christ. Several villages and a cemetery, the latter including a magnificent warrior burial, lay in close association with the bog, which proved to contain one of our finest finds from the Iron Age. In a massive Iron Age peat cutting, two wagons, magnificently equipped with the finest bronze-work, were discovered at the beginning of the 1880s. They were four-wheeled vehicles with wooden bodies and decorated with open-work bronze. The wagons had been dismantled and offered in the bog. Animal bones and crushed pottery vessels in the same bog bear witness to the fact that it was repeatedly the site of offerings. The Dejbjerg wagons were either manufactured in Northern Gaul, in the Middle Rhine area, or in the Teutonic area, perhaps near Holstein.

Foreign valuables brought from Etruscan, Celtic and Roman areas to Denmark by the growing warrior aristocracy were placed in the same locations in the landscape as agriculture's fertility offerings. Often it was small kettle-hole bogs that were selected for deposition of these offerings. The offered valuables were, just like other offerings at this time, destroyed, damaged or dismantled prior to being deposited. The small glimpses the offerings provide of Iron Age cosmology, are all expressions of profound and complicated negotiations with the spirit world. The bog and its water provided a common portal for the village community, its warriors and the growing economic elite for their contacts with the supernatural powers in another world. We have no sources to tell us about these supernatural powers who intervened in people's lives, and who were appeased and worshipped in wetland areas. It is to the archaeological records of the offering rituals that we must look in order to gain insight into contacts between people and spirits in the Iron Age.

The religion of the Iron Age

*Sacrificial offerings of animals and humans are perhaps
the most dramatic form of communication between
people and the supernatural world and, at the same time,
also the most enigmatic.*

Not one, but several gods or spirits reigned over people, animals and the whole of nature. There was no common and absolute religion that applied to everyone. The offerings and the burial rituals do, however, have many general features in common, but
there were local and individual variations on a common religious theme.

According to religious historian Jens Peter Schjødt, religion should be seen as a perception of the world as existing of two fundamentally different worlds, "this world" and
"the other world". It is in the communication between these two worlds that religion
unfolds. Humans live in this world, and it is comprehensible to the people who inhabit
it because it is defined through a pragmatic and technological relationship with the
environment. People need to know when to sow and when to harvest, how to build a
seaworthy boat, and where to find game. Everyone has the opportunity to acquire skills
necessary to exist in society. But not everything goes according to plan. The harvest can
fail, the boat can leak, and the game can fail to materialise. People have no control over
these types of irregularities and in a religious perception of the world they will be
ascribed to the other world. In many respects, the latter is the counterpart of this world.
The beings who live there are usually immortal, and they can decide elements of
people's fate that cannot be controlled from this world, for example the weather. The
other world is divided up into a series of "other worlds" (those of the gods, ancestors,
and demons). Each can have different properties, but all contain aspects that are the
"opposite" of the situation in this world. An exchange takes place between the two
worlds in that spirits in the other world can influence the human world. They can cause
or prevent good or bad events. People carry out rituals in order to win favour with the
other world. For example, a sacrificial animal is sent to the other world in expectation
that the senders will hereby acquire a good relationship with the supernatural powers
such that these powers, in return, will ensure the harvest gives a good yield. Every

The rituals in the bogs took place in communication between two worlds – the world of humans and that of the gods. Lille Vildmose, Himmerland, Jutland.

Human sacrifice or rebirth.
The Gundestrup cauldron.

irregularity, a lightning strike, a threat of war, a loss and all forms of accident, can be interpreted as a sign from the beings in the other world. If a battle is won, the you have the favour of the gods. If the battle is lost, you do not. Offering is carried out in order to acquire tangible advantages such as victory in battle, a good harvest, the birth of healthy children and the avoidance of illness. It is also to ensure that the sun returns after winter and the reappearance of the moon every month.

On the basis of the archaeological record, we can form an impression of the offering rituals of the Iron Age. We can see that people worshipped male and female deities, that they worshipped nature and the powers that ruled over agriculture, animal husbandry and human life. But who the gods were, and precisely with which motives the super-natural powers were worshipped, the archaeological finds do not reveal. It is true that contemporary Iron Age and later authors from the Greek and the Roman worlds, including Tacitus and Strabo, describe the offering rituals, together with other religious traditions among the barbaric Gauls to the north. But these sources can only be used to lift a small corner of the ideology that lay behind the offerings. Historians of the classical world do not cover all aspects of the offerings objectively, but they do provide a basis for an explanation.

The reason Grauballe Man and the other bog bodies are interpreted as sacrifices is

People sent offerings to the other world in intercession for the return of the sun and the moon.

because we presume that Iron Age religion was like religions of other societies, which can be compared with that of the Iron Age. If, for example, we only knew Christianity, and did not have written sources from other contemporary societies, it would probably not even occur to us that the killing of these people could represent a phenomenon linked to the world of the gods.

Life to the gods

Dedication of offerings of flesh, either of humans of animals, to the supernatural powers is significantly different from the offering of inert objects such as, for example, weapons and ornaments. The difference lies fundamentally in the presence of a spirit and the breath of life, and in the transformation from living organism to corpse. Sacrificial death contains an energy, a spiritual power. It was not exclusively a gift to the gods that was involved when humans and animals were slaughtered. Also inherent in the sacrifice was the release of the blood of life, which possessed a unique and mystical power.

Animal sacrifices are widespread in many societies, both in the past and today, and it is probably not possible to arrive at a universal explanation for this phenomenon. In Greek religion, an important element of the killing was the shedding of blood, which was seen as a cleansing process. The gushing, pulsating, and later seeping blood of the sacrifice connects the living in one world with dead souls in the other. The offering has the paradoxical ability to drain life. And where the blood flows the earth is also drained. Or the blood, also the symbol of life, is collected and shed elsewhere.

A ritual sacrifice is a sacred bond between the divine recipient of the sacrifice and the people who execute the act. Animal sacrifice is a ritual in which both the gods and their worshippers participate and consume the offering together. Ritual meals have both a practical and a symbolic significance, in which the offering feast contains a spiritual transformation process when people consume parts of the sacrificed animal. Other animals were offered whole.

By burning, the sacrifice was carried to the gods of the other world in the smoke and ash, or deposited in the earth or in the water in order to provide nourishment to the earth and the underworld. Both burning and ritual celebrations are mentioned in the Judaism of the Old Testament and in Greek and Roman rituals. They are also evident in the archaeological record from Northern Europe's bogs, with ritual sites speaking in their own clear language of similar rituals.

A clear distinction is made between domesticated and wild animals in the offerings. In the examples already mentioned from Fuglsøgård bog and Bukkerup, it is apparent that it was the meat of tame animals that was sacrificed. These animals were more closely associated with people. In the European Iron Age as a whole, the preferred sacrificial animals were horses, dogs and cattle, and this is also reflected at Danish sites. Now and then the links with people were consummated at the offering ceremonies, like those at Hedelisker where human bones were also included. At an offering site at Gournay in Picardy, people and animals were complementary in the offering ritual. Here a newborn baby lay together with a young calf, and the skulls of horses and humans were deposited side by side, as were femurs of both horses and humans. Perhaps the animal bones were intended to replace those of humans, or the sacrifice expressed reciprocal connections between people and their animals.

People also use animals as symbolic negotiators with the other world. For example, when the shaman takes on the form of the animal, with horns, feathers and fur, and establishes connections between the worlds of humans and spirits. This form of shamanism is known from hunting and farming cultures across the whole world, from Siberia in the north to Australia in the south. In the archaeological record, we are able to glimpse traces of such religious beings. For example, one of the inner plates of the Gundestrup cauldron shows a seated man with red deer antlers on his head, surrounded by a great diversity of animals – deer, lion, wolf, dolphin and antelope.

Bog bodies and bog skeletons

Grauballe Man lived, as already mentioned, in the part of the Iron Age known as the Pre-Roman Iron Age, 500 BC. This also applies to the majority of Danish bog bodies and most of the more than 300 other examples we know for certain were found in peat cuttings in the bogs of Northwestern Europe. Even though there are bog bodies dating all the way back to the Neolithic, and from as recently as the Middle Ages, the majority originate from the same 700-year period in the Late Bronze Age and the first part of the Iron Age, *i.e.* from the ninth century BC to the first century AD. The three bodies from Borremosen in Himmerland, Tollund Man, Elling Girl, Haraldskær Woman, Huldremose Woman and Grauballe Man, just to mention the best preserved of the Danish bog bodies, all date from this time. English Lindow Man II, Yde Girl from Holland, Windeby Man from Schleswig, Gallagh Man from Ireland and the latest additions to this gallery of characters, Clonycavan Man and Old Croghan Man date from the twelfth century BC to the third century AD.

However, most of them are from the centuries around the birth of Christ. If skeletons found in bogs are also considered as bog bodies, they mostly lie chronologically within the same period, more than doubling the total by far. The distinction is made between bog bodies and bog skeletons according to whether or not soft tissue is preserved. Many of the skeletons found in bogs, and dated to the Early Iron Age, could well have ended up in there for the same reasons as the bog bodies. The difference between the two terms rests solely on the state of preservation.

Men, women, adults, and children were all deposited in the bogs of Northwestern Europe. From Denmark, we have knowledge of approximately equal numbers of men and women, but there are no children among the Danish bog corpses. They were all adults, between 25 and 40 years of age when they met their end in the bog. The bodies had almost all been laid naked in the bog, a few were, however, wrapped in woollen cloth or a leather cape, such as Huldremose Woman and Haraldskær Woman. Tollund Man wore only a belt and a cap.

These sacrificed people did not die a natural death, and they were apparently healthy when they died. Most were put to death by hanging or strangulation, and a few, like Grauballe Man, had their throats cut. The exaggerated violence it was previously thought these people had been subjected to is no longer securely supported by the evidence.

The deceased were, with a few exceptions, deposited in old, water-filled peat cuttings. When, much later, they were found as bog bodies, remains of branches rammed down into the bog were in many cases also encountered, as well as lumps of peat. The branches and the peat were used to ensure that the body remained submersed under the

*Tollund Man was wearing a cap
and a belt when he was laid in
the bog.*

cold water. Haraldskær Woman's arms were fixed to the bog with bent hazel sticks, which was initially taken as indicating that she was submerged alive and had drowned. This interpretation has since been dismissed. Haraldskær Woman was dead when she was placed in the bog.

Perhaps it was the tradition of depositing and securing the sacrifices in the water-filled peat cuttings that ensured their preservation for posterity, as this practice became widespread at the same time as farmers in the Late Bronze Age began to extract peat from the bogs. Skeletons found in bogs from the same time are, on the other hand, not found in association with peat cuttingss and were perhaps not secured in the water with the same care.

Human sacrifice

We all tend immediately to associate bog bodies with terrifying dark forces. Murder victims, laid naked in the cold water of the bog. We can still see traces of the cruelty of the killings today – the gaping wound in Grauballe Man's neck and the strangulating rope around the neck of Tollund Man. In the cases of those who are even more disfigured, whether this took place before or after death, the macabre expression of death awakens thoughts of a bestial murder. This was one of the reasons that bog bodies were previously interpreted as the victims of murderous robbers or unrest, or that they were punished criminals or bewitched people with special supernatural powers.

The term overkill is mentioned by classical authors as the use of excessive violence in sacrifices, where aggression was significant in particular rituals or in contact with the gods – for example animals which were bound head and foot and cut open in connection with being killed. The English bog body Lindow Man II suffered, as it is termed, a triple death. In addition to having a fractured skull resulting from a blow, he had been strangled and had his throat cut. This excessive violence has been interpreted as a collective act, in which the ritual violence imparts energy to this gift to the gods and reinforces its value, both for the giver and the recipient. Whether Lindow Man's "blow" to the head was in reality due to the pressure of peat masses, future investigations may clarify. This has proved to be the case with the renewed investigations of Danish bog bodies, and it is no longer possible to speak convincingly of overkill.

Tollund Man's serene face with his delectable smile, and Grauballe Man's manicured nails and delicate hands, led Glob to the interpretation of these people as noble sacrifices to the goddess of love. Tacitus' reference to the myth of Nerthus, goddess of agriculture and the crops of the land, and her servants, belongs to a later time. Today, we are much more careful about drawing parallels with prehistory's fabled deities. The archaeological record shows that a fertility cult has been practised as long as there has been agriculture, and it has always had its spirits.

Tacitus writes in one of his many interpretations of the Teutons' human sacrifices that they "submerged cowardly men and such who had indulged in shameful lust, in bogs and morasses and covered them with wattles." And of the actual offering act, he writes: "Of gods, they worship in particular Mercury, to whom they see it as a sacred duty to bring human sacrifices on particular days. Hercules and Mars, on the other hand, are appeased only with the permitted animal sacrifices." Tacitus lived from AD 56 to AD 120, *i.e.* 400 years after Grauballe Man and most of the other bog bodies. Mercury was, in the world of the Roman gods, the people's messenger. Tacitus' accounts of the barbaric and alien Teutons was interpreted and retold in the 15th century, and enjoys little respect as an objective historical testament to the truth. On the other hand, his accounts, and those of his contemporary historians, may well contain elements of historical objectivity.

The classical authors mention both Roman and Greek human sacrifices, and offerings form part of contemporary theatre, for example the tragedy Iphigenia by Euripides, in which King Agamemnon must follow the priest's prophesies and sacrifice his daughter Iphigenia to the gods in order for the wind to carry his army to Troy and ensure the recovery of Helen and the honour and freedom of Greece.

Offering of Iphigenia to the gods, for victory in battle and the honour and freedom of Greece. On this vase painting, Iphigenia avoids a sacrificial death at the last moment, the offering being completed by the sacrificing of a deer.

Human sacrifice was forbidden in Rome in 97 BC and is rarely mentioned in the literature. Marcellus Plutarch, who died in AD 120, does, however, describe a human sacrifice from the end of the First Punic War (265-241 BC). While the Romans were engaged in the war in Carthage, the Gauls saw their opportunity to invade Italy. The Gallic advance weakened the Romans, and they brought an offering of two Greeks, a man and a woman, and two Gauls, also a man and a woman. This was in obedience of a prophetical text by the female prophet Sibylla, whose role it was to negotiate between people and gods and convey in her predictions messages from the deities. Plutarch remarks on the offering that it happened "in remembrance of the winners, who still carry out mystical and secret ceremonies." He, and other contemporary authors, clearly felt an aversion and revulsion towards human sacrifice, which arose at a time when the survival of Rome was threatened. He describes the act as un-Roman and strangely alien behaviour. Descriptions of the Roman offering, whereby those sacrificed were buried alive at the central cattle market in Rome, Forum Boarium, similarly express revulsion and aversion. This form of divisive sacrifice is the opposite of that in which the aim is to engender and maintain the relationship with beings in the other world.

The ultimate sacrifice

Human life is the ultimate sacrifice a person can make. The expression "to offer" comes from the Latin, "Sacrare" – "to make sacred or holy" and has in its origins nothing to do with either to give or to lose. Offering ceremonies are celebrations that involve both people and gods in a sacred partnership, where bonds are established between people in this world and gods in the other world. We have a tendency to associate the offering of life with sorrow, misfortune and abandonment. The Greek and Roman authors, and Tacitus, describe under which dark and terrifying circumstances these rituals took place, perhaps in order to reinforce the drama of their descriptions of the alien and murderous barbarians.

A sacred gift, dedicated to the supernatural powers, must be physically or metaphorically removed from the world of humans. This happens by eliminating the function of the object or by destroying it. In this way, it becomes recreated in the other world. For animals and humans, destruction equalled actual slaughter. Removal of the offerings from this world also means that the sight of them should be removed, for example by depositing them in a bog. In this process of transfer, the location is an important aspect of the offering. For example the bog, which is half land, half water – half this world, half the other world. Places such as bogs represented a boundary between the two worlds, and served to mark an earthly manifestation of the supernatural world.

In evaluating human sacrifices in Europe in the centuries just prior to the birth of Christ we must eliminate completely our own views on, and perception of, the act of sacrificing a human being. In the absence of an understanding of human sacrifice in practice in ancient Europe at this time, we must conquer our natural and understandable perception of ritual murder, which prompts completely different thoughts concerning the status of human life.

The death of the victim is a kind of life insurance for the survivor. Pragmatism is subordinate to the actual offering and the gift can be replaced with a surrogate, for

Axe offering. Frieze in the
Parthenon, wed to the goddess
Athena. Athens, Greece.

example a child for an adult, an animal for a human, as mentioned by the Roman authors. In the Old Testament we find a corresponding account of Abraham's sacrifice of Isaac, who is replaced by a lamb. From ethnography, there are several examples of surrogate offerings, which, in the actual act of offering, are ascribed the same value as the beings they replace. Among Siberian reindeer hunters, for example, surrogate offerings to the ancestors are still performed today, for example a piece of meat with twigs stuck in it to represent the reindeer's antlers. A surrogate for a human life is of less value, of less importance for people and therefore more dispensable than the person it replaces. If the surrogate is a human life of less value, this is perhaps the reason why the classical historians write of the Gauls that the victims of their ritual murders were people of low social status, criminals, prisoners, poor, slaves and strangers.

If the replacement sacrifice is to function effectively, the choice of the victim is important. The surrogate must, in some way or other, stand out from the crowd, differ from the norm, the expected in society, and could be a marginalised individual such as a criminal, a stranger or a slave.

Offerings involving the slaughtering of animals and humans are perhaps the most dramatic form of communication between people and the supernatural world and, at the same time, also the most enigmatic. In the case of the Iron Age, we have only the archaeological record on which to base our explanations. Against this background it is difficult to distinguish between murder, punishment, violence and sacrifice. The Old Testament contains descriptions of the complex rules and circumstances surrounding cultic activities and offering. The people who wrote these were a part of society and they understood the rules. These descriptions include offerings of grain, fire and blood – all with different intentions and circumstances.

The interaction between spirits and people forms the foundation for the offering rituals, but there are many reasons for ritual behaviour. The necessity of killing as part of the communal spirit, whether the body is eaten or not, involves two cruel and related scenarios: performance and violence. The process of offering, the drama, plays an important role in the communication between people and the supernatural. The preparations for the offering would have involved processions including offerings and the victim. Prayers, music, dancing and adornment of the victim would probably have been involved in building up tension towards the climax of the ritual, and subsequent release. The whole event comprised a drama aimed at enriching the central act, the offering, just as a sacred meal concluded the offering ritual. The Greek offerings involved three such elements – preparation, sacrifice, and epilogue.

The Greek historian Strabo, who lived in the first century BC, writes of an incident among the Cimbrians in which the women went sword in hand to prisoners in the military camp. They led them to a bronze cauldron which could hold 20 measures. One of

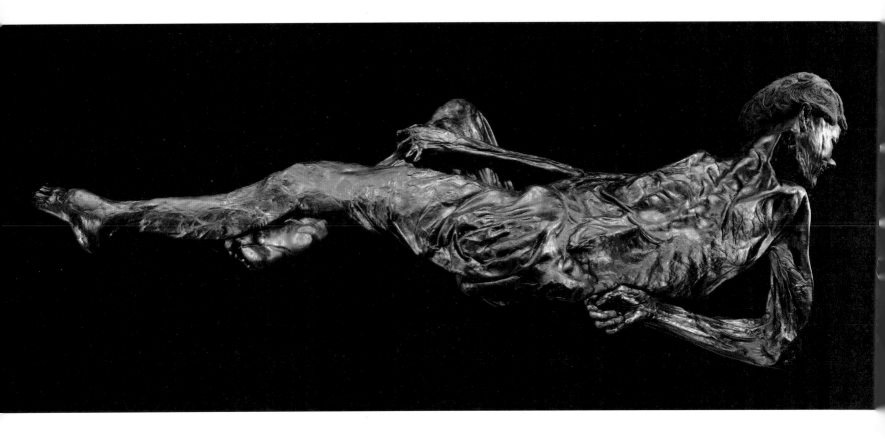

the women cut the throat of one of the prisoners, who was then held over the rim of the cauldron. Others cut up his body, and made prophesies of victory for their countrymen.

The great bronze cauldrons that came to Denmark from foreign parts, for example the Brå cauldron and the silver Gundestrup cauldron, had, by way of their enormous volume, originally a cultural function. Here, in the north, where they ended up as burial urns for warriors or as offerings, their original function had probably been lost. It could be that they were reserved for sacred fluids and Strabo's story leads our thoughts in the direction of offering vessels at blood sacrifices. On one of the Gundestrup cauldron's inner plates, a company of soldiers is seen marching forwards with their shields in their hands cf. p. 219. They are accompanied by an officer, whose higher rank is denoted by the bird decoration on his helmet and by three buglers. To the left, there is a giant figure holding a person over something similar to the Gundestrup cauldron. A platoon of cavalry is riding away from the cauldron led by a snake with ram's horns. The motif can be perceived as a human sacrifice, linked to a procession of warriors. A classical Roman source recounts how the Gauls sacrificed people to the god Teutates by dipping their heads into a cauldron with water until they died from drowning. Another possibility is that this is a resuscitation cauldron – a reincarnation, symbolised by the transformation from infantry to cavalry.

Human sacrifices across the whole world are linked with mysteries concerning the preparation of food. The offerings should be perceived as a cognitive reaction to a world perceived as being inhabited by supernatural powers that are either evil or friendly, depending on how they are treated. Ritual murder was practised in times of stress, crisis and hardship in order to appease or control the spirits in the supernatural world.

The lack of sources results in a corresponding lack of secure evidence relative to the Iron Age. We are not able to identify the spirits, but finds from wetland areas lead us to believe that the latter, with their divine receptivity, were perceived as places that inspired religious veneration and divine personification.

The symbolic significance of preservation must have been valued. The handing over of human and animal bodies, and of wooden figures, to the water could have been intended as an attempt to delay decay. Such a choice must have been significant both in relation to the offering and as remembrance and survival beyond the domain of this world, where Grauballe Man, in a spiritual sense, now finds himself.

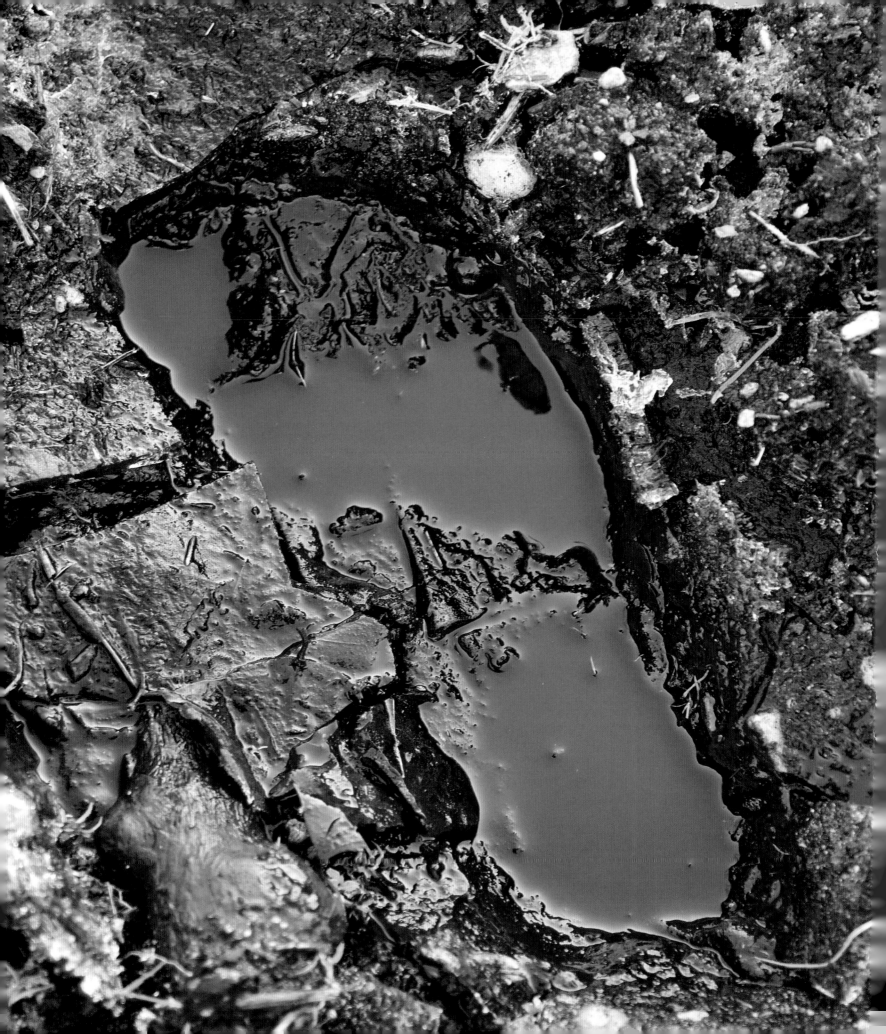

Bibliography

Ahrenholdt-Bindslev, D. 2007: Grauballe Man's Teeth and Jaws. In: P. Asingh & N. Lynnerup (eds.): *Grauballe Man. An Iron Age Bog Body Revisited*. Jysk Arkæologisk Selskab. Højbjerg, pp. 140-153.

Allin, M. 1999: *Zarafa. Den sande historie om giraffen fra det mørke Afrika der endte i Paris*. Borgen. Copenhagen.

Andersen H. 1961: Hun er moder jord. *Skalk* vol. 4, pp. 4-11. Højbjerg.

Aftenposten 17.6.1955, 30.5.1956.

Andersen, C.H. Vogelius 1956: Forhistoriske fingeraftryk. *Kuml. Årbog for Jysk Arkæologisk Selskab* 1956. Århus, pp. 151-154.

Asingh, P. 1988: Diverhøj – a complex burial mound and a Neolithic settlement. In: *Journal of Danish Archaeology* 6, pp. 130-154.

Asingh, P. 2007: The Man in the Bog. In: P. Asingh & N. Lynnerup (eds.): *Grauballe Man. An Iron Age Bog Body Revisited*. Jysk Arkæologisk Selskab. Højbjerg, pp. 14-31.

Asingh, P. 2007: New Scientific Investigations. In: P. Asingh & N. Lynnerup (eds.): *Grauballe Man. An Iron Age Bog Body Revisited*. Jysk Arkæologisk Selskab. Højbjerg, pp. 52-57.

Asingh, P. 2007: The Magical Bog. In: P. Asingh & N. Lynnerup (eds.): *Grauballe Man. An Iron Age Bog Body Revisited*. Jysk Arkæologisk Selskab. Højbjerg, pp. 174-289.

Asingh, P. 2007: The Bog People. In: P. Asingh & N. Lynnerup (eds.): *Grauballe Man. An Iron Age Bog Body Revisited*. Jysk Arkæologisk Selskab. Højbjerg, pp. 290-314.

Asingh, P. 2007: Conclusion. In: P. Asingh & N. Lynnerup (eds.): *Grauballe Man. An Iron Age Bog Body Revisited*. Jysk Arkæologisk Selskab. Højbjerg, pp. 316-323.

Aarhus Amtstidende 8.11.1952.

Aarhuus Stiftstidende 28.4.1952, 1.5.1952, 15.5.1952, 7.11.1952 and 29.10.1953.

Becker, C.J. 1948: Tørvegravning i ældre jernalder. *Fra Nationalmuseets Arbejdsmark* 1948, pp. 92-100.

Becker, C.J. 1972: "Mosepotter" fra Danmarks Jernalder. Problemer omkring mosefundne lerkar og deres tolkning. *Årbøger for nordisk Oldkyndighed og Historie* 1971. Copenhagen.

Bennike, P 1985: *Paleopathology of Danish skeletons*. Akademisk Forlag. Copenhagen.

Berlingske Tidende 12.10.1952 and 22.5.1955.

Boel, L.W. & M. Dalstra: Microscopical Analysis of Bone Specimens; Structural Changes Related to Chronological Age and Possible Diseases. In: P. Asingh & N. Lynnerup (eds.): *Grauballe Man. An Iron Age Bog Body Revisited*. Jysk Arkæologisk Selskab. Højbjerg, pp. 130-139.

Brandt, J. 1951:Planterester fra et moselig fra ældre jernalder. *Årbøger for Nordisk Oldkyndighed og Historie* 1951. Copenhagen.

Briggs, C.S. 1995: The Meaning and Myth of Bog Bodies. Did They Fall or Were They Pushed? Some Unresolved Questions about Bog Bodies. In: R.C. Turner & R.G. Scaife (eds.) *Bog Bodies. New Discoveries and New Perspectives. London,* pp. 168-182.

Demokraten 28.4.1952 and 7.11.1952.

Brothwell, D. 1995: Recent Research on the Lindow Bodies in the Context of Five Years of World Studies. In: Turner, R.C. and Scaife, R.G. (eds.) *Bog Bodies. New Discoveries and New Perspectives*. London, pp. 100-103.

Brothwell, D. & K. Dobney 1986: Studies on the hair and nails of Lindow Man and comparative specimens. In: I.M. Stead, J.B. Bourke & D. Brothwell (Eds.): *Lindow Man. The Body in the Bog*. London, pp. 66-70.

Brothwell, D., D. Liversage, B. Gottleib, 1992: Radiographic and forensic aspects of the female Huldremose body. *Journal of Danish Archaeology*, 9, 1990. Odense. pp. 157-78.

Brothwell, D.T. & Bourke, J.B 1995: The Human Remains from Lindow Moss 1987-88. In: R.C. Turner & R.G. Scaife (eds.) *Bog Bodies. New Discoveries and New Perspectives.* London, pp. 52-58.

Brøndegaard, V.J. 1987: *Folk og Flora. Dansk etnobotanik.* Copenhagen.

Christensen, L.B. & S.B. Sveen (eds.) 1998: *Religion og materiel kultur.* Aarhus University Press, Århus.

Christensen, C & R. Fiedel 2003: Tørvegravning i forhistorisk tid. *Nationalmuseets Arbejdsmark* 2003. Copenhagen, pp. 85-100.

Cleveland Plain Dealer 3.5.1952.

Demokraten 28.2.1952.

Ekstra Bladet 28.4.1952. København.

Feddersen A. 1881: To Mosefund. *Aarbøger for Nordisk Oldkyndighed og Historie* 1881. Copenhagen, pp. 369-389.

Fischer, C. 1980: Moseligene fra Bjældskovdal. *Kuml. Årbog for Jysk Arkæologisk Selskab* 1979. Højbjerg, pp. 7-44.

Fischer, C. 1999: The Tollund Man and the Elling Woman and other bog bodies from Central Jutland. In: B. Coles, J. Coles, M.S. Jørgensen (eds.): *Bog Bodies, Sacred Sites and Wetland Archaeology,* pp. 93-98. WARP, Exeter.

Fischer, C. 2007: *Tollundmanden. Gaven til guderne. Mosefund fra Danmarks forhistorie.* Hovedland, Århus.

Frederiksen, J. & J. Glastrup 2007: Conservation and Analysis of Grauballe Man 2001-2002. In: P. Asingh & N. Lynnerup (eds.): *Grauballe Man. An Iron Age Bog Body Revisited*. Jysk Arkæologisk Selskab. Højbjerg pp. 58-76.

Frolich, B. 2007: The Search for Grauballe Man's Missing Vertebrae. In: P. Asingh & N. Lynnerup (eds.): *Grauballe Man. An Iron Age Bog Body Revisited*. Jysk Arkæologisk Selskab. Højbjerg, pp. 218-225..

Geel, B.V., J.v.d. Plith, M.R. Lillian, E.R. Klaver, J.H.M. Kouwenberg, H. Renssen, I. Reynauld-Farrera, H.T. Waterbolk 1998: The sharp rise of 14C ca. 800 cal. BC: Possible causes, related climatic teleconnections and the impact on human environments. In: Proceedings of the 16th International 14C Conference. W.G. Mook and J. van der Plicht. *RADIOCARBON*, Vol. 40, No. 1, 1998, pp. 535-550.

Glob, P.V. 1956. Jernaldermanden fra Grauballe. *Kuml. Årbog for Jysk Arkæologisk Selskab* 1956. Århus, pp. 99-113.

Glob, P.V. 1965: *Mosefolket. Jernalderens mennesker bevaret i 2000 år*, (1st ed). Gyldendal, Copenhagen.

Green, M.A. 1998: Humans as Ritual Victims in the Later Prehistory of Western Europe. *Oxford Journal of Archaeology* 17, 1998, Oxford, pp. 169-189.

Green, M.A. 2001. Dying for the Gods. Human Sacrifice in Iron Age & Roman Europe. Tempus Publishing Ltd. Charleston.

Gregersen, M., A.G. Jurik & N. Lynnnerup 2007: Forensic Evidence, Injuries and Cause og Death.

P. Asingh & N. Lynnerup (red.): *Grauballe Man. An Iron Age Bog body Revisited*. Jysk Arkæologisk Selskab, s. 234-258.

Grüner, O. 1979: Die 'Moorleiche' von Windeby. *Offa* 36, 1979, pp. 116-118.

Hansen, H-O. 1979: *Danske Naturområder*. Fredningsstyrelsen og Politiken. Copenhagen.

Hansen, M.A. 1965. *Orm og Tyr*. Copenhagen

Harild, J.A., D.E. Robinson & J. Hudlebusch 2007: New Analyses of Grauballe Man's Gut Contents. In: P. Asingh & N. Lynnerup (eds.): *Grauballe Man. An Iron Age Bog Body Revisited*. Jysk Arkæologisk Selskab. Højbjerg, pp. 154-187.

Heinemeier, J. & P. Asingh 2007: Dating of Grauballe Man. In: P. Asingh & N. Lynnerup (eds.): *Grauballe Man. An Iron Age Bog Body Revisited*. Jysk Arkæologisk Selskab. Højbjerg, pp. 196-201.

Helbæk, H. 1950: Tollundmandens sidste måltid. *Årbøger for nordisk Oldkyndighed og Historie* 1950, Copenhagen, pp. 311-341.

Helbæk, H. 1958: Grauballemandens sidste Måltid. *Kuml. Årbog for Jysk Arkæologisk Selskab* 1958. Højbjerg, pp. 83-116.

Henriksen, M.B. 1998: "Pars pro toto"-begravelser i romersk jernalder – et aspekt af jernalderens begravelsesritualer. In: Petersen, A.B. & Sommer, A-L. (eds.). *Dødens Rum*. Odense Universitetsforlag.

Henriksen, M.B. 2007. Brudagergravpladsen. Odense Universitetsforlag, pp. 62-85.

Henriksen, M.B. 2005: Danske kogegruber og kogegrubefelter fra yngre bronzealder og ældre jernalder. In: Gustafson, L., T. Heibreen & J. Martens (eds.) *De gåtefulle kokegroper*. Varia 58, pp. 77-102. Kulturhistorisk Museum, Fornminneseksjonen, Universitetet i Oslo.

Henriksen, P. S. & Robinson, D. E. 1996: Early Iron Age agriculture: archaeobotanical evidence from an underground granary at Overbygård in northern Jutland, Denmark. *Vegetation History and Archaeobotany* 5, pp. 1-11.

Holbæk Amtstidende 19.11.1954.

Holden, T.G. 1995: The Last Meals of the Lindow Bog Men. In: R.C. Turner & R.G. Scaife (eds.) Bog Bodies. *New Discoveries and New Perspectives*. London, pp. 76-82.

Horsens Folkeblad 28.4.1952.

Hove, Th.Th. 1983.: *Tørvegravning I Danmark. Fra håndgravning til moseindustri. Udvikling og vilkår*. Poul Kristensens Forlag. Herning.

Hvass, Lone. 1998: *Dronning Gunhild – et moselig fra jernalderen*. Sesam, Copenhagen.

Ilkjær, J. 2003. *Mosens Skatkammer. Mellem mennesker og guder i jernalderen*. Højbjerg.

Jensen, J.V. 1952: *Orm og Tyr*. Copenhagen.

Jensen, J. 2001: *Danmarks Oldtid. Stenalder 13.000-2000 f.Kr.* Gyldendal. Copenhagen.

Jensen, J. 2002: *Danmarks Oldtid. Bronzealder 2000-500 f.Kr.* Gyldendal. Copenhagen.

Jensen, J. 2003: *Danmarks Oldtid. Ældre Jernalder 500 f.Kr.-400. e.Kr.* Gyldendal. Copenhagen.

Joy, J. 2009: *Lindow Man*. The British Museum, London.

Jurik, A.G. 2007: New Radiological Examinations. In: P. Asingh & N. Lynnerup (eds.): *Grauballe Man. An Iron Age Bog Body Revisited*. Jysk Arkæologisk Selskab. Højbjerg.

Jyllands-Posten 2.5.1952, 11.5.1952, 24.5.1955.

Jørgensen, S. 1956: Grauballemandens fundsted. *Kuml. Årbog for Jysk Arkæologisk Selskab* 1956. Århus, pp. 114-130.

Kaul, F. 1988: Da våbnene tav. Hjortspringfundet og dets baggrund. National-museet. Copenhagen.

Kaul, F. 1994: Trivselstegnet. *Skalk* vol. 3. Højbjerg.

Kaul, F. 2003: Mosen – porten til den anden verden. In: Jørgensen, L., Storgaard, B., Thomsen, L.G. (eds): *Sejrens Triumf. Norden i skyggen af det romerske Imperium*. Nationalmuseet, Copenhagen, pp.18-42.

Kaul, F. 2004: The religion of the Bronze Age. Studies of the iconography of the Nordic Bronze Age. *Nordiske Fortidsminder*, Serie B, bind 22.

Kelly, E.P.2006: "Kingship and sacrifice: Iron age bog bodies and boundaries," *Archaeology Ireland* – Heritage guide No. 35, September 2006.

Klassen, L. 2000: Frühes Kupfer im Norden. Untersuchungen zu Chronologie, Herkunft und Bedeutung der Kupferfunde der nordgruppe der Trichterbecherkultur. *Jutland Archaeological society Vol. 36*.

Klindt-Jensen, Ole. 1979: Gundestrupkedlen. Nationalmuseet. Copenhagen.

Kløvedal, E.R. 1977: Fæ og Frænde. Syvogenhalv nats fortællinger om vejene til Rom og Danmark. Gyldendal. Copenhagen.

Koch, E. 1998: Neolithic Bog Pots from Zealand, Møn, Lolland and Falster. *Det Kongelige Nordiske Oldskriftselskab*. Copenhagen.

Koch, M. & D.V. Poulsen 2007: Analysis of the Skin. In: P. Asingh & N. Lynnerup (eds.): *Grauballe Man. An Iron Age Bog Body Revisited*. Jysk Arkæologisk Selskab. Højbjerg.

Krebs, C.& Ratjen, E. 1956: De radiologiske fund hos moseliget fra Grauballe. *Kuml. Årbog for Jysk Arkæologisk Selskab*. 1957, pp. 138-150. Århus.

Land og Folk 6.9.1953.

Lange-Kornbak, G. 1952, Grauballemanden i Garveriet, *Aarhuus Stiftstidende* 7.11.1952.

Lange-Kornbak, G. 1956. Konservering af en oldtidsmand. *Kuml. Årbog for Jysk Arkæologisk Selskb. 1956*. Århus, pp. 155-159.

Lange-Kornbak's diary (the edited transcript of the diary notes), Moesgård Museum archives, case number 213. Unpublished.

Larsen, R. & D.V. Poulsen 2007: Analysis of the skin. P. Asingh & N. Lynnerup (eds.): Grauballe Man. An Iron Age Bog Body Revisited. Jysk Arkæologisk Selskab, pp. 84-94.

Larsen, E.B.1995: *Historien om Det store sølvfund fra Gundestrup*. Jysk Arkæologisk Selskab. Højbjerg.

Larsen, P.N., Bjerkhof, S. 2006: *Verden som landskab. Nordisk landskabsmaleri 1840-1910*. Statens Museum for Kunst. Copenhagen.

Lund, A. 2002: *Mumificerede moselig*. Høst & Søn. Copenhagen.

Jund, J. 1984: Nedgravede huse og kældre i ældre jernalder. *Hikuin* 10. Højbjerg.

Lund, J. 2002: Forlev Nymølle. En offerplads fra yngre førromersk jernalder. *Kuml. Årbog for Jysk Arkæologisk Selskab* 2002. Højbjerg, pp. 143-196.

Lynnerup, N., L.B. Boldsen & Anne Gretha Jurik 2007: The Biological Anthropology of Grauballe Man. In: P. Asingh & N. Lynnerup (eds.): *Grauballe Man. An Iron Age Bog Body Revisited*. Jysk Arkæologisk Selskab. Højbjerg, pp. 226-233.

Lynnerup, N., A.G. Jurik & M. Dalstra, R. Bergholdt Hansen 2007: Microscopical

Analysis of Bone Specimens. In: P. Asingh & N. Lynnerup (eds.): *Grauballe Man. An Iron Age Bog Body Revisited*. Jysk Arkæologisk Selskab. Højbjerg, pp. 130-139.

Lynnerup, N., Bennike, P., Iregreen, E. 2008: *Biologisk Antropologi med human osteologi*. Gyldendal. Copenhagen.

Mahler, D.L.D 1996: Forsøg med tørvekul. Upubliceret rapport. Historisk Arkæologisk Forsøgscenter, Lejre.

Mulhall, I., Briggs, E.K. 2006: *Presenting a Past Society to a Present Day Audience: Bog Bodies in Iron Age Ireland*. National Museum, Dublin.

Munck, W. 1956: Patologisk-anatomisk og retsmedicinsk undersøgelse af moseliget fra Grauballe. *Kuml. Årbog for Jysk Arkæologisk Selskab. Århus.* pp. 131-137.

Müller-Wille, M. 1999: Opferkulte der Germanen und Slawen. *Sonderheft der Zeitschrift "Archäoligie in Deutschland".* Stuttgart.

Nordström, N. 2007: *De odödliga. Förhistoriska individer i vetenskap og media*. Nordic Akademic Press. Lund.

Painter, T. 1991: Preservation in Pest. Chemistry & Industry, June 1991, pp. 421-424.

Painter, T. J. 1995: Chemical and Microbiological Aspects of the Preservation Process in Sphagnum Peat. In: R.C. Turner & R.G. Scaife (eds.) *Bog Bodies. New Discoveries and New Perspectives*. London, pp. 88-99.

Pearson, M.P., A. Chamberlai, O. Craig, P. Marshall, J. Mulville, H. Smithh, C. Chenery, M.Collins, G. Cook, G. Craig, J. Evans, J. Hiller, J. Mongomery, J-L. Schwenninger, G. Tailor & T. Wess 2005: Evidence for mummification in Bronze Age Britain. In: *Antiquity* 79, pp. 529-546.

Politiken 8.5.1956.

Sanden, W. van der 1996a: *Udødeliggjorte i mosen. Historierne om de nordvesteuropæiske moselig*. Batavian Lion International, Amsterdam.

Schjødt, J.P. in press: Religion i jernalderen og kilder fra middelalderen: Kontinuitet og brud. I: Katalog til udstillingen: Tollundmandens Rejse, Silkeborg Museum.

Schlabow, K., W. Hage, H. Jankuhn, H et al. 1958: Zwei Moorleichenfunde aus dem Domlandsmoor. *Praehistorische Zeitschrift* XXXVI.

Silkeborg Soc.-Demokrat 28.4.1952.

Silkeborg Avis 28.4.1952, 9.5.1953.

Smith, B.K. & W. Doniger 1989: Sacrifice and Substitution: Ritual Mystification and Mythical Demystification. I: *Numen*, Vol. 36, Fasc. 2., pp.189-224. BRILL.

Stoltze, M. 2007: *Dansk Natur*. Gyldendal. København.

Strehle, H. 2007: The Conservation of Grauballe Man. In: P. Asingh & N. Lynnerup (eds.): *Grauballe Man. An Iron Age Bog Body Revisited*. Jysk Arkæologisk Selskab. Højbjerg.

Stoker, B. 2006. *The Snake's Pass*. Valancourt Books. Dublin.

Tanaka, S. & L. Mcgaw, L. 1997: Die Welt des Gletschermanns. Carlsen. Hamburg.

Tauber, H 1956: Tidsfæstelse af Grauballemanden ved kulstof-14 måling. *Kuml. Årbog for Jysk Arkæologisk Selskab 1956*. Århus, pp.160-163.

Tauber, H. 1980. Kulstof-14 datering af moselig. *Kuml. Årbog for Jysk Arkæologisk Selskab 1979*. Århus, pp. 73-78.

Tauber, H. 1981: Kostvaner i forhistorisk tid – belyst ved C-13 målinger. In: R. Egevang (ed.): *Det Skabende Menneske*. Nationalmuseet, pp. 112-126.

Thorvildsen, K. 1947: Moseliget fra Borremose i Himmerland. *Fra Nationalmuseets Arbejdsmark*. Copenhagen, pp. 57-67.

Thorvildsen, K. 1950: Moseliget fra Tollund. *Aarbøger for nordisk Oldkyndighed og Historie 1950*. Copenhagen, pp. 302-310.

Thorvildsen, E. 1952: Menneskeofringer i oldtiden. Jernalderligene fra Borremose i Himmerland. *Kuml. Årbog for Jysk Arkæologisk Selskab 1952, Århus.* pp. 32-48.

Turner, R. 1999: Dating the Lindow Moss and other British bog bodies and the problems of assigning their cultural context. In: B. Coles, J. Coles & M.S. Jørgensen (eds.): *Bog Bodies, Sacred Sites and Wetland Archaeology*. Exeter, pp. 227-234.

Vebæk, C.L. 1944: En østjysk offermose fra keltisk jernalder. *Nationalmuseets Arbejdsmark 1944*. Copenhagen, pp. 21-28.

Vebæk, C.L. 1945: Smederup. An Early Iron Age sacrificial bog in East Jutland. *Acta Archaeologica* XVI. Copenhagen, pp. 195-211.

Vogelius Andersen, C.H. 1956: Forhistoriske fingeraftryk. *Kuml. Årbog for Jysk Arkæologisk Selskab,* Århus, pp. 151-54.

Warrer, E.& Leth, H. 1971: En odontologisk undersøgelse af moseliget fra landsbyen Grauballe i Jylland. *Tandlægebladet* 75, pp. 592-605.

Wilkinson, C.M. 2004: *Forensic Facial Reconstruction*. Cambridge.

Wilkinson, C.M. 2007: Facial Reconstruction of Grauballe Man. In: P. Asingh & N. Lynnerup (eds.): *Grauballe Man. An Iron Age Bog Body Revisited*. Jysk Arkæologisk Selskab. Højbjerg, pp. 260-271.

Willis, R. 1993: *World mythology*. Duncan Baird Publishers. London.

Wilson A.S, & M.T.P. Gilbert. 2006: Identification from hair and nail. In: T. Thompson & S. Black (eds.): Introduction to Biological Human Identification. Boca Raton, pp.147-174.

Wilson, A.S., M.P. Richards, B. Stern, R.C. Janaway, A.M. Pollard & D.J. Tobin 2007: Information on Grauballe Man from his Hair. In: P. Asingh & N. Lynnerup (eds.): *Grauballe Man. An Iron Age Bog Body Revisited*. Jysk Arkæologisk Selskab, Højbjerg, pp. 188-195.

Index of names, places and subjects

Photo credits

Page 2. Sam Vangstrup, Hadsund.

Page 8. P.V. Glob, Moesgård Museum.

Page 10. Sven Türck, Copenhagen.

Page 13. Moesgård Museum.

Page 14. Moesgård Museum.

Page 15. P.V. Glob, Moesgård Museum.

Page 17. Sven Türck, Copenhagen.

Page 19. Moesgård Museum.

Page 20. Aarhus Stiftstidende.

Page 21. Aarhus Stiftstidende.

Page 22. Moesgård Museum.

Page 25. The National Museum, Copenhagen.

Page 28. Sam Vangstrup, Hadsund.

Page 30 Above. P.V. Glob, Moesgård Museum

Page 30 Below. Moesgård Museum.

Page 32. Aarhus Stiftstidende.

Page 33. Aarhus Stiftstidende.

Page 34. Aarhus Stiftstidende.

Page 35. Carl Krebs and Erling Ratjen, Århus District Hospital

Page 36. Moesgård Museum.

Page 37. Aarhus Stiftstidende.

Page 38. Kaj Josephsen, University of Århus.

Page 39. Kaj Josephsen, University of Århus.

Page 42. The National Museum, Copenhagen.

Page 45. Aarhus Stiftstidende.

Page 46. Sam Vangstrup, Hadsund

Page 48. Roberto Fortuna, The National Museum, Copenhagen.

Page 49. The National Museum, Copenhagen.

Page 50. The National Museum, Copenhagen.

Page 52. Moesgård Museum.

Page 53. The National Museum, Copenhagen.

Page 54. Moesgård Museum.

Page 55. Aarhus Stiftstidende.

Page 56. Ib Hansen, Aarhus Stiftstidende.

Page 57. Ib Hansen, Aarhus Stiftstidende.

Page 58. Børge Venge, Aarhus Stiftstidende.

Page 59. Moesgård Museum Archives.

Page 60. Bjarke Larsen, Aarhus Stiftstidende.

Page 61. Børge Venge, Aarhus Stiftstidende.

Page 62. Børge Venge, Aarhus Stiftstidende.

Page 63. Børge Venge, Aarhus Stiftstidende.

Page 64. Børge Venge, Aarhus Stiftstidende.

Page 66. Sam Vangstrup, Hadsund.

Page 69. Preben Delholm, Moesgård Museum.

Page 70. Jens Thaysen, Aarhus Stiftstidende.

Page 72. Anne Grethe Jurik, Århus University Hospital.

Page 73 Above. Preben Delholm, Moesgård Museum.

Page 73 Below. Bruno Frolich, National Museum of Natural History, Washington D.C.

Page 74. Anne Grethe Jurik, Århus University Hospital.

Page 76. Anne Grethe Jurik, Århus University Hospital.

Page 77. Niels Lynnerup, University of Copenhagen.

Page 78. Ib Hansen, Aarhus Stiftstidende.

Page 79 Left. State Archaeological Museum, Gottorp Castle, Schleswig.

Page 79 Right. Robert Clark, New York City.

Page 81. The National Museum, Copenhagen.

Page 82. National Museum of Ireland, Dublin.

Page 84. Lene Warner Boel, Århus University Hospital.

Page 87. Preben Delholm, Moesgård Museum.

Page 88. Kaj Josephsen, University of Århus.

Page 89. Kaj Josephsen, University of Århus.

Page 90. The National Museum, Copenhagen.

Page 91. Peter Steen Henriksen, Copenhagen.

Page 93. Jan Andreas Harild, The National Museum, Copenhagen.

Page 94. David Earle Robinson and Jan Andreas Harild, The National Museum, Copenhagen after Hans Helbæk, Kuml 1958.

Page 95. Jan Andreas Harild, The National Museum, Copenhagen.

Page 97. Jan Andreas Harild, The National Museum, Copenhagen.

Page 98. Peter Steen Henriksen, Copenhagen.

Page 99. Jens Kirkeby, Moesgård Museum.

Page 100 Left. Moesgård Museum.

Page 100 Right. Arnold Mikkelsen, Copenhagen.

Page 101. Jan Andreas Harild, The National Museum, Copenhagen.

Page 104. Moesgård Museum.

Page 105. Jens Kirkeby, Moesgård Museum.

Page 107. Jan Andreas Harild, The National Museum, Copenhagen.

Page 108. Sam Vangstrup, Hadsund.

Page 110 Above. P.V. Glob, Moesgård Museum.

Page 110 Below. Robert Clark, New York City.

Page 111. Jens Kirkeby, Moesgård Museum.

Page 112 Left. Niels Lynnerup, University of Copenhagen.

Page 112 Right Preben Delholm, Moesgård Museum.

Page 114. Jens Kirkeby, Moesgård Museum.

Page 115. Jens Kirkeby, Moesgård Museum.

Page 116. Robert Clark, New York City.

Page 117. Jens Kirkeby, Moesgård Museum.

Page 118. Jens Kirkeby, Moesgård Museum.

Page 120. Robert Clark, New York City.

Page 121. University of Manchester.

Page 122. John Lee, The National Museum, Copenhagen.

Page 124. Jens Kirkeby, Moesgård Museum.

Page 125. Jens Kirkeby, Moesgård Museum.

Page 126. Eilif Peterssen, The National Museum of Art, Architecture and Design, Oslo.

Page 128. Robert Clark, New York City.

Page 129. Jens Kirkeby, Moesgård museum.

Page 130. Jens Kirkeby, Moesgård Museum.

Page 131. Jens Kirkeby, Moesgård Museum.

Page 132. Jens Kirkeby, Moesgård Museum.

Page 134. Robert Clark, New York City.

Page 135. National Museum of Ireland, Dublin.

Page 137. Niels Fabæk, Skørping.

Page 138. Jens Kirkeby, Moesgård Museum.

Page 139. Jens Kirkeby, Moesgård Museum.

Page 140 Above. Poul-Erik Lillholm Rosenbaum, Scanpix

Page 140 Below. Niels Fabæk, Skørping.

Page 142. The National Museum of Art, Architecture and Design, Oslo.

Page 143. The National Museum, Stockholm.

Page 144. Sam Vangstrup, Hadsund.

Page 146 Above. Pål Brenre, Scanpix.

Page 146 Below. Jens Kirkeby, Moesgård Museum.

Page 147 Above. Lennart Larsen, The National Museum, Copenhagen.

Page 147 Below. Moesgård Museum.

Page 148. Lars Gejl, Scanpix.

Page 149. Jesper Weng, The National Museum, Copenhagen.

Page 150. Moesgård Museum.

Page 151. Jens Kirkeby, Moesgård Museum.

Page 152. Anders Tvevad, Scanpix.

Page 153 Above. Lennart Larsen, The National Museum, Copenhagen.

Page 153 Below. The National Museum, Copenhagen.

Page 155. John Lee, The National Museum, Copenhagen.

Page 156. Lennart Larsen, The National Museum, Copenhagen.

Page 158. The National Museum, Copenhagen.

Page 160. Jens-Henrik Bech, Museum for Thy and Vester Hanherred.

Page 161 Above. Ernst Stidsing, Cultural-Historical Museum, Randers.

Page 161. Below. Pauline Asingh, Moesgård Museum.

Page 163. John Olsen, Ringe.

Page 164. Roberto Fortuna, The National Museum, Copenhagen.

Page 165. Lennart Larsen, The National Museum, Copenhagen.

Page 166. Lennart Larsen, The National Museum, Copenhagen.

Page 167. The National Museum.

Page 168. Rógvi Nolsøe Johansen, Moesgård Museum.

Page 169. John Lee, The National Museum, Copenhagen.

Page 170. Sam Vangstrup, Hadsund.

Page 172. Ann Sullivan, Scanpix.

Page 173 Above. Vojtek Buss, Scanpix.

Page 173 Below. Ann Ronan, Scanpix.

Page 175. Niels Fabæk, Skørping.

Page 176. Jens Kirkeby, Moesgård Museum.

Page 177. Ole Malling, Hvalsø.

Page 179. Jens Kirkeby, Moesgård Museum.

Page 180. Robert Clark, New York City.

Page 181. Kristian Søgaard.

Page 182. Rógvi Nolsøe Johansen, Moesgård Museum.

Page 184. Ole Malling, Hvalsø

Page 185. Flemming Bau, Århus.

Page 186. Reno Fiedel, Cultural-Historical Museum, Randers.

Page 188. The National Museum, Copenhagen.

Page 189. The National Museum, Copenhagen.

Page 190. Ditlev Mahler, Historical-Archaeological Experimental Centre, Lejre.

Page 192. Sam Vangstrup, Hadsund

Page 194. Reno Fiedel, Cultural-Historical Museum, Randers.

Page 195. Reno Fiedel, Cultural-Historical Museum, Randers.

Page 196. Flemming Kaul, The National Museum, Copenhagen.

Page 197. Lennart Larsen, The National Museum, Copenhagen.

Page 198. Ilse Rasmussen.

Page 199. The National Museum, Copenhagen.

Page 200. Jens Kirkeby, Moesgård Museum.

Page 201. The National Museum, Copenhagen.

Page 202. Jørgen Kragelund, Højbjerg. After Jørgen Jensen 2003: *Danmarks Oldtid, ældre jernalder 500 f.Kr-400 e. Kr.,* p. 191.

Page 203 Left. P.V.Glob, Moesgård Museum.

Page 203 Right Louise Hilmar, Moesgård Museum.

Page 204. After P.V. Glob. 1965: Mosefolket, p. 161.

Page 206. Rógvi Nolsøe Johansen, Moesgård Museum.

Page 208. The National Museum, Copenhagen.

Page 209. The National Museum, Copenhagen.

Page 211. Kitt Weiss, The National Museum, Copenhagen.

Page 212. John Lee, The National Museum, Copenhagen.

Page 213. John Lee, The National Museum, Copenhagen.

Page 214. The National Museum, Copenhagen.

Page 216. Sam Vangstrup, Hadsund.

Page 218. Sam Vangstrup, Hadsund.

Page 219. John Lee, The National Museum, Copenhagen.

Page 220. Sam Vangstrup, Hadsund.

Page 223. State Archaeological Museum, Gottorp Castle, Schleswig.

Page 224. The National Museum, Copenhagen.

Page 226. British Museum, London.

Page 228. British Museum, London.

Page 230. Robert Clark, New York City.

Page 232. Sam Vangstrup, Hadsund.

Thanks

Many thanks to the competent team of researchers responsible for the new scientific investigations of Grauballe Man, Dorthe Ahrenholdt-Bindslev, Lene Wagner Boel, Jesper Lier Boldsen, Michel Dalstra, Frey Eberholst, Jesper Frederiksen, Bruno Frolich, Markil Gregersen, Jan Andreas Harild, Jan Heinemeier, Finn Taagehøj Jensen, Anne Grethe Jurik, Mogens S. Koch, Aksel Kruse, René Larsen, Christian Brahe Pedersen, Dorthe V. Poulsen, David Earle Robinson, Mikkel Sharff, Hans Stødkilde-Jørgensen, Helle Strehle, Caroline Wilkinson and Andrew Wilson and for their contributions to the scientific publication *Grauballe Man – An Iron Age Bog Body Revisited,* published in 2007. The sections on new scientific investigations are based on the results of their research. Jens Peter Skjødt, Lisbeth Bredholdt Christensen, Mogens Bo Henriksen, Rane Willerslev, Pernille Plaetner, Annette Damm, Jes Damm and Ginna Marie Sørensen are thanked for professional inspiration and comments on the manuscript for this book.

Bog sites from the Pre-Roman Iron Age

Grauballe Man's time

Localities mentioned in this book

1. Nebelgaard bog. Grauballe Man
2. Bjældskovdal bog. Tollund Man
3. Bjældskovdal bog. Ellinge Girl.
4. Borremosen. Three bog bodies.
5. Huldremosen, Huldremose Woman.
6. Haraldskær bog. Haraldskær Woman.
7. Dejbjerg bog. Dejbjerg wagons.
8. Rævemosen. Gundestrup cauldron
9. Mosbæk. Bronze cauldron.
10. Falling bog. Ring offering.
11. Smederup bog. Ring offering.
12. Sattrup bog. Ring offering
13. Forlev Nymølle. Wooden idol, offerings.
14. Nørre Smedeby. Peat cutting, offerings.
15. Fuglsøgård bog. Peat cutting, offerings.
16. Hjortspring bog. Hjortspring boat.
17. Bråddenbjerg. Wooden idol, offerings.
18. Hedelisker. Phallus, offerings
19. Bukkerup. Animal sacrifices.
20. Årre. Ring offering.